THE BEST OF THE
ARKANSAS TRAVELER
1956-1986

Publisher's Note: During the years in which the Arkansas Traveler column has appeared, stylistic guidelines have undergone numerous changes, to the end that the columns included herein have been composed and published under varying assumptions about the use of numerals, of quotes and italics, and of capitalization. In preparing this book, we have imposed consistency in these elements only when we felt that not doing so would result in confusion to the reader.

As seen in the Arkansas Gazette.

THE BEST OF THE
ARKANSAS TRAVELER
1956-1986

Ernie Deane   Mike Trimble
Bob Lancaster   Charles Allbright

Edited by Maylon T. Rice

August House / Little Rock

P U B L I S H E R S

Printed in the United States of America
10 9 8 7 6 5 4 3 2 1

LIBRARY OF CONGRESS CATALOGING-IN-PUBLICATION DATA
The Best of the Arkansas traveler, 1956–1986.

1. Arkansas—Social life and customs.
2. Arkansas—Description and travel—1951–1980.
3. Arkansas—Description and travel—1981-   .
I. Deane, Ernie. II. Rice, Maylon T., 1955-   .
III. Arkansas gazette (Little Rock, Ark. : 1889)
IV. Title: Arkansas traveler, 1956–1986.
F415.B47   1986   917.67   86-70048
ISBN 0-87483-004-4

First Edition, 1986

Cover illustration and design by Carol Spencer Morris
Production artwork by Byron Taylor
Typography by Arrow Connection, Pollock Pines, CA
Design direction by Ted Parkhurst
Project direction by Liz Parkhurst

This book is printed on archival-quality paper which
meets the guidelines for performance and durability of
the Committee on Production Guidelines for Book
Longevity of the Council on Library Resources.

AUGUST HOUSE, INC. • PUBLISHERS • LITTLE ROCK

To the memory of
John David Rice
April 19, 1984

for his eleven hours on this earth
that changed my life

Acknowledgments

Special thanks are due to my wife, Donna, and daughters, Katie and Laura Jan, who have endured this project and my absences from home in working on it; to Alfred Thomas and the staff of the Arkansas Gazette library; to Susie Miles, the newspaper's Marketing Communications Manager; and to all the other Gazette employees who lent their support to this project.

M. T. R.

Contents

Foreword

Since 1956, the *Arkansas Gazette*, through the Arkansas Traveler column, has profiled our state in a unique fashion—with wit, personal anecdotes, travelogues and features involving the truly natural folk and state around us.

This book is designed to celebrate not only the 30th anniversary of the Arkansas Traveler column but the 150th anniversary of Arkansas's statehood. This book (and the Arkansas Traveler column) is neither a serious history nor a political commentary on our state; many other fine publications have served and will continue to serve those purposes. This book does, however, chronicle those events which are best left out of textbooks but which nonetheless have much to tell about the Arkansas character.

We at the *Gazette* are happy to contribute to a book which reflects, with charm and good humor, our readers' daily lives. No better reflection, we feel, can be found than in *The Best of the Arkansas Traveler: 1956–1986.*

Along with August House, Inc., we hope you will read and enjoy the discoveries of our four Arkansas Travelers as they have appeared in the *Gazette* over the last thirty years.

Hugh B. Patterson   Carrick Patterson
PUBLISHER   EDITOR

Introduction

Deane, Lancaster, Trimble and Allbright. Travelers all. Alike but different; very different.

Twenty inches, five days a week or so. A snap, a two-hour-a-day creampuff of a job. It all flows so well in the newspaper, that column, leaving the reader many times with a feeling of a personal relationship with the Arkansas Traveler column.

The words did flow from the Travelers, but many times seeing them at work was not unlike looking into the eyes of a grunt soldier going into battle for the first time.

Ernie Deane, a man of the military with self-confidence and somewhat of an appreciated Texas brashness, brought to the job an ability to be a good listener and to make himself at home anywhere. A not-so-kind copy editor once headlined one of Deane's articles: "Columnist Stands on River Bottom, Stays Dry."

Truth is, Deane wrote the column with more ease than any of his successors, and he would go anywhere, anytime to get a column. He was a familiar figure in the newsroom, checking the little parking meter reminder that told him how long he had to beat the ticket metermaid to his car on Louisiana Street.

Bob Lancaster, his nasal twang betraying roots deep in Arkansas, brought to the column thoughts of what is and what should be that sometimes tormented his soul.

But for Lancaster the column also brought personal torment. At times it was difficult to put in a column of space the message he wanted to impart. He honed each sentence, and his style revealed his deep feelings about the subjects on which he wrote.

Mike Trimble, as clever a mind, as accomplished a writer as any in grace in any newsroom anywhere. From hilarious happenings to poignant tales of life and death of man and beast, Trimble was a master. Organization, he would tell you, was not his forte. He knew well the blank-stare battle of copy paper and writer. His columns, however, never betrayed that secret battle.

Charles Allbright is a survivor. His prose flows, and his feeling for the people who reveal their lives to him is genuine and sincere. But he, too, knows the agony of hours of staring at blank paper and empty VDT screens.

The handwrenching, the fingers massaging the tired brow,

the frantic gum chewing when the cigarettes had been given up once again, and the nervous trip through the newsroom to the coffee machine. It was all in a day's work.

Allbright, as much as any Traveler, has left with the reader thoughts and messages that last long beyond the last word of the column.

William K. Rutherford
NEWS EDITOR

Ernie Deane

Ernie Deane, a native Arkansan who hails from the Red River Valley of the southwest portion of the state, became the first modern-day Arkansas Traveler in 1956. He had occupied the editorial writer's chair while *Gazette* editor Harry Ashmore was away hoping to extend Adlai Stevenson's run at a Presidential bid. When Ashmore returned to his desk, Deane was given an assignment.

"Get out. Cover the state. Tell us what is going on out there. And," Ashmore concluded, "write it in the first person."

And for the balance of ten years, Deane did so. And he did so more regularly than any other Traveler columnist to date.

His columns first appeared on the *Gazette*'s editorial page and were later moved to Page 1B during the week and the paper's Sunday *Magazine* on the weekend. Later still, the Sunday column appeared in the Editorial section.

Deane, in his own way, also started the "Arkansas Press" column that quotes weekly and daily newspapers across the state in a weekly sampling of editorial opinions. That feature now covers almost an entire page in the paper's Editorial section every Sunday.

After what he refers to as "a hop-skip-and-jump life as a journalist," Deane now lives in Fayetteville, having retired from teaching at the University of Arkansas there.

Moonshine Era Apparently Isn't Quite Over Yet

"Arkansas has 37 counties which are completely dry legally, but illegally you can buy a drink in any of them ... a gallon of moonshine whiskey can be bought for $10."—Associated Press report by Tom Dygard.

Well it sets a fellow to remembering—if he's old enough, and I am—the late Twenties and early Thirties.

That was when national prohibition was staggering along to its end. And the stagger as a style of locomotion was much in vogue among the upper as well as the lower crusts of society in that period.

The AP report does help to show that time brings changes in some things and none in others.

Somewhat the same situation seems to exist now as it did when the revenooers were hunting moonshiners along the creeks and chasing down bootleggers in the cities and towns. That is to say, white lightning is still being distilled, peddled, and consumed.

But that $10 a gallon figure is jolting.

"Good" likker in Arkansas could be bought for $4 to $5 a gallon in the last years of Prohibition.

"Good" likker, of course, was stuff that could be taken into the human innards with fair assurance that the innards wouldn't reject it forthwith.

It might leave a fellow with a head as big as a Hempstead County watermelon the next morning, but his lips wouldn't break out in blisters that afternoon.

The manufacture of this kind of hootch was a fine art of which there were numerous practitioners.

Down in my home country in Southwest Arkansas there was—and still is—a difference of opinion as to whether the Garland City or the Fouke area distilleries turned out the best stuff.

"Garland Pride," however, was the only Arkansas moonshine that I ever heard of that was nationally distributed under its own label.

"Bad" likker was something else, and it sold considerably cheaper than "good" likker.

It often was so fresh from the still that the feet of the man who plowed the corn could be smelled in it. At least, that's what folks used to say.

Moonshine of this kind had all sorts of nicknames, many of them unprintable even now when public sensibilities are not quite so easily shocked as they used to be.

There was "Squirrel Whiskey" for one. Three drinks of it made a man want to climb trees.

A woodland retreat in the Ozarks known as Bear Hollow, somewhere in the vicinity of Fayetteville, was notorious for the manufacture of this kind of booze.

It had a high content of tobacco juice, which didn't improve the flavor any but gave a bit of color.

All sorts of means were concocted to enable guzzlers to get it down.

There was the "nose dive" for one.

A shot glass filled with likker was lowered gently to the bottom of a water glass. Then orange juice or some other kind of chaser was poured around the shot glass and up to its rim.

The trick then was to lift the big glass to the lips and to tilt it carefully so that the chaser entered the mouth with the likker riding along on top of it. Thus the tummy got the first shock and everybody knows the stomach can take more punishment than the goozle.

Nose dives generally were employed only in the earlier stages of a bout with the bottle. After a few drinks nobody had enough co-ordination left to handle one of the things.

But whatever means people employed to get the stuff down it often wouldn't stay there. It generally stayed long enough, however, to get folks powerful drunk and that seemed to be the principal purpose of drinking in those days.

Moonshining and bootlegging quite often proved to be a mighty violent kind of a business.

Not only did those engaged directly in manufacturing and distribution ends of the game fight their own kind on occasion, but they fought the cops and the federals too.

Arkansas, so far as I ever knew, never had organized gangs of the type that ran things around Chicago but there was a certain degree of rivalry that broke into gunfire from time to time.

This was an era in which the makers of quart and half-gallon fruit jars had a gold mine, and so did those who made flat pints and hip flasks.

While the professionals pretty well took care of the moonshine likker making during Prohibition, there was a nation-wide "do it yourself" in the brewing and bottling of home-made beer.

The swapping of recipes was a common practice. There were serious debates over such questions as whether the addition of a raisin or a couple of grains of rice to each bottle would give greater "kick."

Many folks became quite adept at the art and were held in considerable esteem by neighbors and friends whose own products often blew up all over the basement.

"Home brew" was produced commercially too. Every community had one or more places where it could be procured—two bits a bottle, give or take a nickel.

Bathtub gin, which enjoyed great popularity up North and in the East, never caught on well in Arkansas. But it was a "do it yourself" product too, made from alcohol with a bit of juniper extract added.

An interesting era, Prohibition. And still with us, apparently, in places.

Wondering Who Said the South Will Rise Again

In traveling around to gather material for this space I often come across items which taken alone won't quite make enough "copy"—as we call it in the newspaper game—for a full article.

Call 'em jottings from a traveling reporter's notebook or whatever, here are some samples of what I mean:

Over the kitchen door in a Morrilton restaurant is a sign which reads, "Rest Rooms Strait Back."

Of course when you gotta go you don't care how good or bad the spelling may be.

Something that has puzzled me for years concerning such facilities, however, is how they ever came to be called "rest" rooms.

And another thing that sort of gets me occasionally is to see a sign, usually in front of a onetime magnificent mansion, "funeral home."

How come it's a "home"?

Certainly the principal character of the drama that takes place inside of it isn't going to stay there, and neither is anybody else if he can help it.

All my life I've heard the unpleasantness of the 1860s between the Union and the South referred to as the Civil War or the War Between the States.

I picked up a new one the other day while walking over some historic ground on the Memphis side of the Mississippi River.

A marker near the east end of the Memphis-Arkansas Bridge informs those who stop—and not many do—that Fort Pickering was established at the site in 1801 by Captain Zebulon M. Pike of the United States Army.

"Federal defenses were extensive here during the Confederate War," the sign also reports.

Well, boys, no matter what the right name of that War happens to be, "save your Confederate money, the South will rise again." (I wonder who first coined that rallying cry?)

This marker, by the way, is on a bluff overlooking the mighty Mississippi at a spot where Memphis folks like to think that DeSoto got his first look at the great River.

The last I heard, the momentous event took place farther downstream somewhere below the present locations of Helena, Arkansas, and Friars Point, Mississippi.

While standing on the bluff and letting my imagination run free I got to thinking of all the history that has been made thereabouts since Marquette and Joliet, the Frenchmen, passed by almost 300 years ago.

A tugboat was making its way up river. A jet fighter plane zipped by overhead. And a freight train and hundreds of autos and trucks roared across the nearby bridges.

Not a canoe or an Indian in sight, however, and no Frenchman either.

Over in Hot Springs on another trip I picked up a bit of information that is of no particular import unless you happen to be a race horse or a friend of one.

However life these days is too full of things of great import and to help balance them off slightly here's what I learned.

Steel shoes for race horses are made from a strip of metal seven inches long and one-half to three-sixteenths of an inch thick, and a dozen men are kept busy during the Hot Springs racing season fashioning such shoes and putting them on the horses.

Shoes of aluminum are also used but they're made in Maryland and California—out of Arkansas aluminum, let's hope. In fact more aluminum shoes are used at Oaklawn Park than steel ones.

Horseshoes come in sizes 3 through 7—no quadruple A's or such even for the most fastidious of fillies.

A set will last about 30 days under average conditions, less if there are rocky conditions around the stables and track.

Depending on a lot of things, including the way the horse is feeling at the time, it takes about 45 minutes' work to put a set of shoes on a thoroughbred—which gets his, or her, first set at 18 or 19 months of age.

Most men doing horseshoeing start with the animal's left front foot. From that point there's no exact route for getting around to the other three, some taking the left hind foot next and some the right front.

The big thing I'd presume is to avoid getting kicked.

For these tidbits of off-the-track data I'm indebted to H. A. Lloyd of Hot Springs, who learned blacksmithing at his dad's shop in Texas, and to R. L. Wadleigh of Cambridge, Kansas, who got into the game as a kid on a ranch on the prairies.

Neither had any suggestions on a sure thing in the seventh.

Worry Not That Chicago Paper Hits "Hillbillies"

A man thinking out about some things that have been troubling some fellow Arkansans recently:

Our migrant citizens now working for the Yankee dollar in the Chicago area needn't have been surprised when the *Chicago Tribune* turned on them as "hillbillies" who allegedly are damaging the culture and economy of that one-time home of Al Capone.

The *Tribune*—which modestly bills itself as "The World's Greatest Newspaper"—never has let the truth stand in the way of a campaign to attract reader interest.

I had some small experience with the "World's Greatest" during one unpleasant period of my military service overseas, catching a sideswipe from its bullwhip during a lashing it gave a general I was working for.

My advice to the ex-Arkansans whose pride has been wounded by the *Tribune's* words about "hillbillies" is this:

(1) Ignore it.

(2) Come on home to Arkansas where you'll be welcome, and appreciated.

There's a little moral for the rest of us in what the Chicago newspaper did, and how our folks in that vicinity reacted.

It's this: If we want to attract new people, new industries, and new money we ought not to make a practice of taking shots at "outsiders" in our midst.

Quite naturally those who are hit are pained by it, just the same as a good many decent and hard-working Arkansans in Chicago have been troubled by the *Tribune's* indignant words on "hillbillies."

This is not to say of course that Arkansas would welcome gangsters and the like, some of which Chicago has sent us as "tourists" and "health seekers" in times past.

That wasn't the Civil Defense Agency's air raid siren in North Little Rock you heard breaking the sound barrier the other day.

That was a wail from the Little Rock

Chamber of Commerce.

My friend Bill Shepherd's radar detection apparatus picked up some blips that looked suspiciously like the Industrial Committee of the Hot Springs Chamber of Commerce.

They seemed to be making a fast approach toward the headquarters of the burned out boat factory of Bowman Manufacturers, Inc.

Bill, whose talk normally follows the win-friends-and-influence-people line, let fly with a barrage that made some interesting reading even though it didn't seem to wing any of the invaders from Bathhouse Row.

Well you can't blame the Little Rock C of C president for jumping to the defense of the local economy, although I thought the Hot Springs people gave a pretty good explanation of their move.

They said they'd heard that the Bowman firm might re-locate in another state.

I've got a word or two for Little Rock's civic boosters—born and raised as I was in border counties and traveling much of the state as I do to earn my keep.

Rightly or otherwise, Little Rock has a reputation around the state for grabbing off everything that it can, whether some other Arkansas community wants and could use it or not.

Editor Al Rose of the Camden *Daily News* touched on this recently. He protested against the taxpayers of the state being touched for $700,000 to make improvements to the Coliseum at the state Livestock Show grounds.

Little Rock gets most of the benefits of what goes on at the Coliseum, Editor Rose held.

Could be that he's right. But whether he is or not, his comments are indicative of a considerable body of sentiment in the far reaches of the state.

At least some alumni of the University of Arkansas are watching with a suspicious eye Little Rock's efforts to expand its Junior College to a four-year school.

They see in this and in recurrent moves to split the University Medical School away from its parent institution, and in the creation of the Graduate Institute of Technology, a long-range plot to establish the state's No. 1 university in Little Rock.

Little Rock shouldn't be too greatly surprised if other communities in the state occasionally consider the capital city a fair target—and instead of spending time wailing about it, might well step up its efforts to create good will for the state's only metropolis.

The Day Comes When a Man Is Tired of Hokum

A man grousing just a bit over some of the irritants he encounters in this high-pressured modern world:

We're caught up in the numbers racket.

A cigarette company's hucksters assail the ear and eye with "20,000 filters" hokum.

A deodorant maker takes up a similar line.

His—or is it her?—perspiration neutralizer *swooshes* out of its bottle with *millions* more misty little bubbles of underarm sweetener than do "ordinary" brands.

The motorist—already badly baffled by conflicting claims of greater fuel power, has more mileage and such—wheels into the filling station to be confronted with a choice of not one, not two, but "three billiant gasolines."

Einstein died too soon.

He might have been able to make sense out of the barrage of mathematical mumbo-jumbo to which we lesser brains are being subjected these days.

It saddens me to stand by helplessly and watch a perfectly good word like "ordinary" worked to death in the frantic scramble for customer approval—and dollars—that's going on in the world of trade.

An "ordinary" product these days is one put to the vital test before the TV camera during that period of the program customarily presented as the time to receive "a message of importance from our sponsor."

"Our sponsor" can be expected to come through with something that makes the "ordinary" and otherwise unidentified lard or gasoline or hair set look rather inferior indeed.

Sometimes the pitch is made on a slightly different level.

This is when "other leading brands" take a beating, "our sponsor" being gentleman—or lady—enough to confess that there are others in the field above the "ordinary" class.

Lovers of the ordinary in this world, arise. We are being deluged with quality products and who among us knows for sure what is a quality product?

For want of anybody to discuss the passing scene with when I'm traveling around Arkansas, I turn on my car radio—a sensitive and chrome-trimmed gadget I didn't intend to buy with the car but the salesman threw it in extra to close the deal.

That's what he said he was doing and, boy, do I believe auto salesmen.

Anyhow, I get to wondering sometimes what sort of folks the radio people think the rest of us are.

Who among us really appreciates, for example, what is "electronic news"?

That's what the voices at the microphones tell us they're just about to give us from time to time.

I listen to it and danged if it sounds much different from what I'd read that morning in the *Gazette*.

Maybe we newspaper folks are dispensing "electronic news" too and just don't realize it.

Another mystery of major consequence which ought to be cleared up, in connection with radio "commercials," is this:

Just what are "low, low prices"?

I know what a "low price" is. That's what you pay for "ordinary" products and "other leading brands" items.

There's another trend which has every possibility of getting out of hand, the classifying of people as this or that, usually in a laudatory light.

We've had "All Something or Other" football teams for years, and also the Social Register and Who's Who in America.

Now we're swamped with an increasing number of Men of the Year, All-American Families, and the like.

And just recently I noticed that somebody has come out with a "Who's Who in Baton Twirling."

J. Edgar Hoover's "Ten Most Wanted Men" is just about the only list left that nobody wants to get on, although there's a possibility that some of the elite in bank robbing and safe-cracking circles might aspire to that.

ERNIE DEANE   17

An Orphan Doll And an Ozarks Woman's Hobby

'Tilda was a doll and somebody left her hanging in the fork of an apple tree in Michigan many a year ago.

You might not think that this would be much of a start to fame, but it was.

I heard the tale of 'Tilda while in Mountain Home recently, this from the lady who loved her during childhood and who now works to put little 'Tildas in the hands of doll collectors all across the nation.

The lady is Mrs. Neil Eatman, a housewife whose parlor is her workshop and whose skill of hand and artistry of eye have delighted little girls and big ones, too, for quite a long time.

She was a little girl herself when one of her cousins found the original 'Tilda hanging in the apple tree and made her a present of it. She brought the doll to Arkansas when her family moved south, then suffered a typical child's heartbreak when 'Tilda's porcelain head was smashed in the collapse of a barn roof on the doll house.

But through the years Mrs. Eatman designed and made doll dresses for lots of little girls and developed a technique which now is recognized as exceptional.

The original 'Tilda was about 20 inches tall and was dressed in the style of the early 1890s, pantaloons and bonnet included.

Mrs. Eatman never forgot her face nor the way she was attired.

Then, just a few years ago, she spotted a miniature 'Tilda, only three or four inches tall but with the same hand-painted porcelain features.

It was German-made, and, as she learned later, was of pre-World War II manufacture and one of a small supply which had been stored away for protection against the bombs of that War.

Mrs. Eatman happily dressed her new 'Tilda in calico and put her in a place of honor in the parlor of her tree-shaded white frame home.

Mrs. Tom Lyle at the time was operating a gift shop in Mountain Home and suggested that Mrs. Eatman dress more tiny 'Tildas and put them up for sale in the shop.

Mrs. Eatman obtained only twelve of the German imports at first but they quickly sold. The next time she bought and dressed a hundred and Mrs. Lyle took some of them to Marshall Field's in Chicago where they were just as quickly bought.

And that's when the national travels of the modern 'Tildas started. Mrs. Eatman knows that they're now considered collector's items in at least 25 states, that some are on display in doll museums, and that one sits on a marble mantle in an old mansion in the nation's capital.

Mrs. Eatman suffered a broken hip not so long ago. While this has handicapped her somewhat in getting around it hasn't dampened her enthusiasm for her hobby which has become a commercial enterprise.

However, as she told me, she only creates dress designs and does the minute and intricate handwork when she "feels like it."

A day's labor goes into each tiny costume—sleeves three-quarters of an inch in length, petticoats one and five-eighths inches long.

She started out, she said, asking two dollars each for the fully-dressed dolls, having paid one dollar for their heads and bodies. Orders piled up so rapidly she decided to raise the price to five dollars each, thinking to reduce the demand.

"But five-dollar bills and checks came right on," she told me with a smile.

Mrs. Eatman's principal concern—other than that of trying to meet the orders for her handiwork—is that the supply of heads and bodies won't last.

The ones she has been using were made at a place she doesn't know. She has been told that German housewives painted the little faces in their spare time for a manufacturer. She doesn't know if they're made now, and of such excellent quality.

Mrs. Eatman's work is attracting the interest of various publications as well as doll collectors.

Bonnie Lela Crump's article on her 'Tildas was given national distribution in

Spinning Wheel, a magazine of antiques which appears monthly. *Doll Talk* magazine has also told its readers about them.

Mrs. Eatman, of course, is not the only artist at work in the doll field in the mountains of Arkansas.

Author Crump, who lives and writes in Eureka Springs, published a booklet earlier this year entitled "Dolls of Ozarkland" in which she gave accounts of several doll-making enterprises, as well as some touching personal accounts by a number of women concerning favorite dolls of their childhoods.

Mrs. Crump's booklet tells of dolls with heads made from apples and from nuts, from corn cobs and from wood.

The "Ozarkland" collection of facts also lists three doll collections in that region which attract many visitors: At Zoe Harp's Native Doll Shop and the Bracken Museum, both in Eureka Springs, and the third at Katie's Doll House in Fayetteville.

The Bracken Museum, incidentally, contains a dozen of Mrs. Eatman's 'Tildas.

"Arkansas is noted for her 'character dolls'," Mrs. Crump wrote, "[and] these are selling all over America and well they should be for they are works of art."

The Oldtimers Had Hog, Also Hominy Aplenty

If I hadn't made a trip over to Helena I probably never would have learned that at least some Arkansans didn't lack for hog and hominy back in the winter of 1871.

My journey to the banks of the Mississippi wasn't made for the purpose of checking into the state agricultural situation of 86 years ago. I just picked up this little detail accidentally.

I was hiding from the East Arkansas heat at the time, sitting around the air-conditioned office of the *Helena–West Helena World* and gabbing with C. M. Young, veteran publisher of that newspaper, and his sons Jack and Porter.

He showed me some photostats of the original edition of the *World*, first published on December 5, 1871.

The front page fare was a trifle dull that day—consisting principally of a lengthy synopsis of the War Department's annual report. So I turned to the inside and came across an account of the White River Conference of the Methodist Church which had been held at Batesville.

I'm not much of a hand to get excited over church conference reports but this one was different.

The bishop, a gentleman identified only by the name McTyerle, evidently had traveled over a good bit of Arkansas to get to Batesville.

The article didn't say whence he came nor where he went, but indicated that he had been to Little Rock and points between there and Batesville.

The good brother's eye took in quite a few details along the way.

The *World*'s summary of the gathering quoted part of a letter the bishop wrote, and I found his observations rather interesting.

"Arkansas," he said, "has been more traveled over and preached over episcopally than any other state embraced within our connection, Tennessee not excepted."

Maybe Arkansas needed more preaching over than Tennessee in those days.

Bishop McTyerle also wrote that the character of the Arkansas people had been "misconceived and misrepresented."

"Instead of violence," he reported, "and brawls and pistols and 'tooth-picks' I have everywhere found a quiet, industrious, intelligent population, much given to church going and to hospitality."

That's certainly a welcome description, considering the reputation which Arkansas has had at some periods in our past.

As for that complimentary note on hospitality, I'd guess it resulted from the work of Arkansas wimmen folks making sure the bishop's plate was heaped with fried chicken at every stop.

Mr. McTyerle noticed that there was a

plentitude of hog and hominy, and also of mast.

This latter, for the information of the uninformed, is a word meaning nuts of various kinds, but whether he meant mast for people or for those hogs isn't clear.

The question of how to pronounce "Arkansas" must have been a matter of some importance in those times.

The bishop's letter took up this, too.

"Refined men and women" of Arkansas, he said, pronounced the name "Arkansaw."

There've been occasions in my life when I wished the spelling was that way also.

Well, so much for the bishop, a man with a good eye for details and a way with words.

I get to wondering sometimes as I travel through the state just how the oldtimers might react if they could see Arkansas today.

So many things they knew intimately as a part of their daily lives have disappeared, so many others of which they never dreamed are now commonplace.

At least the pronunciation of Arkansas has stuck, and there's still hog and hominy to be had in the land.

The original *Helena World*, I found while looking through it, was published by William S. Burnett and Company.

Its editorial department was declared to be "under the management of the Democratic Conservative Committees in Phillips County."

The Democratic Conservative Party platform was given and included these points:

The Party "stands before the country the advocate and protector of civil and religious liberty.

"The teachings of the [Civil] War have not been lost upon [the Party].

"We recognize the Constitution of the United States as the supreme law of the land. . . . We deny the right of any state or body of citizens to nullify the law passed by constituted authorities."

Taxes should "be reduced to the lowest possible rate."

As I read these, I thought to myself that in some respects things don't change much with the years after all.

Others do, certainly.

A *World* advertiser offered shoes for ladies at a dollar a pair and boots for men at $2.75. Five thousand boxes of "gent's" paper collars were on sale at five cents a box.

And the War Department's report mentioned previously showed that Uncle Sam had made beef purchases for the Army in 41 states and territories, the average price in Texas being 4½ cents a pound and in Delaware 16 cents.

No price given on hog and hominy.

Boys Are Boys In Arkansas And All Is Well

Anybody looking for evidence that the world isn't going to pieces after all? Then take heart, folks. There is reason to believe that here in the happy land of Arkansas boys continue to be boys. And so long as that condition prevails there's hope for mankind.

This thought is based on happenings at Pine Bluff, as reported by Jack Bradley in his front page column, "On the City Hall Beat," in the *Commercial*. Let's let Mr. Bradley tell it:

Recently the last of the swimmers climbed out of the water at the Oakland Park swimming pool and claimed their wire baskets of clothes at the window. There was one basket of clothes left over, and pool attendants quickly checked the premises. There were a little boy's clothes in the basket, but no little boy.

Startled pool officials did the logical thing—they drained the pool hoping that they wouldn't find a body. They didn't, but 350,000 gallons of water had gone down the drain.

The following morning, a little boy who had gone home in his bathing suit the night before, showed up in search of his clothes.

Another day about two weeks ago, a mother bought dressing room tickets for herself and for her little boy. She went to the right to the women's dressing room and he went to the left to the men's dressing room.

When the mother arrived at the pool in her swim suit, she couldn't spot her little boy about the pool so she had an attendant to go in the men's side to fetch him. There was no little boy in the men's side.

The mother became frantic. They searched the premises quickly, and said they could not find the little boy. Everybody turned to and they started draining the pool. But before all of the 350,000 gallons of water was gone, the little boy showed up—outside the fence.

It seems that he was more anxious to see the fun at the rides concession in another section of the park than to go swimming. He had waited until his mother had time to go into the women's dressing room and then turned on his heel and headed for the rides.

The swimming pool acquired a big water bill from the two incidents, and two little boys acquired red bottoms.

Well, if we're to believe statistics, the loss of the water is a minor thing because Pine Bluff has a whopping supply of the stuff that makes the grass grow green and cities prosper. But we do hope that Mr. Bradley's report that the lads "acquired red bottoms" isn't entirely correct because it's not everybody who can drain a swimming pool without so much as touching a faucet.

Not only in Pine Bluff are youngsters confusing the grownups. The "Round the Town" column of the *Advance Monticellonian* at Monticello tells of experiences that local families are having with children away at summer camps. Here's a typical case:

A little girl who abbreviates quite liberally in her letters home said, "Send me my TR." The father said that was an easy one. It was tennis racket.

It was the one they had to decipher last year that all but bested them. The little girl wrote: "Send me a SP and a bottle of DCSP." The family worked on the riddle for hours. Finally, the father worked it out to be a "Spoon and a bottle of Dr. Caldwell's Syrup of Pepsin." That was right.

You'll note that the father appears to be the one who deciphered the TR message. That's not surprising for man through the ages has had to condition himself to dealing with the non-specifics of woman-talk. All due credit to the male of the species, he has done rather well at developing a sort of mind-reading ability to fathom the depths of female thought—not nearly so well as the ladies have done in developing their "sixth sense" but sufficient to get by on much of the time.

The Monticello father ought to find some joy in the fact that the message didn't say: "Send MM." In short, more money.

ERNIE DEANE   *21*

About People, Places and A Thirsty Turtle

An excellent spot from which to look down on a sea of growing corn: the long bridge across the valley and the White River, approaching Batesville from the south.

Enjoyed an extended conversation with Mrs. Josephine Jones, publisher, and Paul Buchanan, editor, of the *Batesville Daily Guard*.

Mrs. Jones is one of the few wimmen folks in Arkansas I know who's publishing both a daily and a weekly newspaper.

Editor Buchanan turns up more human interest stories—and tall tales—about folks in his area than you'll find in many papers in the state.

He urged me to go out in the country a few miles and check on a tame terrapin there which makes regular trips to a cross-roads store for water and soda crackers.

The terrapin's hours are badly irregular, however, and there's never any knowing when he'll report in for chow.

I was in too big a hurry to sit around and wait for anything as slow as an Ozarks terrapin—and besides, Paul said the danged thing is unfriendly to everybody except the storekeeper.

Stray cattle notes:

On this trip of more than 420 miles I saw only one bunch of livestock wandering along a public highway and creating a traffic hazard.

This was near St. James in Stone County, on State Highway 14, about a dozen better-than-average whiteface beef animals. Something for the county sheriff and the state Highway Patrol to look into.

How to mar the beauty of a scenic stretch of Ozarks highway: let a town dump keep on growing alongside of it.

That's what's being done just north of Hardy on U.S. 63, right about where Sharp and Fulton Counties join.

The Mammoth Spring-Hardy drive, 16 miles or so, is a truly attractive one which brings a lot of out-of-state visitors into Arkansas.

Seems to me the good folks of the tourist-conscious towns of Hardy would get rid of that public eyesore pronto—a terrible advertisement for their community and our state.

Bargains do exist even though we are living in a period of 10-cent coffee and over-priced hamburgers.

I spent a comfortable night in a tourist court at Salem for $2.50 plus state tax. Usual price I've found around Arkansas for similar accommodations: four bucks, often more.

Then at Mammoth Spring I saw a "gas war" on, making prices even better than they usually are—and they're usually cheaper than regular Arkansas prices because border country station operators meet the lower Missouri figures.

"Ethyl" gas was 26.4 cents a gallon, "regular" was 22.9 cents.

Hardy is a picturesque town of about 600 people, with the Spring River—created by Mammoth Spring—flowing alongside it.

The local newspaper publisher is Ben Daulton of the *Sharp County Independent*. He's past 70 and true to the name of his paper he's sharp and independent, too.

Publisher Daulton gets up at 4 a.m. every day of the week and walks all over town, up hills and down, delivering the *Gazette*.

Mrs. Daulton, a gentle-voiced lady whose diploma from a famous French University helps adorn the *Independent*'s front office wall, is *Gazette* correspondent. Their newspaper plant is one of the cleanest in Arkansas, by the way.

Mr. Daulton learned the printer's trade from his father in the 1890s. His father was Francis M. Daulton who numbered Mark Twain among his friends and who published the *Greene County Events* at Old Gainesville back in 1883.

In the *Independent* plant he showed me a printing press—still in useable condition—which was manufactured about 80 years ago in Cincinnati. Its trade name was "Nonpareil" and it has surely lived up to the name.

Dress Factory In West Helena Opened A Door

If Victor A. Juengel Sr. of Helena ever asks me to write a rhyming commercial for his business I'm going to borrow a bit of verse which appeared in *Harper's Weekly* a hundred years ago:

> *Dresses for breakfast and dinners and balls;*
> *Dresses to sit in, and stand in, and walk in;*
> *Dresses to dance in, and flirt in, and talk in;*
> *Dresses in which to do nothing at all;*
> *Dresses for Winter, Spring, Summer, and Fall.*

Mr. Juengel (pronounced jingle) and his son, Vic Jr., are a pair of pleasant and enterprising gentlemen who head the Helena Garment Company, one of several divisions of a Cleveland corporation which manufactures and markets Bobbie Brooks dresses.

Their plant in West Helena keeps some 500 employees—mostly women—busy making about 300 dozen dresses a day. And they're talking of further expansions which eventually will require a working force of 750 people.

The plant, with its weekly payroll of around $26,000, is an important one in the improving industrial picture of Phillips County, and this in more ways than one.

The injection of that much payroll cash into the local economy naturally has welcome effects.

But there's another aspect of the Helena Garment Company story which has broader significance in the sustained effort which the twin cities of this longtime agricultural area are making to get a sounder balance between farming and manufacturing.

Harry J. McCarty, a hardware and appliance merchant who is head of the Helena–West Helena Industrial Development Corporation, pointed it out to me.

First, he said, the community has obtained "a wealth of experience" in dealing with the problems of industrial progress.

And then, he added, the success of the plant operation itself has given the Corporation an excellent talking point when going out to sell the area's advantages to other manufacturers.

Mr. McCarty also said that the Juengels themselves are first class boosters for their adopted home community.

Whatever it is that Helena–West Helena are doing to get industry, the effort is paying off—three new plants brought into operation since the dress factory and a fourth one recently announced.

Back in 1951 the community was hurting for enterprises which would provide jobs. An industrial development group was incorporated to try to do something about the need.

Arkansas at that time didn't have the present state Industrial Development Commission nor laws enabling local organizations to obtain financial backing through the state.

It took six months, Mr. McCarty told me, to raise $50,000 with which to purchase land and a former plant building—converted to county fair use—to bring in the Bobbie Brooks firm.

Since getting into production on a small scale late in the fall of '51, the Helena Garment Company has made several substantial enlargements and improvements to its facilities.

Mr. Juengel informed me that the present plant, with equipment, represents an investment of approximately $700,000. He said proudly that—based on what he knows about the garment manufacturing business after a lifetime in it—he believes the factory is "one of the most modern in the nation."

I asked him how he and the firm he represents happened to choose an Arkansas location.

He replied that he had known about the favorable experience of other manufacturers in the state and this set him to thinking about Arkansas. The Helena–West Helena area proved to have an available building and the community was willing to put its money where its mouth was, so to speak, to make arrangements for the dress factory.

Vic Juengel Jr. took me all through the plant and explained step by step the rather complicated process during which cloth, buttons, zippers, and such become a dress.

Fifty different styles of dresses are manufactured and the styles are changed five times a year, he said. Right now clothing for fall is being produced, but the plant is busiest when making clothing for the spring and summer markets.

Some innovations in streamlining the operation have caught the attention of other manufacturers and they drop in from time to time to see how things are done here, he told me.

One of these is a conveyor system, using an endless rubber belt which passes along overhead framework, to move materials from one working area to another and finally to the storage room to await shipment.

Oil and grease are a curse in the garment industry, he explained, and the great improvement achieved in this particular machinery is that it works without lubrication.

The Juengels are enthusiastic over the progress of their company in Helena–West Helena, and, as Vic Sr. expressed it, much credit is due their employees—practically all of whom come from East Arkansas.

Another pleasing thing about the operation: most of the cloth used in the plant is cotton, and much of this is Arkansas-grown.

Jake's Tongue Was Unhitched By Will Rogers

To suggest other reading material—except what's in the *Gazette*—is not even one of my minor purposes in filling this space each day but for once an exception seems in order.

Especially is this recommendation—of "How Will Rogers Changed My Life," on Page 143 of the August issue of the *Reader's Digest*—directed to parents of handicapped children or to children themselves if they are old enough to understand.

The article runs only about 500 words in length. It was written by J. Q. Mahaffey, editor of the *Texarkana Gazette*, and it should prove interesting to almost everybody.

"Jake" Mahaffey tells how the noted cowboy humorist, actor and all-around American encouraged him to overcome a problem of stammering which he says was so bad he could hardly talk. The incident happened in Texarkana in the early '30s when Mr. Mahaffey was a cub reporter and Will Rogers was one of the most famous and best-loved men of the day.

I knew Jake Mahaffey then, for we were boys together in the Texarkana of the '20s, and what an exciting town it was. I can't remember anybody figuring at that time that Jake could ever untie the hitch in his tongue sufficiently to become a first class newspaper reporter, much less an excellent editor. He did it though, and in his touching and inspiring report in the *Digest* he relates how Will Rogers helped him over the speech hurdle when such help was what he needed.

(In brief, Will told him that people worth meeting wouldn't pay any attention to the stammer and that Jake wouldn't miss anything by not talking to the other kind.)

Texarkana is an unusual city. In fact it is two unusual cities, for the Arkansas-Texas state line runs smack north and south, and that makes for all sorts of complications. Two city governments, for one thing. Two sets of local, county and state laws for another. And the Texas side of town has the most folks, some of whom will recite for you the hoary legend that long ago on the corner of Broad Street and State Line Avenue stood a sign that read, "Entering Texas."

(The legend, Texas version, is that all the pioneers who could read went on west to settle the Land of the Big Rich and those who couldn't read stayed behind and settled Arkansas. A colossal lie, of course, but a favorite among the descendants of Sam Houston and Jim Bowie.)

I mention the uniqueness of Texarkana, Ark-Texas, as Uncle Sam's post office designates it, to indicate that news-papering there can be complicated enough for a man with unhampered speech. Jake Mahaffey took on the complications, stammer and all, and has made a name for himself among newspapermen while serving his community well.

Incidentally, Mr. Mahaffey is not only an editor and civic leader but has become a public speaker of note in more recent years. I heard him down in Texas a year or two ago at a newspapermen's gathering, laying 'em in the aisles with tales of typographical boners that drive editors crazy.

I thought at the time that Jake had climbed a long and difficult grade but I didn't know until I read his story about Will Rogers just how and when he got the inspiration to do it. Read the article and get the full flavor of his case first hand. It's a pity that the great Oklahoman—part Indian, he was—isn't around to read it too.

Editors Mourn As the Circus Folds Its Tents

It's easy to "travel" around Arkansas without ever leaving home. Just read a couple of dozen, or more, weekly and daily newspapers regularly and you'll get most of the news that's fit to print and some that isn't. And you'll also get a pretty fair cross-section of Arkansas editorial thinking.

That's what I've been doing for some time in preparing the weekly "Arkansas Press" roundup on this page. Now this column will contain the roundup, usually on Fridays.

Numerous Arkansas newspaper people wept into their typewriters (and rightfully so) when word came that the Ringling Brothers, Barnum & Bailey Circus was folding.

Members of our craft—or call it profession if you wish to compliment us—nearly always were favored with the gift of a ticket or two by the circus advance man. And the same as folks who had to pay their way, members of the press found enjoyment in the performers, sights, sounds and smells that made the circus what it was.

Louis Graves of the *Nashville News* recalled, among many other circus wonders, the calliope:

It was the Pied Piper's horn and he who did not respond was hopelessly tangled in the tedium of daily living, blind to the rainbow hues and deaf to the mystic sounds of a world that came only once a year after the cotton crop had piled its money in the area.

Well, Louis, our generation (and many before it) had the calliope and the present one has the juke box and that fellow Presley. I'll take the calliope. (History note: the instrument was named for the muse Calliope—pronounced with a long "i"— who presided over eloquence and heroic poetry.)

John R. Newman of the *Harrison Times* observed that not only the circus but the opera is fading and added that seldom did either enter the smaller towns. Most of us folks of small town origin will take the circus, anytime.

The *Osceola Times*, of which Sam Hodges is publisher, is "trying to be philosophical" about the current rock-and-roll music craze and recalls a bit of history:

Every generation seems to have its own way of expressing revolt against the established order of things. Going back not too far, we can remember "Mairzy Doats." In the 1930s every youth thought "Three Little Fishes" was the ultimate in music. And, somewhat farther back, we never did understand what they meant when saxaphones wailed just as objectionably as they do now and a trio sang "Jada."

And Sam, how about "Barney Google" and "Yes, We Have No Bananas"?

Editorial doings from all over the place:

Dorothy Stuck of the *Marked Tree Tribune* reports that husband Howard is recuperating excellently from the broken leg he suffered while chasing a news item.

The *Lincoln Ledger* of Star City says with sound reasoning that a community "will grow more if we grow toward a goal and we will grow better if we grow with a plan."

Woody Woodliff in the *Trumann Democrat* was surprised at the speed with which readers snapped up his offer to give away five puppies. (Dear Woody: It's good to know that there's at least one newspaperman who can still suffer surprise at public response to a "free dog" offer.)

The *Batesville Guard* opines: "Gall is divided into three parts—Republican, Democratic and Southern Democratic." (Well put.)

The "Casual Chat" editor (unidentified) of the *Wynne Progress* made an empty beer can count on highways in "dry" and "wet" counties and came to the conclusion that "people in 'wet' counties can throw a beer can farther than people in 'dry' counties."

The *Crossett Observer*, the *Marked Tree Tribune* and the *Eagle-Democrat* of Warren are campaigning for improved traffic law enforcement. (Power to you all.)

State's People Disturbed By Bad Publicity

Many Arkansans are disturbed by the adverse treatment our state is getting in much of the nation's press in connection with the Little Rock school mess.

We have reason to be distressed.

Bad publicity is costly.

Arkansas has been in serious need of friendly and understanding notice in newspapers and magazines of the country for generations. The same with respect to radio, and in more recent times, television.

Thanks to a number of things, we had been getting some pretty favorable attention—"a good press" as it's called—over the past few years.

Improved highways helped to obtain this.

So did the spending of a considerable amount of taxpayer's money in an agressive publicity and advertising campaign.

Improved recreational facilities—including state-owned parks—and accommodations for travelers contributed their share.

No less important—and perhaps most important—was the up-by-our-bootstraps struggle to achieve a sounder economy for Arkansas's people through industrial development.

And nobody attempting to analyze the trend toward better national appreciation of Arkansas can discount the tremendous asset which Winthrop Rockefeller's personal participation in this state's effort has been.

Now—only temporarily let us hope—the publicity which Arkansas is getting nationally is anything but good.

Arkansans can blame this on out-of-state editors and reporters, or the ill-advised actions of our governor, or to a dozen other factors, just depending on personal viewpoint.

But whatever the underlying causes, or the events which touched off a wave of criticism against Arkansas, there's nothing to be gained by arguing this particular aspect of the matter.

And certainly there's nothing to be gained by cussing and shoving visiting representatives of the press, radio, and TV.

Neither is there anything to be gained by any display by Arkansans of a persecution complex—that we're just getting picked on by a bunch of Yankees and other people who don't like us.

It's over what to do for the long pull, during which Arkansas must continue to try to move ahead economically, educationally, and otherwise, that Arkansans generally must concern ourselves.

How costly the present bad publicity is going to be in the loss of tourist business, in new industries, in home seekers, in national political influence, and in other ways can't be accurately predicted.

But make no mistake, there are going to be some losses. The lower Arkansans can keep these the better for every citizen, and the sooner a move is made to reverse the present trend of unfavorable publicity the lower the costs will be.

The first big opportunity Arkansas will have to make such a move will come within the next few days.

Into Hot Springs from points throughout America will come men and women members of the National Association of Travel Organizations.

Several hundred of them who have great influence where it counts among millions of tourists and recreation seekers will be on hand, many making their first visit to our state.

With them will be travel editors and reporters from quite a few of the principal newspapers and magazines of the country.

An excellent program of entertainment and information has been arranged for them.

Governor Faubus is listed as one of the principal speakers. If he appears he will have a ready-made audience before which to dispel the highly unfortunate impression he gave TV viewers nationally recently, that Arkansas people aren't friendly to strangers. This is the least the governor can seek to do.

The chairman of the state Publicity and Parks Commission is on the program. So is the president of the Arkansas State Chamber of Commerce. And so is C. Hamilton Moses who in his time has traveled many thousands of miles across this country to spread good words about Arkansas.

By means of their expressions, and by a display of real Arkansas hospitality and good will, perhaps some success can be achieved toward diminishing the damage which Arkansas's reputation has suffered recently.

ERNIE DEANE   27

The Big Story And the Voice Of Our People

In this past month, during which too many Arkansans have been on an emotional jag and so much unfortunate history has been made, I've continued traveling in quest of the type of material this column customarily carries.

But while I've not been out "on the story," as we say in the newspaper game, there's been no avoiding running into the biggest one in many a year in Arkansas—the Little Rock mess.

Talk about it has been—and still is—everywhere.

There's no escaping hearing the people of my native Arkansas having their say.

There's no direction in which to look without seeing puzzlement, dismay, and anger too.

When it's all done—as surely it will be—and we all give ourselves time to think about what has happened and what must be done down the long road ahead, there'll be things to remember and things to forget.

Which of my own memories of this turbulent month will remain and which will fade—as so many others have stayed or gone away—I don't know.

It's not given to a man to pick what he'll remember any more than it's given to him to select his parents.

But at the moment, on what I hope will be a quiet autumn Sabbath, there are some things fresh on my mind after journeys of the past four weeks.

These trips have taken me to the Mississippi River in east Arkansas, almost to the Louisiana line in south Arkansas, close to Missouri in north Arkansas, almost to the Texas border in southwest Arkansas.

Old friends' voices, strangers' voices, irate voices, worried voices, I've heard them all, and more besides.

Questions, answers, arguments, misinformation, bad logic, and insults, too—all shaped as they inevitably must be by a man's raising, his present environment, the pressures of business, a thousand other influences.

There was my long-time friend whose talk is so Southern you hear Confederate bugles when he speaks.

And he said something along this line: "My old grandpappy would turn over in his grave if he heard me, but the South over the years hasn't given the Negro a fair shake."

There was the east Arkansas legislator who told me that in his section, judging by the sentiment of the people, there just isn't going to be any integration anytime.

There was the mother in north Arkansas, in an area almost devoid of colored people, who expressed genuine concern that there will be inter-marriage of the races if their children grow up together in public schools.

The editor of a small town newspaper in east Arkansas told of pressure from planters—so far resisted—to support the governor's actions. Can't seriously support President Eisenhower's action, either, "so what does this make me, a Whig?"

There was the man in the know in Little Rock business affairs who told of economic retaliation from out-of-state firms, threats to quit buying Arkansas products.

There was the loaded question behind which some Southerners take refuge when there's nothing else left to take refuge behind: "You wouldn't want your daughter to marry a nigger, would you?"

And the usual answer: "No, and I wouldn't want her to marry po' white trash, either."

And neither the question nor the answer seems to solve anything whatever, leaving tempers frayed just a bit more than they already were.

There's the suggestion that folks on both sides "are going to have to give just a little" to work things out. And this seems to make at least a little more sense than some other proposals.

Out of it all the people of Arkansas can perhaps learn a lesson or two—expensive though these will be—and apply what we've learned in working for a better tomorrow for our state.

First, to get to the business quickly of binding up the wounds we've inflicted upon ourselves, Arkansan against Arkansan.

And then, to go out through the nation—which had been watching us with favorable interest until recent weeks—and renew our very worthy effort to sell Arkansas and its attractions and resources to the people of America.

The Lord helping us, we can't afford to do otherwise.

Fish Net Hoops And the Story Of Slim Collins

Cabot—If Editor Cone Magie of the *Cabot Herald* hadn't taken me to see "Slim" Collins and his fish net hoop factory I'd never have learned about Slim or his factory either.

And unless Slim had showed me a froe I reckon I'd have gone plumb through life without ever knowing what one of the things is.

But either way, the O. E. Collins Net Hoop factory and the froes, draw knives and hammers used in it play an important part in the nation's commercial fishing business.

And in case you've overlooked—as I had—the importance of commercial fishing, take the word of the state Game and Fish Commission in Little Rock that in Arkansas alone there are some 4,000 commercial fishermen. (They're individuals who are licensed to catch and to sell such finny critters as catfish, drum, buffalo and carp.)

How many commercial fishermen there are in the U.S.A. is a question on which I'd never win even a little TV payoff but Slim Collins sells hoops for their nets at points all over the country. And he sells more in Maryland, Tennessee and Louisiana than in most other states. In our own state fishermen use Collins hoops on the Arkansas, White, Red and Little Red Rivers.

You might not believe that this is a factory of national reputation just from looking at the ramshackle corrugated tin building and shed in which it is housed. But Mr. Collins—that's Slim—has the look of Abe Lincoln about him and he isn't a fisherman so I'm content to accept his tale the way he tells it.

And this is the way he tells it:

Back in the Depression days of 1934 he quit the carpentering trade which was bringing him about 75 cents a day income and went to work in the fish net hoop plant in Cabot for 12½ cents an hour. Work days were 10 hours long and that 50 cents additional income was good for groceries he'd been doing without.

The factory had been opened in 1913 by I. J. Martin to meet a demand of commercial fishermen for strong oak hoops to which their nets could be attached. B. G. Byrd gave Slim a job splitting white oak logs just brought in from the nearby forests.

Slim was 20 at the time and he learned to use a froe to split the tough, green oak rails into smaller strips. And for the benefit of those folks who until now didn't know any more about a froe than I previously did, let me explain: It is a cleaving tool with a flat steel head about eight inches long and two inches wide that is attached at a right angle to a stout wooden handle about half as long as a baseball bat. In days gone by stave and shingle makers used this tool and probably still do for all I know.

Then he learned to use a draw knife to trim the oak strips to proper thickness for eventual bending into hoops. (It takes strength in the arms, a steady hand and a good eye to follow the grain exactly with a sharp draw knife). And he learned how to steam the strips and bend them into a loop and nail the ends together with just the exact amount of overlap. (Some of the hoops are made from strips 11 feet long.)

Everything in the plant was done by hand then and it is today. Can't mechanize, says Slim, because a machine can't follow that grain and if you cut across the grain the hoops will break under the weight of fish and the pull of moving water.

He bought out Byrd in 1948 and has

operated the factory since. In the months of rush business, usually January to June, he employs up to 20 men. Six were at work when I visited the plant.

He spends about $11,000 on white oak logs brought in from an area bounded roughly by De Vall's Bluff, Conway, Searcy and Benton and the annual payroll of the plant is around $15,000. So the operation is no small factor in this small town.

Slim Collins, as his nickname implies, is a tall, lank man. He is the father of three children and, so he told me, happy with his hoop factory and glad he quit that six bits a day carpentering to pick up a froe.

And just before I left him he gave an indication of his way of overcoming trouble. One of his employees was cussing the knots in an especially tough piece of oak. "Go eat yourself some lunch," advised Slim, "and when you get back they'll probably all be gone."

Pogonotrophy: It's Sweeping Phillips County

Helena—At least one practitioner of pogonotrophy in this historic Mississippi River community has suffered a singed upper lip for the sake of his art and many of his fellow "Brothers of the Brush" are smoking with greater caution these days.

Lest anyone be completely confused by this report on doings in the Delta, let me explain that pogonotrophy is a legal, moral activity whose name is derived from Greek words meaning "beard" and "nourishment." In short, pogonotrophy is beard-growing.

There is a mass movement of it underway among male residents of Helena, West Helena and Phillips County these days in preparation for the celebration to be held August 17–22 marking Helena's 100 years as an incorporated city.

Some 1,300 "Brothers of the Brush" are led by Jack Young, of the *Helena World* publishing family, and they are the pogonotrophers. Local talk has it that the Brother who scorched his lip forgot himself for a moment, let his cigaret burn down too short and set his mustache afire.

There's a great deal more to the Centennial observance than the mere cultivation of an impressive face full of whiskers, for the people of Phillips County have a long and proud history that they intend to recall. Excellent crop prospects this year, in addition to continued industrial development, give added incentive for a "come all" week that will include five evening presentations of a historic pageant, with a cast of 500, tours of pre-Civil War homes and wartime battle sites, and all special welcoming activities for former residents who are expected to return home from points throughout the nation.

Fifty committees are at work preparing Centennial events. The general chairman is Porter C. Young, a newspaperman, assisted by these steering committee members: Harry McCarty, a furniture dealer, vice chairman; Mrs. Ruth Clopton, a printing firm owner, secretary; and Harlan Ross, a banker, treasurer. Some 500 enthusiastic men and women are members of the various committees.

The known history of Helena and vicinity goes back to the 16th century when two Indian tribes, the Pacha and Casqui, were living hereabouts. Hernando de Soto and his band of Spaniards are generally believed to have visited the tribes in 1541. (Of course there are many towns in Arkansas that say de Soto came their way but Helena's "brag" sounds more authentic than most.) In the next century the French were around and in 1763 Father Marquette and Joliet came by.

The first white settlers included William Patterson, who in 1800 built a rude warehouse for storage of goods and provisions. (Some people define "goods" as food and clothing and "provisions" as gunpowder and likker, but every man to his own definition.)

The steamer *New Orleans* made her first call in 1811 and Helena, which later became "Arkansas's Only Seaport" by Chamber of Commerce decree, grew into quite a river town. Also in the year 1811 the New Madrid earthquake changed the topography of the county—named Phillips in honor of a pioneer settler—and helped form what are now called Old Town Lake and Long Lake.

Helena got its name from a daughter of Mr. Phillips. The town furnished seven generals to the Confederacy and was the site of some bloody fighting when Southern forces tried to dislodge Union troops that occupied the tactically important community and its heights.

All of this and much more will be recalled during the Centennial week. Although nobody is expecting any Mississippi River showboats or Indians to register in there is every indication locally that the celebration is going to be a real ball.

Underground Is Where This Man Gets His Thrills

Roger Bottoms of Forrest City is a sandy-haired fellow who doesn't look a thing like a cave-man, and he isn't, but he knows a lot about caves.

He had been described to me as an outstanding spelunker—explorer of caves—by a man much interested in the potential uses of Arkansas caverns as bomb shelters in case of atomic war.

Richard Antrim of Mountain Home, a retired rear admiral of the United States Navy, was the civil-defense minded individual who suggested I talk with Mr. Bottoms for some authentic information on caves.

So when passing through Forrest City the other day I stopped by the Arkansas Power & Light Company's generating plant west of town and got acquainted with him.

Mr. Bottoms is assistant superintendent of the plant, at one time AP&L's biggest.

I caught him on duty so we sat in his office and talked while boilers roared and machinery hummed and jolly little kilowatts went zipping out over the wires to goodness knows where.

Not a single stalactite or stalagmite in sight, although I'd thought surely he'd have one around for a door stop.

I never can remember, by the way, which it is that hangs from the ceiling and which rises from the floor, but no matter.

He picked up the spelunking hobby as a high school lad, he told me, and went in for it quite vigorously during his college years in Virginia.

Where's the thrill? I asked him.

Spelunkers, he replied, "enjoy going places underground where nobody has been before," for one thing.

There's a lot to be learned about the earth from cave exploration, too, he added.

It's not true spelunking, incidentally, to go wandering around a commercially developed cave with a guide.

After he and his wife moved to Arkansas they took a look at a map one day and spotted a cave location near Melbourne in Izard County. That was the first he entered in the state and he has been in quite a few since and is looking for more.

Mrs. Bottoms is a spelunker, too, and they're both members of the National Speleological Society.

"Ever get lost?" I inquired.

Only once, he smiled, and that was when he broke a fundamental safety rule and went into a cave alone. He crawled through a narrow passage into a big room and neglected to mark it with his carbide light which makes a black smudge on the rocks when properly applied.

On preparing to leave he discovered half a dozen exits and experienced a feeling which he says there's nothing like, that of being lost in a cave. He finally got out after some mighty careful searching for the proper passage.

How about snakes?

Other than at the very entrance to Arkansas caves he has never encountered any, Mr. Bottoms said. He has heard of snake-infested caves in other states, however.

Bats?

Plenty of them live underground in Arkansas, he said, but none has ever attacked him or members of his party. Bone Cave near Batesville for one has quite a colony of the spooky little critters.

Any exciting discoveries, skeletons and the like?

In the big Half Mile Cave near Blanchard Springs (Stone County) he and companions found a flattened human skull and thought they'd come on evidence of prehistoric man.

Study by experts resulted in disappointment. It was only that of an Indian, one of many whose heads had been deliberately misshapened as a baby.

Half Mile Cave is a whopper, he told me. The ceiling of one room in it is more than 100 feet high.

He believes he and spelunking friends have laid to rest a legend about Blowing Cave near Cushman which tells of a boy disappearing into it and then his parents doing the same while in search of the child.

Mr. Bottoms and companions have carefully searched the area below a drop-off over which the people supposedly fell to their deaths and found no bones or other evidence.

And what about using Arkansas caves as bomb shelters and temporary dwellings in case of World War III?

Those near towns could be useful, in his opinion, with necessary improvements made but even so there would be some disadvantages to be considered.

Many have air currents which rush out of the known exits, he explained, this indicating that air is getting into them from somewhere else. What this would mean in terms of air polluted by atomic dust and fallout he said he doesn't know, but it could be a factor.

Inactivity over any prolonged period in the 55- to 60-degree chill—often damp— would have a bad effect on individuals and steps would have to be taken to keep them warm. It doesn't take much of a fire to do this, he added.

Food in tins would have to be specially protected, he said. And there's a number of other things, sanitation for one.

Meanwhile, the information he and other spelunkers are gathering about Arkansas caves could very well prove of life saving value eventually, as Admiral Antrim has been pointing out to folks in the northern part of the state.

Why Fritz Kuhn Has Postponed His 'Gator Hunt

Magnolia—An Arkansas alligator hunt that never came off brought Fritz Kuhn of North Dakota to south Arkansas and therein lies a tale from which all sorts of conclusions—inspirational as well as otherwise—might be drawn.

Fritz Kuhn is a wiry little man of 40, quick to laugh, philosophical about the times he has been flat broke, and maybe a little superstitious too. (He never tells his wife Candy good-bye on the telephone.) He's one of these fellows you've heard about from time to time, one about whom somebody "ought to write a book." And here briefly are some highlights of his tale.

His folks were Germans who came to the Dakota wheat country as children. Depression and drouth put Fritz into the Civilian Conservation Corps in his 'teens, working in the badlands on park projects. Then he went into Uncle Sam's Air Force in 1939 as a ground crewman and had a tour of duty at St. Petersburg, Florida, where he married at war's end.

He and Sara—that's her real name—bought a motorcycle with a side car and took out for San Francisco in the winter of '45. He became a cabinet maker—"because," says Fritz, "that's the only job I could find." Too much traffic, too much confusion in California so he and Candy crossed the continent on the motorcycle—camping out along the way and met a fellow from Arkansas who convinced Fritz that there was money as well as fun to be had in catching alligators in the Arkansas swamps.

The alligator hunt never came off because Fritz and Candy hit Magnolia one afternoon in September of 1947 with about 15 cents between them and no groceries. That was the end of the line until they could work awhile and get some more money together.

Fritz got a job as a carpenter in Magnolia and Candy went to work as a nurse at the local hospital. And what with one thing and another, including Fritz's love of building things with his hands, they're still here and doing well. At least, that's what W. C. Blewster, president of the First National Bank, told me, and he is in a position to know.

At Mr. Blewster's summons Fritz left his factory and Candy left the hospital operating room and we met in the banker's office. Fritz was in overalls, covered with sawdust, and Candy—a bright and cheerful lady of 32—was in operating room gown and cap.

Their first month in Magnolia was marked by incidents they remember with particular warmth. The owner of a small grocery store let them have food on credit and the owner of a trailer house gave them a place to live on the cuff.

Fritz went from carpentering to cabinet and furniture making and in 1953 he and Gaylord Christie, a Magnolia veteran of both World War II and the Korean thing, formed a partnership in the woodworking trade. Their enterprise has grown until they now have a small plant in Magnolia's industrial district that is grossing around $100,000 annually and keeping three employees besides the partners busy.

The Firestone Tire and Rubber Company came along a while back and established a factory in some of the old Magnolia textile mill buildings, making portable water tanks, life rafts and whatnot for the Armed Services. Fritz and "Gay," as he calls his partner, began bidding for and getting orders from Firestone for such things as shipping boxes, staves for the huge rubberized tanks, tent stakes and such.

The Magnolia Wood Products Company, as the Kuhn and Christie firm is now known, buys beech, hickory, elm and pine boards from mills in this vicinity; one new mill has been set up, employing eight men, just to cut special stock for the tank staves. (Here's a good example, by the way, of how one major industry locating in an Arkansas community creates a demand for satellite industries that use Arkansas raw materials and labor.)

The partners continue to do cabinet work and are rather proud of the fact that they made all the furniture for a hotel in nearby El Dorado and have built store and home fixtures throughout Magnolia.

Fritz occasionally turns his hand to fancy woodcarving or to drawing and painting but there's little time for that these days.

I later stood in the plant with Mr. and Mrs. Kuhn and asked Fritz, among other things, about his feelings as a busy and successful man after all of the hard knocks he has had and the times when he and Candy were broke and hungry. He answered by telling me what he expects of his employees: "a good day's work and a real desire to better himself." With those things, he suggested, how can a man miss—even if he never catches an alligator?

Rural Symbols Of Earlier Day Not So Plentiful

In traveling around Arkansas I see evidence of change almost everywhere and of course a lot of it is in the rural areas.

There's the near disappearance of the mule for one thing, something on which I had a bit to report in this column awhile back.

More recently I've been noticing that at least three symbols of the rural Arkansas of yesterday are getting fewer and fewer. These are farm cabins, especially in the cotton areas, snuff signs all over, and "chill tonic" signs all through the malaria belt.

The type of cabin I mean has one room, with a high roof at the front sloping sharply towards the rear. A front porch inevitably is a part of the design. And during my boyhood some chimneys were still being built out of clay.

All through the cotton country these cabins could be seen by the hundreds until a few years ago. Often they were lined up for half a mile or so on the larger plantations. They were nearly always of frame construction, sometimes whitewashed and sometimes painted red but often not painted at all.

These are fast disappearing along with the tenant farmers who once lived in them, although I do see a few occasionally and on rare occasions even spot a row of them.

Most are in disrepair or on the verge of falling down.

At least one typical farm cabin ought to be preserved somewhere in Arkansas, with furnishings typical of the times inside. This should well be a personal project for an enterprising and history-minded planter, if not a county historical society.

These cabins played an important part in the agricultural development of Arkansas, almost as important a part as the middle-buster plow and the mule. Folks in the generations to come will never see such a cabin unless some effort is made to keep one intact.

Time was, too, when signs advertising the various brands of snuff were everywhere, on the sides of barns, nailed to fence posts, painted on the outside walls of country stores.

Quite a few are still to be seen but not nearly so many as a few years ago.

I got to inquiring around among the wholesale grocery and tobacco firms about this, thinking that perhaps the use of snuff was going the way of the mule and the farm cabin and that was why there were not as many signs.

Judging from what I was told by people in the business of selling snuff, however, my analysis of the situation was incorrect.

It's true that there isn't as much outdoor advertising of the dipper's delight as formerly. But the majority opinion is that snuff sales are holding their own, and in fact gaining a little in places.

City folks are snuff users just the same as their country cousins, I was told. Women use it the same as men. And one man in the trade told me that you can take any given number of snuff users and find that about half of them also smoke cigarettes or pipes or like chewing tobacco.

Snuff has been around a long time and one popular brand has been on the market since 1782.

High society and royalty back in the 17th and 18th centuries were big users of it. Their gold, silver and jeweled snuff boxes are collector's items today. Sniffing rather than dipping was the thing to do in those times.

I asked one tobacco wholesaler why there aren't as many snuff signs to be seen around the countryside as there used to be. He blamed the situation on the politicians.

"Every campaign," he said, "they'd go out and nail their signs over ours or tear ours down to make room for theirs."

Used to be also, he said, that farmers were glad to swap a little barn or fence post space for a big can or two of snuff. Now they want cash, he informed me.

Historical note: Arkansas once was quite a producer of tobacco, especially in the mountains, and grew a million-pound crop in 1860. (Whether we ever had a snuff factory I don't know.)

As for "chill tonic," if the stuff is disappearing as fast as the signs that's okay with me.

In my time in South Arkansas, before the war against the mosquito and malaria turned in favor of suffering humanity, I reckon I consumed a barrel of the nasty tasting stuff.

On the other hand, the only "wonder drugs" of the day that I can remember were quinine and calomel. (Come to think of it that hasn't been so many years ago.) So I suppose a fellow ought to hold at least a little gratitude in his heart for the people who concocted, bottled and sold the medicine that was designed to offset the chills and fever.

Nobody who bothers to look can travel over Arkansas these days without seeing evidence of change. Some of it indicates progress but unfortunately some does not.

The Hillbillies Had Their Day But It's Fading

For a hundred years or more there was a hardy and individualistic breed of folks in Arkansas known best as "hillbillies," who had little contact with the rest of the world.

Their log cabin ways, their talk, and their outlook on life sort of baffled folks on the outside, including a lot of writers whose reports were read with glee all over the country.

Well if there ever was a misunderstood fellow it was the hillbilly.

His disinterest in fancy dress earned him a reputation for slovenliness.

His lack of desire for the latest luxuries won him an undeserved tag of "lazy."

His failure to travel to far places, or to read the literary output of city people, led the sophisticated elements of society to consider him ignorant.

Hillbillies were, in the words of Vance Randolph of Eureka Springs—observer, friend, and Boswell of the mountain folks—"the most deliberately unprogressive people in the United States."

But this does not mean that the hillbilly was the low type of fellow that so many thought him to be. Rather his philosophy was closely patterned after that of Henry David Thoreau, the 19th century naturalist and one-time hermit who held that "a man is rich in proportion to the number of things he can afford to leave alone."

While the hillbillies were going their chosen route, a lot of other Arkansans were taking a different path.

They were lapping up book learning, exerting themselves mightily in quest of currency, and living by standards they considered to be as good as anybody's anywhere.

Somewhere along the way a vast segment of the American public got the notion that most Arkansans were hillbillies in heart and mind if not actually in appearance.

This continues to be a painful matter to Arkansas patriots who leave home without having acquired the ability to laugh off the jibes of Texans or of residents of the asphalt jungles of Brooklyn and other cultural centers.

I've known the pain myself on occasion.

But as I've moved around the country and observed how folks live and look in other sections, I've come to realize that an Arkansan need not get his dander up if somebody mistakes him for a hillbilly.

ERNIE DEANE   35

I've learned to ignore those jokers who think it's funny to comment at some high-faluting gathering or tea-sipping soiree, "here's a man from Arkansas who's wearing shoes."

For one thing I'm too fat to fight such folks on a fair and equal basis and my knees are now much too kinky for me to hit and run.

In any event, be happy or sad about the situation as you will, the oldtime Arkansas hillbilly is disappearing.

I have this on good authority, the word of Paul Faris of the Hendrix College faculty at Conway.

Mr. Faris has studied the hillbilly in his native habitat, especially in the Ozarks, and has made some really striking photographs of log cabins that are hillbilly homes.

He tells me that the type of existence followed for so many generations by the hillbillies is all but gone and that some real searching is called for in trying to find a log cabin inhabited by a typical hillbilly family.

Paved roads and automobiles, radio, and television more recently, have brought the outside world into the hills. It doesn't take much looking to see the changes they've caused.

"World War II was a major factor, too," Mr. Faris, a slender, graying and scholarly gent, reminded me.

The draft reached into every valley and behind every hill and carried the young men away for a taste of life in points all over the world. The young women left for work in the cities. Members of that generation haven't come back home in any great numbers and those who did return didn't take up the old ways of living.

It won't be long before a sure-enough hillbilly will be as rare a sight as a steam locomotive or a mule with plow.

Appraise this change in the Arkansas hill country any way you care. As for myself, having known a few hillbillies fairly well and rather liking the flavor that they gave to the Arkansas scene, I consider their passing to be a matter of regret.

With Arkansas now into the tourist business on a grand scale, and hillbillies being almost as interesting to the touring public as Indians, perhaps some provision could be made to establish a colony of them at a strategic spot in the Ozarks or Ouachitas.

If I weren't so accustomed to what we city dwelling folks call "the finer things of life" I might consider starting one myself.

Czar's Captain Makes Cheese At Arkansas Plant

Morrilton—Is there any merit to the notion that a better understanding between individuals of the nations of the world will help the cause for peace?

In Morrilton there's a man of almost unbelievable experiences in international work and travel who believes there is.

He is Albert ("Pappy") Steffen, one of a long line of Swiss cheesemakers who has operated a factory in this community since 1945.

I heard about him through Jimmy Sinnott of El Dorado. He told me a former cavalry officer of the army of the last czar of imperial Russia, a friend of Mongolian princes, a linguist, an author and an artist, lived here.

I found Steffen busy in his plant, turning out the cheddar cheese that is sold nationally under Kraft labels. He welcomed me with a hand as big as I ever shook and in a friendly rumbling voice tinged with a Germanic accent.

Then in his comfortably furnished home nearby I listened to tales of adventure as exciting as any that ever went into a book or a movie. And I heard some simple but persuasive words about the good that can come to the world through friendly contact between peoples.

Pappy Steffen is a broad-shouldered, powerful man, three inches over six feet in height and well past 200 pounds. His hair is gray and his sharp brown eyes are heavily shaded by jet-black brows. If he hadn't told me I'd never have guessed that he is in his 60s for he moves with the agility of an athlete of far fewer years.

He was born of German and Italian parents near Bern, Switzerland, and orphaned as a child. An uncle with business in Siberia took him as a youth on visits to that faraway province of the czar's empire. Then after learning the cheesemaking trade in Switzerland, he returned to Siberia in 1910 to organize cheese factories and creameries there.

The Russians kept him in the country when World War I broke out and because of his fluency in languages made him an interpreter. He volunteered for line duty and became a captain of cavalry and for a time fought as a guerrilla. The Bolsheviks would have executed him after the revolution except for the influence of a friend.

In 1920 the Reds sent him to Mongolia as their first ambassador. He sickened at their brutalities and other ways of doing things and, in his own words, "deserted" within a year, making his way to Peking.

At one point he was lined up with more than 20 men to be executed by a firing squad but learned by chance that their commander was a former acquaintance from the Balkans. This saved his life.

He later spent several years among Mongolian tribesmen in a cheesemaking venture in which he was associated with the princes of that strange and remote land. While there he made numerous photos and did some beautiful oil paintings of native subjects that he showed me.

The Communist invasion of 1927 put him on the run and he escaped with American assistance to the United States, arriving broke but with a valuable stamp collection which he sold. He went to work for Kraft in Wisconsin and in the course of time came to Morrilton.

Steffen is the author of three books in German, all published in Switzerland. The latest, *In 40 Years Around the World*, seeks to foster a clearer understanding of the countries and the peoples he has known.

For example, he complimented American women on their home-making abilities, hoping, he said, to dispel to some extent the European notion that they are idlers who spend most of their time smoking cigarettes and drinking cocktails.

Through Morrilton Rotary Club contacts he encourages friends to correspond with men in other nations and carries on an extensive letter-writing project himself. Such a person-to-person exchange of ideas, he feels, does much to offset false impressions that hamper the efforts to achieve a peaceful world.

More recently he was elected president of the Morrilton Rotary Club and will represent it next spring at the gathering in Lucerne, Switzerland, of men from some 90 nations.

I asked him about that nickname of

ERNIE DEANE 37

"Pappy."

When he and his wife and young daughter moved to Morrilton most acquaintances called him "Mister," he told me. The child, now an attractive junior in the local high school, suggested that they refer to him "the way we do at home." The nickname stuck.

Pappy Steffen is an enthusiastic supporter of international student exchange programs. And being fluent in many tongues he strongly believes that foreign languages should be taught in American public schools.

I'm with him on both of these points, although I speak only one language, an uncertain brand of Arkansas English.

Henry Dugan: 55 Years With The Alligators

Hot Springs—Every now and then a big alligator takes out after a bandy-legged little man here and the crowd gets itself a thrill as the man outruns the beast.

Henry Dugan has been outrunning and side-stepping 'gators for a long time and by his own admission it hasn't been easy.

"Folks have been coming back here regularly year after year to see that alligator catch me," he says, "but I know 'gators and I ain't fixing to let one get ahold of me."

He pointed out a bob-tailed member of the Hot Springs Alligator Farm herd to illustrate what can happen when a 'gator gets his wicked teeth into something and starts to twist and roll.

This particular animal lost a couple of feet of appendage in a fight in the pen. As Henry explained, somewhat unnecessarily, an alligator's tail is a danged sight tougher than a man's leg.

As for that "alligator chases man" event, Henry admits that it's all a part of an act he has worked up to excite tourists.

Just as readily he confesses that he is scared of most of the several dozen 'gators that he feeds and cares for and he isn't going to give them a chance at him.

"The Outlaw" is one of the latter, 13 feet long and 830 pounds in weight. By Henry's estimate this one is more than 400 years old, just past middle age as 'gators go, he says. (You don't count an alligator's teeth to learn his age, but keep a record of his annual growth for a few years and figure it from there.)

This rugged old meanie was caught in the Arkansas River bottoms near Pine Bluff and has been on display here since 1902.

Henry got here ahead of The Outlaw, having started to work for "Alligator Joe" Campbell in 1901. Outside of a couple of years Army duty in World War I he has been handling 'gators ever since. Only one ever side-swiped him with his tail, years ago—"nearly broke my ankle."

Henry Dugan is 67, short in stature, ruddy complexioned, white-haired, and soft of voice except when he delivers his spiel to the paying customers.

His father was a National Park employee and Henry as a kid trapped minnows in a creek next to Alligator Joe's establishment and sold them to fishermen. He went to work for the Farm as a general handy man and graduated, so to speak, to alligator trainer, keeper, and crowd astonisher.

Here are some bits on 'gators he gave me:

They never forget what they have once learned, although their brains are mighty small. They have no sense of smell, but their eyesight and hearing are acute. Being reptiles, their body temperature changes according to changes in their surroundings. They can live under water for months, and during the six-month hibernation period in the fall and winter eat nothing at all but don't lose weight.

Females lay eggs every other year, 25 to 50 at a time. These hatch in eight weeks in nests of leaves and grass. Females are just as adept at fighting as the males and equally as dangerous.

Some folks who step up to the fences to observe the 'gators think the motionless animals are dead.

"They ain't dead. They ain't lazy. It's Nature's plan that they be the way they are," Henry explains.

Henry has had some experience with snakes too and he'll take alligators every time.

Back in the days when Alligator Joe was his employer the Farm took a lot of snakes to the fair in Little Rock, and Henry's part of the act was to dress as a "wild woman" and get in the pit with the snakes.

He over fortified himself with a well-known type of snake poison antidote and—take Henry's word for it, not mine—he just went right to sleep down there in the pit.

"Next morning," says Henry, "I woke up with snakes, real snakes, crawling all over me. That's when I quit the act."

(Were they poisonous snakes? Yep, says Henry, but their fangs had been removed, but even so, who wants to sleep with snakes?)

I asked Henry if alligators have a language. He cupped his hands to his mouth and gave some short, high grunts. In the nearest pit a dozen young 'gators raised their heads and started toward us.

"That's the sound they make when they find food," he explained. "They also grunt for a change in the weather."

And that's where I left Henry Dugan—may his legs stay nimble and his eyesight sharp.

Damsel Sought For Dulcimer: Must Be Pretty

Eureka Springs—Wanted: beautiful, talented, conscientious young woman; to make a career out of dulcimer playing.

Now young ladies, hold everything.

Do not rush in to see me.

I'm not the one who's hunting candidates for this job. Until recently I didn't even know whether a dulcimer is something to eat or something to wear in case of wet weather.

Now I know it's a musical instrument of ancient ancestry. And I also know the lady's looking for somebody to take up where she's figuring to leave off one of these days—playing the dulcimer, that is.

She is Ruth M. Tyler of Neosho, Missouri, a spirited and clever blonde who by her own admission is on the far side of 60.

She's a tall tale teller, an expert in hillbilly cookery, a writer of Ozarks dialect, and a "hear a tune once, play it forever" musician.

We got acquainted at the annual Ozark Folk Festival here, where she performs to the delight of those who dig dulcimer music—and there seems to be quite a few.

Her instrument is of heavy mahogany, about 150 years old, and is about the size and shape of a suit box. It has 47 steel strings tightly stretched over three bridges.

Sounds are produced by striking the strings with little mallets made of balsa wood and corset stays, one mallet to each hand.

Her specialty is folk music, played from the memory she has developed over a 20-year period as a piano accompanist to movies in the old "silent" days.

So far as history is concerned, the dulcimer is mentioned in the third chapter of the Book of David, in connection with Nebuchadnezzar's decree that music would be played and everybody would worship his gold image.

(Shadrach, Meshach and Abednigo held out and were tossed into the fiery pit, remember?)

What's more, the dulcimer is the grand-pappy of today's piano.

The poet Coleridge mentioned the instrument in his rather wild and confusing "Kubla Khan," which he never finished and perhaps it's just as well he didn't. Anyhow, here's what he wrote and I think it's right pretty:

A damsel with a dulcimer
In a vision once I saw:
It was an Abyssinian maid
And on her dulcimer she played
Singing of Mount Abora.

Miss Tyler tapped out "Skip to My Lou" and similar ditties in a private demonstration she gave me and a friend at her hotel. And in her high-pitched Ozarks twang she bemoaned the fact that dulcimer playing is in danger of becoming a lost art.

"I must teach somebody before it's too late," she said. And that's when she laid down the requirement that the "somebody" be young, beautiful, talented, and so on.

Well, girls, you can get ahold of her at Neosho, over in the southwest corner of Missouri near Joplin and the Oklahoma border. Tell'er I sent you.

I ran into another musical shortage while talking to Adolph Kukler and his wife Augusta, a quiet-spoken, gentle Austrian-born couple who have lived in the United States for over half a century and who performed at the Festival. Mr. Kukler is a retired crane operator who is a talented zither player and the owner of several of the beautifully made instruments that date back in history to the Greeks.

He is getting short on strings and can't find any in the United States, or in Europe either at the moment. The zither is a favorite music-making instrument in the Alps of Switzerland and Bavaria, however, and he is hopeful of obtaining some strings soon.

The Kuklers live in a neat, white-painted frame house on Main Street and welcome the passing public into their parlor.

Mr. Kukler plays from the classics and from his collection of Austrian folk songs. Judging from the rapt attention I saw visitors give him, zither music has charms.

On Sunday mornings he plays at services in the local Catholic Church. He is also making recordings which he rather modestly offers for sale.

Mr. and Mrs. Kukler have been Arkansas citizens seven years and have put their thoughts into a state song, "Oh You My Homeland."

One of the Kukler zithers was made of tulip wood in a Washington, Missouri, factory in the early 1800s and later won an international prize in Vienna.

It is inlaid with gold, mother-of-pearl and ivory. From its 42 strings he produces music that inspired one visitor to write in the registration book that Mr. Kukler knows "how to transmit from wood and metal the music of the wind, of colors, of birds, of all nature."

That's such a well-composed and pertinent line I wish I'd thought it up myself.

The Hucksters And Pitch Men Under His Hide

A man grumbling softly to himself over some of the petty confusions and absurdities of the day:

Wonder how much longer the great TV-watching public is going to have to suffer through cigarette commercials that run to such a high content of hokum?

And don't the fag makers really trust their video salesmen to get the "important message from our sponsor" across with one recitation of the merits?

Why, for example, should "tastes great straight"—whatever that means—have to be repeated half a dozen times in a single shot of sales slush?

Why rhyme things anyhow in a period when prose is far more popular than verse? I'm thinking of "Stinkers Taste Good—[pause for two hand claps]—Like a Cigarette Should."

Those carefully rehearsed, loving little glances the pitch man gives the cigarette in his fingers seem to be copied after the old familiar daddy-looks-at-sleeping-babe routine.

I'm plumb baffled by the battle of the filters.

Do Old Stiflers really have twice as many filters as the other two leading brands? And if so, what's the difference?

I don't smoke but I'd surely like to know the answers to such questions that creep into my thoughts when I manage to stick with the TV for an evening.

No point in asking my cigarette-smoking friends because I don't believe they sit through the tobacco commercials.

As for radio, there's a fellow in that game I'd like to meet sometime.

He's the one who dreamed up the notion that "wherever you go there's radio."

I want to take him on some of my travels around Arkansas and let him try to get the radio in my car to function when we're riding along in the vicinity of high voltage electric lines.

There are more miles of these wires in Arkansas than I'd ever have guessed possible until I took to the road earlier this year.

Great thing, radio—but after all of these years it's still inclined to fall back on the bad old habit of using a lot of ballyhoo and fast talk.

I'm just a trifle confused, incidentally, as to what is meant by "big radio."

I picked up a Greenville, Mississippi, station that was using the term while I was down in Southeast Arkansas a while back and more recently have heard one of our Little Rock stations using the same pitch.

There's at least one thing about radio that beats TV: a fellow doesn't have to keep his eyes on the set to take in its offerings.

My radio listening goes back to the time when teenaged boys and a lot of grown men built their own crystal sets and figured they'd done something remarkable when they managed to tune in KDKA from Pittsburgh, Pennsylvania.

As a matter of fact, it was remarkable.

I'd miss radio, ballyhoo and all, if it passed on. Can't say as much yet for TV and those simpering chaps peddling the newest products of the tobacconists' art.

Lest these comments pain some of my friends in the electronics field, let me say that despite a lifetime of being around newspapers I don't always dig what they mean either.

Abbreviationitis has taken hold of this fine old profession in recent years and it's a befuddling business at best.

This is a disease which deprives its victim of the ability or desire to write out the name of an organization, agency, or even a military installation.

The unfortunate results are frequently seen.

There are PSC, AIDC, GACE, NCCA, NAACP, and even SPEBQSIA (or something like that which means Society for the Preservation and Encouragement of Barbershop Quartet Singing in America).

Nobody has yet fallen so completely under the ravages of abbreviationitis, so far as I know, to shorten Senate Office Building to its component initials. But they will if the trend continues.

State Newsmen To Hold Winter Press Meeting

Some of my favorite people will be in Little Rock tomorrow for their annual mid-winter business and social gathering.

They're editors, publishers and other folks associated with the newspapers of Arkansas.

They're members of a hardy breed that has had a hand in the affairs of Arkansas communities ever since William E. Woodruff set up shop at Arkansas Post in 1819 and started printing the *Gazette*.

Newspaper folks have to get together at some central point occasionally to swap information and, when things get tough as they sometimes do, to cry on a friendly shoulder.

There aren't as many newspapers as there used to be in Arkansas, but whether there are as many newspaper people I don't know.

Anyhow, half a century ago, there were more than 300 newspapers published in this state. Today there are only 168, of which 128 come out once a week, four appear twice a week, and 36 are dailies. Among the dailies are eight published on Sundays.

Fewer though they may be, by most counts today's newspapers do a far better job of informing the public than they possibly could have done even 25 or 30 years ago.

That's partly because the methods of gathering and distributing news and pictures have been vastly improved, and so have the machines that are used to do the job.

And newspaper people these days are generally better trained than they once were.

I took a run through the records of the Arkansas Press Association and found a thing or two that might be of interest.

If I counted right, the word "News" is the favorite name for Arkansas papers, 26 using it either singly or in combination with something else—such as the *News Observer* at Crossett.

"Democrat" follows closely behind, 24 papers having that as their name or as part of their name.

"Times," "Herald," "Record," "Star" and "Journal" are also favorites.

The happiest combinations of town names and newspaper names in Arkansas, to my mind, are the *DeQueen Bee* and the *Hope Star*.

As for unusual newspaper names, how about the *Log Cabin Democrat* at Conway, the *Arkansas Plaindealer* at Hampton, the *Siftings Herald* at Arkadelphia, the *Picayune* at Prescott, the *Mountain Echo* at Yellville or the *Mountain Wave* at Marshall?

The *Advance Monticellonian* has one of the longest names and incidentally both its publisher and its editor are ladies—Mrs. M. R. Whittington and Mrs. Frances Jaggers.

Every county in Arkansas has at least one home published newspaper but there are two county seats with no local paper. The two are Desha, of which Arkansas City is seat, and Crittenden, of which Marion is the seat. However two weekly newspapers are published in Desha County and a weekly, a twice-a-week, and a daily are published in Crittenden County.

Things are a lot tamer now than they once were for Arkansas newspaper men— there were few if any newspaper women in the early days.

Editors used to slug it out through their columns with rival editors and others of different opinion in a manner that isn't followed in this more polite age.

These typographical duels occasionally ended in gunsmoke, and every now and then in a funeral.

Fred W. Allsopp in his *History of the Arkansas Press for a Hundred Years and More*, published in 1922, recorded details of several incidents in which tempers were cooled only by hot lead.

In one of these duels, fought in 1845 by the editors of competing Van Buren papers, rifles were used instead of pistols. Neither of the hostile journalists was much of a shot, however, for each missed his target although the distance was only 60 paces.

Maybe they'd both fortified themselves with a slug or two of type cleaner before stepping into the fray and couldn't see past the end of their gun barrels. Mr. Allsopp didn't say.

In my time I've known and worked with a lot of newspaper people whose talents ran from exceptionally good to rather poor.

I've seen some of them—war correspondents—show personal courage of a high degree when death waited around the next corner or over the next hedgerow.

A man is expected to show his courage in a war, however.

All across the land in times of peace there are examples of personal courage to be found on the part of newspaper people—courage that doesn't seem like much at first thought but is true courage nevertheless.

It takes courage, for example, for an editor in a community to buck those elements who have things going their own way—sometimes a crooked way—and don't want them changed.

It takes courage for a newspaper man—or woman—to set down in print the shortcomings of the school board, or city council, folks who'll be met face to face at the local coffee bar or the church supper next day.

It also takes courage for the publisher of a struggling little daily or weekly to turn down the demand of an important advertiser that he lay off a touchy local subject.

Many show such courage and among them are Arkansas newspaper people of my acquaintance. That's why, among other reasons, I say they're some of my favorite folks.

At The Race He Learned Never Brag On A Nag

Spend a day or a lifetime around a race track and what do you learn about horses?

The answer is "many things" but there's one in particular: don't brag on a nag.

I base this profound observation upon details of a true and somewhat sad chapter in the story of Ray Thompson of Hot Springs.

In the past 25 years or so he has spent more time aboard horses than most of us have spent on our feet.

In his bright red jacket, his white shirt and riding breeches, black boots, bow tie and cap he's a familiar figure and an important man at tracks around the country.

He's an outrider, the fellow who leads the thoroughbreds past the stands and to the starting post, and chases the recalcitrant ones of which there are a goodly number.

Without him, or others doing the same work, there couldn't very well be a horse race. (Suggestion to anti-horse race readers: liquidate outriders and you've got it made.)

Mr. Thompson is a wiry, sun-tanned, blue-eyed and friendly man just six inches over five feet in height, also a native of Missouri which is more famed for mules than horses.

He sat in the restaurant in the stable area at Oaklawn Park and told me about horses and especially about one named "Shorty"—now dead—and another he was to ride that day whose name he couldn't quite remember.

Before the day was over he was wishing he had old Shorty back again. That other horse done him wrong.

Part of an outrider's job is to chase down runaway bangtails and bring 'em to the starting point so the race can begin.

Let a runaway get plumb loose and the track management has to refund all bets made on that particular horse. Since the track would keep 10 per cent of those bets, the expense can be pretty heavy. What's more, a runaway can cause a lot of trouble that might bring injuries to other horses and their riders.

To chase down the wild ones the outrider uses a fast-breaking, highly trained animal—quarter horses being good for the work and that's what Shorty was, Thompson explained. In three years' time together they failed only three times to catch a runaway, and they worked 1,443 races all the way from the Kentucky Derby to California.

Shorty took down with the lockjaw recently and had to be destroyed.

On the day I watched Mr. Thompson work he was using a borrowed horse that made his owner some good money last year as a calf-roping pony at rodeos. A plenty fast, dependable horse, Mr. Thompson said, one that knew just what to do, the kind the exercise boys could bet on to catch runaways—as they sometimes do—and figure to pick up a little easy money.

Then came the very first race of the day, five and a half furlongs for three-year-old maidens, a skittish lot indeed.

It was a pretty afternoon and a sizeable crowd watched Mr. Thompson lead the racers up to the starting post.

And then just before the "they're off!" was about to be called, a horse broke the barrier, spilled its rider, and tore out with Mr. Thompson and his rodeo roper in hot pursuit. They almost made the catch but not quite. The runaway circled the track to the cheers of the crowd, riderless, wild-eyed, and scratched from the board.

That's when I came to the conclusion that there's little gained by bragging on a horse, even if it's just one that's used to chase other horses.

Next time I see Ray Thompson I figure he'll be riding a hoss whose name he knows.

Down in the stable area I came across one of those cases that make a non-horse owner wonder what it is that keeps folks in the racing game in the face of all its heartbreaks.

I found Mr. and Mrs. D. T. Crabtree of Owensboro, Kentucky, working away on a beautiful big black horse named Gunner Lad.

Mrs. Crabtree, a petite lady almost dwarfed by the animal she was ministering to, was on the floor of the stall doctoring Gunner Lad's legs and hoofs.

Mr. Crabtree, who turned out to be something of a philosopher, had the horse by the halter and was calming him down from time to time with a word or two. He has been around horses all his life and he and Mrs. Crabtree have their own string and train racers for other owners.

Gunner Lad is now seven years old and the best thoroughbred they've ever had, Mr. Crabtree told me.

The horse won six races as a two-year-old and seven as a three-year-old and at one time there was an offer for $50,000 on him.

Then hard luck began to dog him.

In Denver in 1954 Gunner Lad slipped in his stall and injured a front leg and he hasn't raced since.

The Crabtrees keep working with him however and are hopeful concerning his future.

"He can run at any distance," Mr. Crabtree said.

Being rather ignorant about such matters, I asked Mr. Crabtree if leg injuries made much trouble for horses and horse owners.

"If it wasn't for leg injuries," he said without a trace of a smile, "everybody would be rich." And he handed Mrs. Crabtree the bottle of horse liniment.

State's History Isn't Taught In Enough Schools

A wise and good friend of mine, born up North but a resident of Arkansas for many years and one of Arkansas's greatest boosters, was talking to me about "the damnable inferiority complex," as he called it, that Arkansans have toward our own state.

Whatever it's called it does exist—the old feeling that if a thing is done in Arkansas it's somehow inferior to what's done elsewhere.

My friend didn't recommend that we adopt the bragging practices that Texans use—apparently with success—in building up their own state.

But he did recommend strongly, almost passionately, that Arkansans learn more about Arkansas—not only its present but its past.

And that entails the study of Arkansas history, he pointed out, a study that ought to be emphasized and encouraged in our public schools and especially in the high schools.

I'm in full agreement with that and imagine that a great many other Arkansans feel the same, although little seems to have been accomplished to put such feelings into effect.

Somebody correct me if I'm wrong, but as I get the story the study of Arkansas history isn't required in the state as part of a student's work to obtain a high school diploma.

Arkansas history isn't even offered as an alternative course for credit in most of our high schools.

Nor is it required to obtain a degree from any of the state colleges or the University.

Perhaps making the study of state history mandatory wouldn't be a widely popular or a proper step to take. But at least such study ought to be encouraged and I'm told that this isn't being done on anything like a broad scale.

The question naturally arises, what good is the study of history anyhow?

People in the business of education, and others with whom I've talked, agree that better knowledge of our state's past—especially its accomplishments—would serve to instill a greater sense of pride in Arkansas among Arkansans.

Goodness knows that has been needed for a long time.

Most of Arkansas's difficulties of today stem from conditions and actions—or lack of actions—of days gone by. Better knowledge of the past could well serve to guide Arkansas in the days to come.

Study of our state's history also could bring greater appreciation by Arkansans of the possibilities which exist for progress. History will surely show that we haven't capitalized on our opportunities, and might help explain why.

And if no other good reason existed for such study, nobody ought to grow up in our state ignorant of the colorful, dramatic, and significant events of the past.

At least one high school to my knowledge is making an effort to afford young Arkansans an opportunity to learn about their state.

That's at Batesville, where Al Harris, the superintendent of schools, has organized the course and teaches it personally.

I had a talk with him about it the other day, sitting in his office in a structure that has quite a history itself—the first brick school building in Batesville, he told me, erected in 1882 and now used as a junior high school.

Arkansas history is offered as a one-semester fall course, he said, having been started in the 1955–56 term as an elective subject—that is, not required.

For a text he uses *The Arkansas Story*, written by O. E. McKnight, professor of education at Henderson State Teachers College at Arkadelphia, and Boyd W. Johnson, superintendent of schools at Green Forest. It was published in 1955 by an Oklahoma City firm.

Mr. Harris supplements the text with materials gathered from numerous sources: *The Arkansas Almanac*, the *Gazette*'s Other Days feature, material from the state Publicity and Parks Commission and from the regional library in Batesville, for example.

To add interest to the course, he had his students dig into local history as well and

ERNIE DEANE   45

there is a great deal of it around Batesville.

Among material used in this phase of the course is a 38-page booklet, published in 1919 by the Senior Class of Batesville High and entitled "History of Batesville." In itself the booklet is a rather remarkable publication, coming as it did from student pens.

I asked Mr. Harris how he came to start the course.

"I realized my own lack of knowledge of my native state," he replied.

And what about the students?

"They just don't know much about Arkansas," he said. Judging from the work they do in preparing end-of-term papers, he said, now they're at least getting a better understanding of Arkansas.

And how to get more schools to offer Arkansas history?

My own notion is that the same should be said for Arkansas generally—more of us should take a personal interest in making sure that our young people get a better knowledge of their home state.

Melvin Endsley: An Ozarks Boy Singing "Blues"

A heavy drizzle sent water rolling red down the Ozark slopes and there was a murky quietness over the hills when I stopped at a crossroads store in the Cleburne County village of Drasco the other day.

I was looking for Melvin Endsley, Arkansas's newly famous composer of "country style" music whose "Singing the Blues" has lifted him out of obscurity and hard times.

"Go up the gravel road about two miles and a quarter and turn left at the mailbox," a man in the store told me, "he's at the first house."

Like many other people, I'd been wondering what sort of a person is this 22-year-old son of a hill farmer, struck by polio at three, who wrote tunes in his head for 14 years before he scored in the highly competitive game of song making.

I found him in his wheelchair in the parlor of the family's modest frame house, listening to a radio.

Beneath the home-made table that held the radio and a TV set were two well-worn guitars. A boiling kettle on the wood stove in the middle of the room was singing its own ballad.

Some people have the ability to wear fame and newfound fortune modestly. Melvin Endsley has that ability.

A more unassuming, friendly, and straightforward person than this boy with the handsome, smiling face and wavy blonde hair would be hard to find.

Polio cost him the use of his legs and much of the use of his shoulders and arms. But inside of him there has always been music and he has been trying ever since he was a kid to make it come out in song. And he finally did it without a music lesson of any kind.

What "Singing the Blues" has done on various "shows" in the past three or four months is well known—11 straight weeks as No. 1 on the Lucky Strike Hit Parade for example.

It's still going strong on radio and TV and in record sales. About a million and a quarter platters have been sold so far, the reports say.

His more recent "Knee Deep in the Blues," sung by Marty Robbins as was "Singing," is in the top 25 bracket.

Melvin's recordings of his own voice and guitar in "I Ain't Getting Nowhere With You" and "Bringing the Blues to My Door" are doing well too. He's mighty grateful to disc jockeys, and especially to those in Arkansas, for helping to push these two numbers.

His "Too Many Times," out about two months with Billy Worth doing the singing, could be doing better but Melvin isn't complaining.

On the day I talked with him he reached another "first" in his musical career.

His "I Love You Still" came out simultaneously under two labels. Bud Deckleman does the singing country style on an MGM record and The Four Voices do the "pop" version for Columbia.

More of his compositions are already being prepared for release by his publishers, Acuff-Rose of Nashville, and Melvin is working on some new ones.

He is under exclusive contract to the Nashville firm and gets a percentage cut in the sale of all his songs, both those on records and on sheet music.

I asked him the inevitable question, how about the money that folks generally think comes rolling in by the barrel for the writer of a "hit."

"Let's say that if everything goes well the rest of this year, I hope to be set up pretty good financially," he replied.

My guess is that those of us who are uninformed in such things would figure his income considerably higher than it is. Nothing about him or his home surroundings indicates any desire to live it up lavishly at the moment.

And where does he do his work, and at what times of the day?

"Mostly around home," Melvin said as to location, "and sometimes when I'm riding along in my car."

As for time, "I can't ever tell when the mood will come."

It used to be that he would compose an entire song—words and music—and just keep it in his head. Now he has a tape recorder into which he sings, listens to the results and makes improvements, and then when satisfied mails the tape to his publishers.

"Singing the Blues," incidentally, had been running through his thoughts for some time but when it finally came to him he put it together in 45 minutes.

Melvin is getting lots of mail these days, including letters from other hopeful writers seeking advice and offers from others to join them in composing songs. His contract precludes the making of any arrangements with other people, he explained.

Incidentally, his mailing address is Heber Springs. A Conway radio station for which he worked last fall is still receiving mail addressed to him.

I asked him for his opinion on the future of country style music, whether he and other composers believe it's here to stay.

There was a strong trend in its favor in the days of Hank Williams back in the late '40s and early '50s, he said, but a slump came after Williams died.

Public favor turned heavily back to it last year, under the impact of three songs.

One was Marty Robbins's "Walking in the Rain." Another was Johnny Cash's "I'll Walk the Line." (Cash is an Arkansas boy too.)

And not meaning to boast, said Melvin, "Singing the Blues" was the other.

He's hopeful concerning the long pull. Of course an optimistic spirit has been a key factor in bringing him along the rough road he has traveled.

I asked about future plans, where he'll live and so forth.

No plans at present to live anywhere except in the Ozarks, he said, unless his business develops to a point that he might have to move to Nashville, the country music capital of the world.

Meanwhile, he's home with his parents, Mr. and Mrs. Fred Endsley. In the home, too, are his three younger sisters, all students in the consolidated school at Cotter where he completed a four-year course in just three years.

A most remarkable Arkansan is Melvin Endsley.

The High Cost Of Ballyhoo For The Politicians

John Q. Arkansan, who never has bought so much as ten seconds of television time nor a small newspaper advertisement to make a campaign for public office, must wonder occasionally just how much a statewide ballyhoo effort actually costs.

I got curious, too, and questioned some professional advertising men on the matter, men who customarily are hired in election years to guide and assist candidates for major office in the important advertising and publicity operations of the campaign.

The professionals earn their livelihood year-round by promoting the best interests of causes, products and men through use of various "media": Television and radio, newspapers, billboards, direct mail, printed matter, "specialties" such as nail files and paper matches and all the other things that can be used to capture the attention and presumably earn the good will of the public.

Since television is the newest of the mass communication media, let's consider TV in Arkansas politics as some of the professionals explain it. (Expense figures to be used pertain only to those affecting candidates for state office and not to persons seeking local or county offices. Costs aren't as high for the latter candidates.)

More TV stations are now in operation than there were two years ago and there are thousands more TV sets in Arkansas homes. So television necessarily is an important campaign instrument, although it does have its drawbacks and its use does run into money.

While the professionals questioned do not agree on various aspects of TV in Arkansas politics, there does seem to be general agreement on these points:

(1) The evening hours are preferable for political presentations, especially after the children go to bed; (2) care should be taken not to annoy people by replacing popular entertainment programs with political harangues; (3) 30 minutes is just about the maximum for an appearance by a candidate at any one time, and some think this is too long; (4) not everyone shows up at his best before the camera; (5) if a candidate's statewide TV talk goes well he can reach more people in the comfort of their homes in a short time than he could by making an extended tour; (6) TV cannot replace the personal-contact type of campaigning, the hearty handshake and toothy smile routine, but television is replacing old-time mass political rallies.

There are three television stations in Little Rock and one each in El Dorado, Fort Smith and Texarkana. A candidate wishing to blanket the state also has to consider use of stations at Monroe, Louisiana, Springfield, Missouri, and Memphis.

Costs vary according to station and time of day, with evening periods the most expensive. Thirty minutes of evening TV time on Little Rock stations costs $270 and the same time would cost more in Memphis and less at some other points. A "live" broadcast, in which the candidate appears in person, costs more than one in which previously-prepared sound film is used. Preparation of film, however, costs approximately $450 for 30 minutes. Extra film prints, for use on other stations, add to the cost.

A candidate making a 30-minute TV plea by film simultaneously over the nine stations required to completely cover Arkansas will spend about $3,200 or approximately $106 a minute.

Of course time can be bought in smaller (or bigger) lots than 30 minutes, down to and including 10-second "spots." But it's all expensive: one of the Little Rock stations gets $45 for a single broadcast of a 10-second spot during the evening and the other two stations charge $50.

Not much can be presented in 10 seconds except the candidate's face, a very brief message and the name of the office he seeks. But not many viewers can get from the chair to the switch to cut him off in 10 seconds, and that's more than can be said for longer broadcasts.

How effective television politicking actually is remains one of those matters on which everybody is an "expert." Owners of TV sets who also hold poll tax receipts undoubtedly have their own ideas.

Why Not Score The Lassies At Football Games?

Now that the autumn madness is upon us again, and a 50-yard line ticket is as hard to come by as a nickel parking place at the Marion, I feel compelled to comment on a few aspects of modern football.

Ordinarily and rightly so such subjects are left to the *Gazette*'s Mr. O. Henry and his staff, experts all in the intricacies of the pigeon-toed T and the coddling of quarterbacks.

But sports writers are men who make their living by going to the stadium to report on the doings of athletes, while I go to help those very same athletes make a living.

A man who spends most of his working hours in a press box at a football game couldn't have the same viewpoint as the rest of us have. Hence, this piece.

Now what I've got to say shouldn't be taken in any way as the opinion of a man who knows football inside and outside.

In recent years, during which the University of Arkansas Razorbacks have obtained a coaching staff that is bigger than the oldtime squads used to be, I've watched football principally from the outside. That is, due to the scramble for tickets I've been watching it from outside the 20-yard line seats.

The last time I was in a position to see football from the inside was when Tommy Thomsen had Dwight Sloan and Jack Robbins pitching and Jim Benton and Red Hamilton catching.

Those were the days before Jack Mitchell became a "general." In fact he wasn't even a buck private yet and most of his present squad of daring young men weren't even born.

Well anyhow, the way things have changed in football I'm convinced that the scoring system is out of keeping with today's conditions.

The comparative quality of schools cannot be properly judged merely by scores achieved on touchdowns, points after TDs, field goals and safeties.

And let's not be unaware of the fact that it's the reputations of schools, not teams alone, that are at stake these fall afternoons and evenings when the kickoff whistles blow.

So I propose that major modifications be made in the scoring rules to give a more realistic appraisal of these mass spectacles that quaintly enough are still referred to as "games."

Since half-time entertainment on the field is such an integral part of today's gridiron events, I'd suggest that scores be kept on the lovely lassies who cavort so energetically in front of the school bands. The higher they kick the more points their side should have. If a twirler drops her baton, penalize her team half a yard or something.

All drunks showing partisanship should be counted and the school with the most of this type of supporter should be docked a point or two. (Nonpartisan, unruly drunks should be benched below the stadium and kept on warm chaser for the next quarter.)

Schools allowing their fans to bring radios into the stands and to annoy nearby people with broadcasts of other games should be put on probation—and the radios sent to the Goodwill Industries.

Singing of the alma mater in that solemn moment before the kickoff should be scored. A school able to demonstrate that as many as one-tenth of its supporters are familiar with even the first line of the song surely should get some extra points.

And now that coaches appear for their weekly ordeal in the full regalia of successful business executives, they too ought to be judged. A head coach with clashing colors in his sideline ensemble should be dealt with harshly, and no excuses accepted.

These are just some random ideas that occurred to me as I fought my way through the Memorial Stadium traffic last night. The dogs at West Memphis have a better chance to catch the mechanical rabbit than these proposals have to win adoption.

Even so, I'm going to seek the ear of Goldie Jones, the vivacious grandmother on the Razorback business staff, and pass along these thoughts. I knew Goldie before she became a grandma, back when the going price for one of today's second string halfbacks would have bought a whole backfield, with waterboy thrown in.

Maybe Goldie will listen. She's heard a lot of screwball ideas in her time, including the theory that football players ought to attend class and make passing marks.

The Bride Wept And the Groom Made Speeches

Since this is a season that is enlivened both by elections and weddings, this department offers herewith a tale as evidence that to mix politics and romance is to risk disaster.

The details are lifted from a letter dispatched from Little Rock by a Massachusetts gentleman to his brother back East. A copy of the communication fell into my hands too late for publication ahead of the Democratic primary, which in a way is unfortunate but does not detract one whit from the moral of the story.

Here's the account of an eyeball witness:

"The day was fixed for the wedding to take place Friday last. The bridegroom left here about a week before the time he was to take to himself a bride, [to make] an electioneering tour of an adjoining county, telling his intended and her relations to go on and prepare the wedding feast as he would certainly be back on the day appointed.

"Accordingly the guests were invited, the cake baked, the pig roasted, the turkey, deer, bear, buffalo, etc, slaughtered and all good things collected and made ready; the company assembled, the house was crowded, the parson waited, the bride wept, but the bridegroom came not.

"The company waited anxiously awhile longer but to no purpose. However we ate the pig, turkey, cakes and custards and . . . drank the wine to the health of the bride and the confusion of the groom and went home very well satisfied with our part of the wedding.

"About 12 o'clock next day the bridegroom cometh; the frowns were smoothed away, the tears dried up and the bride's face beamed forth like a sunny morning in May.

"And what do you think [the bridegroom's] excuse was for such unheard-of conduct? . . . a little stream of water about five yards wide had detained him two days, and he within 10 miles of his fair one.

"The wedding took place on Saturday and however unpleasant it might have been to the bride that the first time miscarried, it was all to the better for us guests as we attended and feasted twice whilst [the couple] was only married once."

Now as most must have suspected on reading mention of the slaughtering of "turkey, deer, bear and buffalo" in preparation for the wedding feast, this incident could hardly have been of recent occurrence.

As a matter of history, it all happened back in January of 1832, and was reported by one Hiram A. Whittington, an Easterner who had migrated to Arkansas Territory.

Hiram was a printer in the employ of William E. Woodruff, founder of the *Arkansas Gazette*. Over a period of ten years, during which time he moved to Hot Springs and became a pioneer businessman, Hiram wrote many letters to his New England kinfolks to give them information about life, people and customs on the Western frontier.

He wrote his brother Granville that politicians of the day were expected to "treat" their friends often during campaigns and that to make a race "commonly costs twice as much as the office is worth." Apparently some things haven't changed materially in Arkansas politics in more than a century.

Margaret Ross, of the state History Commission staff, is preparing a collection of the Whittington letters for publication by the Pulaski County Historical Society. Take my word for it, based on a sketchy study of their contents, the letters are going to be worth reading.

Anybody Seen Or Heard A Mule Lately?

Batesville—There came a report from over this way recently that two men returned from a fishing hole to find a mule eating the seat covers of their automobile. No details were given as to whether they were more shocked at seeing this demonstration of the animal's lack of gustatory discrimination or at seeing a real-life mule.

As most folks may have noticed, the mule is rapidly disappearing here in Arkansas, a state almost as closely identified with the long-eared cuss as Missouri. It's a long road that affords the present-day motorist an opportunity to dodge a mule-drawn wagon. The tractor has just about taken the mule's place on the farm. In fact, Uncle Sam's agricultural census-takers could find only 18,892 mules and horses on Arkansas farms in 1954, whereas there had been some 36,000 in 1950. (No breakdown given as to mules and horses separately.) In all of the United States in 1954 there were only 1,599,000 mules; the 1910 count was nearly 4,500,000.

Of course the mule cannot be adequately handled as a statistic. He has been man's helper since the earliest times and has won a reputation that is described in phrases both printable and unprintable.

For one thing the mule is credited with possession of the sobriety, patience, endurance and sure-footedness of his father, the ass, and the vigor, strength and courage of his mother, the horse. Immunity from many animal diseases, ability to carry or to pull heavy loads, sense enough not to over-eat, stamina for work in tropical or desert heat, all are counted among his better qualities.

As for some of his less-lovable characteristics, the mule has won some sort of immortality through words that have got into the language: mulish, mule-eared, stubborn-as-a-mule.

Josh Billings, who saw many things as they really were, said that, "The mule is half horse and half jackass and then comes to a full stop, Nature discovering her mistake."

In the early days of World War II, while going through one of those ordeals that the Army so quaintly called a "refresher course," I had occasion to discover that not everyone knows as much about the mule's ancestry as did Josh Billings.

A young lieutenant was lecturing to some of us on the work of the now defunct Remount Service, whose mission was to keep the Army supplied with horses and mules.

"The Army is so anxious to encourage the raising of these animals," he said, with authority ringing in every word, "that it frequently loans out its own fine horses and mules for breeding purposes." He was wide open for a flank attack so I asked him if it could possibly be true that the Army was loaning out its blooded mules for such a purpose. The lad was cagey and said that if I knew anything more about the subject he'd be glad to hear it.

"Well," I said, "we can be sure that if the Army is trying to get mules that way it ain't gonna get very many," and later some of us who knew about the home life of the jackass briefed the looey on the secret of where little mules come from.

So much for the mule: may he never suffer the fate of the prairie hen or the dodo. Perhaps zoos will keep a few of his kind on hand so that the upcoming generations can look upon and marvel at this beast of whom the poet Arthur Guiterman wrote:

> Oh, the Brown Missouri mule
>   has a copper-plated throat,
> and the welkin splits apart
>   when he hits an upper note.

Our State Seen As Happy Land For the Retired

Arkansas as an ideal land for retired people is much on the mind these days of a short, brisk-talking, energetic transplanted Texan who makes his home in Fayetteville.

He's Elgin H. Blalock, a long-time federal employee, a lawyer, and in recent years a sparkplug in a movement which is bringing new citizens to our state.

I saw him for the first time at a meeting on the University of Arkansas campus during which retirement needs and possibilities were discussed.

His humorous labeling of Florida as "the state of romance, rheumatism, and religion" and some of his comments on Arkansas's natural advantages stirred my interest so I went around later to his office just off the Fayetteville square to talk with him.

Mr. Blalock, it turned out, went to work for Uncle Sam in the Shreveport, Louisiana, post office back in 1907 after leaving his home at Marshall, Texas, "too green to be picked" as he put it.

In his federal career, which ended with his retirement in 1950, he served the War Department, the Veterans Administration, did duty in the old Army Air Corps, and traveled much of the United States.

And, he told me with a good-natured chuckle, he took time out twice to run for Congress, once in Texas and once in Oklahoma—dropping out of the Texas race and losing the Oklahoma one. He also got a degree in law.

He'd bought a 40-acre tract of land at West Fork, south of Fayetteville, while working in Oklahoma and "never did anything with it." But it kept his thoughts on Arkansas.

After retirement, and after he and his wife had got their fill of traveling—including nearly two years in Florida—he picked Fayetteville for their permanent home base and they settled there in 1954.

And, figuring that retiring doesn't mean doing nothing, he opened a law office.

It's not practicing law that has kept him busy as much as 16 hours a day, he said.

It's the spreading of the story of Arkansas's advantages among retired civil service people and those about to retire which is taking most of his time and some of his money, too.

He figures he's helping people like himself when he tips them off to what he strongly considers to be a good thing—a pleasant and not too expensive life in Arkansas.

He feels just as strongly, too, that our state is going to miss out on something with real economic potentialities if Arkansans don't reach out and encourage former government workers to move here.

"Around 90,000 civil service employees retire annually," he explained. "Their average annual annuity is $2,100 and they'll spend practically all of it."

Even if Arkansas attracted only a thousand such people a year, he pointed out, the economic gain would be substantial.

What's more, he added, "every known occupation, trade, and profession is represented among government workers."

The mere fact that a person is retired from government service doesn't mean that he cannot continue to perform needed and useful services, he said. Here again Arkansas could gain.

There's one expression you musn't use around him, "government pension."

"That word pension makes me mad," he said, looking just a bit mad.

Since the early 1920s government civil servants have had deductions made from their salaries to finance future retirement annuities, Mr. Blalock explained. What they get on completion of their service costs the taxpayers not at all.

He's plenty unhappy, by the way, over failure of Congress to adjust the annuity payments upwards to offset the rising cost of living.

In actuality, said Mr. Blalock, retired government workers such as himself paid in 100-cent dollars over the years and are now getting 50-cent dollars back in annuities.

Mr. Blalock is an active member of the National Association of Retired Civil

Employees.

He organized a Fayetteville chapter of the organization in 1954 with 15 members, now up to 59, which gives some small indication of the way that Ozarks community is attracting retired people.

A state organization was formed two years ago and its efforts were dedicated, as he expressed it, "to get Arkansas over to civil service people."

He handed me a copy of the July, 1957, issue of *Retirement Life*, the national association's monthly magazine, and pointed to an illustrated article entitled "Arkansas."

This state, the opening paragraph declared, is "a land we know too little about."

Here's part of what the article told the magazine's readers:

"Arkansas offers a reasonable tax system in favor of those in lower income. . . . Its winters are short and heating costs are nominal. . . . Food costs are low. . . . housing costs [are] much lower than elsewhere. . . . It has almost limitless health and recreational facilities."

When I left Mr. Blalock he turned back to his typewriter to complete a letter he was writing to ex-Senator James M. Mead of New York, now living much of the time in Florida.

"An old friend," Mr. Blalock said. "I'm selling him on Arkansas."

Forecasts of 1960s Highlights, Lowlights

The *Gazette*'s sports writers aren't the only ones who can make predictions of things to come.

Here goes with a few of my own forecasts on what to expect in 1960. I'm making these without benefit of astrological charts or the voodoo magic of sorcerers at old Argenta.

Mrs. Dick Nixon's fur coat won't be an issue in the presidential campaign, if her husband can sidestep it.

American journalists accompanying President Eisenhower through Russia will report that he's bearing up under the strain better than they are. The dispatching of such news is customary when the president travels, and there's some truth to it. He gets more sleep than they do.

John L. McClellan will continue as Arkansas's senior senator, without particular difficulty.

Crip Hall will be Arkansas's next secretary of state—and hasn't he been?

A movement will start to raise the salary of Frank Broyles. If it succeeds the new president of the University of Arkansas will also benefit, for the legislature will feel obligated to keep his pay on a level with that of the football coach.

Bruce Bennett won't run for the top job if Our Leader tries for a fourth term—and I believe he will.

A drug manufacturer will come out with a toothpaste that's spotted. It'll contain an unpronounceable ingredient that brightens the teeth, sweetens the breath and seals unglued envelopes.

The scourge of "irregularity" will continue to sweep the land wherever television can reach into parlors, pool halls and play rooms. Fewer than four firms whose products help Americans toward their normal regularity will permit the word constipation to appear in TV commercials.

Somebody at Hot Springs will slip me a hot tip on a horse. The horse will finish out of the money.

The French Army will not recall Brigitte Bardot's husband to the colors. He's too nervous for the service.

Additional miles of roadside vistas in our state will be beautified by the spread of automobile junk yards.

University status for Arkansas State College will be back in the news and deeper in politics than before.

The Shah of Iran will become a daddy again—of a daughter. The fellow obviously is jinxed.

Witt Stephens will add lightning rods to his line of buggies, horse collars, gas lights and rocking chairs—if he can see a way to make 'em pay. And he can see more ways to make a thing pay than almost anybody in Arkansas.

Winthrop Rockefeller would make an excellent governor, but he won't seek the job.

Hollywood will stretch its nudity game until the public reacts against it.

At least a dozen Chambers of Commerce in Arkansas will declare indignantly that the census takers didn't count everybody in their communities. The federal government will then be blamed in some quarters for conspiring against our state.

Sid McMath will be looking for a type of outdoor exercise which doesn't involve a horse.

George of the Marion Hotel's famous Gar Hole will be asked by numerous patrons from "up nawth" if that's a real gar in the pool above the bar. It is, but it's a runt.

Directories in most public telephone booths I step into will have a page torn out. That'll be the page listing the number I'm hunting.

A high percentage of restrooms in bus stations will need cleaning up—and they'll stay that way.

The Russians will shoot another rocket to the moon, and Elvis Presley's return from the Army will generate wild jubila-tion. I won't lose any sleep over either event.

The name of Aransas Pass, Texas, will appear in the papers at least once as Arkansas Pass.

My neighbor, Jim Dildy of Arkansas Power and Light Company, will wage his usual summer war against nut grass in his yard. The nut grass will emerge victorious, as usual.

Cuba will not apply for admission as the 51st American state.

Harry Truman and Gen. Douglas MacArthur will not be guests at the White House for the 15th anniversary of victory in World War II.

A recluse living as a pauper on the edge of a city dump in New Jersey—but believed to have a fortune hidden in his mattress—will be found dead. A search by police will turn up not even a dime. This story will not appear in newspapers, or on radio or television, across the nation.

Well, that's about all I can manage at this seance.

Whether Eddie Fisher and Liz Taylor will stay together, whether a dissatisfied customer will return his empty Geritol bottle for a refund or whether Elder Jerry Shrieves will start writing flawless grammar, I just can't say.

Anybody can make forecasts. Why not make a few of your own?

There's a World of Difference Between Creek and Greek

Every now and then I am jolted to learn—once again—how easily the changing of one letter in a word will completely alter its meaning.

In yesterday's column, in telling of the generosity of the late Thomas Gilcrease of Tulsa, I described him as "part Creek." This came out in print as "part Greek."

The Creek Indians were among the so-called Five Civilized Tribes forcibly moved from their homes in the southeastern region of our country to Indian Territory, in what is now Oklahoma. Gilcrease's mother was half-Creek.

The other Civilized Tribes were Cherokees, Choctaws, Chickasaws, and Seminoles.

Now the Greeks were—and are—somebody else entirely. Their homeland is far from the southeastern region of the United States, away off yonder on the lower end of the Balkan Peninsula, its shores washed by the waters of the Ionian and the Aegean Seas. I do not know whether the Greeks ever met the Creeks, or the Creeks ever went to Hellas—the old name for Greece—but I do know there ain't any Greek Indian tribe in Oklahoma.

Incidentally, I went to Hellas once. They have a national joy drink over there that I can't begin to spell, but it's pronounced "oozoe." Three shots of that Grecian firewater and you can't tell a Creek from a Greek and by then nobody cares anyhow.

In yesterday's column I also reported that Oklahoma's only Republican congressman, Page Belcher, mispronounces Arkansas, calling it "Ark-an-sis," as in Kansas.

I've done a bit of research into this matter, on request of a friend in Tulsa who's an oil company lawyer with an inquisitive mind.

As best I can learn, the Frenchmen who explored this part of the world back in the 1700s are to blame for most of the confusion, including that of Congressman Belcher, and danged near everybody in Kansas.

Quapaw Indians, who lived along the Mississippi River when the white men first came, got their name from a tribal term, Ugakhpa, meaning "downstream people." They were part of a lot of Sioux who had crossed the Mississippi long ago. The Ugakhpa came downstream and the early French explorers referred to them as Akansea or Akansa. Some of the Sioux who went upstream were called Kansa, and that's where the name for Kansas originated. They were also called Kaw; the Akansa and the Kansa names are found closely related in early French records.

Well, there you have it. The proper pronunciation of Kansas actually is Kansaw, and it makes a lot of sense in a lot of ways. How much sweeter and more pleasing to the ear, for example, is Wichita, Kansaw, than is Wichitas, Kan-sis.

For the matter, why not drop Kansas entirely and change the name of the state to Kaw?

Write your congressman today. Let's put an end to the confusion over how to pronounce Arkansas and Kansas, once and for all. Change the name of Kansas. Suh? Not only yes, but heck yes!

In this connection, I stand corrected as to the identity of that noble orator who is credited with preventing a change in the name of Arkansas, back there in the legislature of 1881.

As a boy, I learned one version of his oration and his name stuck in my memory as Senator Hiram Jackson of Johnson County. Now I'm informed that it was Senator Cassius Johnson of Jackson County.

No matter about the identity of the senator, or the county from which he sprang. He was a better man than most in his day, and made a danged sight more sense then some do now.

Bob Lancaster

Grant County has produced two sets of brothers that cause people to sit up and take notice. One is the Stephens brothers—Witt and Jack—whose investment banking firm has made waves in financial circles worldwide.

The other is the Lancaster brothers, Bill and Bob, both highly respected in Arkansas journalism. Bob Lancaster, a tall, quiet country boy whose serious demeanor belies his formal education as a Nieman Fellow at Harvard and the absolutely sidesplitting humor that marks his writing, was the Arkansas Traveler in the early 1970s.

Lancaster is a master at his craft. He worked hard writing columns that said something, and that something stayed with his readers until his next column appeared.

He left the Traveler spot to "be a journalistic missionary in the Pennsylvania Heart of Darkness," he wrote in 1973, when he left to join the staff of the *Philadelphia Inquirer*. He returned to the state in 1976 and is now Senior Editor of the *Arkansas Times* magazine.

Stalking the Wily Mosquito

The color and warmth and aroma of spring are compelling, but the season has its obnoxious aspects, too. For every hour I spend admiring the bloom of the dogwood and the song of the whippoorwill, I spend two waging psychological warfare against a mosquito that has invaded my bedroom in the middle of the night.

I've never learned the secret of fighting a mosquito at two in the morning. He is as elusive and relentless an enemy as a Viet Cong, attacking under cover of darkness and then disappearing when you turn on the light.

Unlike his adversary, a mosquito never gets exasperated. He never goes berserk after a couple of hours and says, "All right, I've got to get up and go to work in the morning and I'm sick and tired of this so let's quit playing games." A mosquito is infinitely patient. He originated protracted, hit-and-run warfare.

He instinctively knows the precise instant to strike—at the exact moment when every part of your body is asleep except the little corner of your mind that sluggishly perceives and identifies his faint and telltale hum. He knows that at that point you'd rather die or take castor oil than have to struggle all the way back into wakefulness. So he feasts for a while on your forehead or on an exposed ankle, until it becomes essential that you slap and curse, and arise and take up arms.

But the instant you switch on the light, he vanishes. He becomes as impossible to find as McGovern supporters or low-priced meat. I've devastated bedrooms in every house we've ever lived in looking for such mosquitoes. In groggy desperation, I've ripped pictures off of walls to look behind them, and rugs up off of floors to look under them. I've dumped the clothes out of bureau drawers and turned socks and gloves inside out looking for such mosquitoes. I've spent hours standing in the dark, with one hand on the light switch and the other clutching a rolled-up newspaper, hoping to outwit and outwait such a mosquito.

But nothing has ever worked, and I don't know the answer.

There are other equally distressing and apparently insoluble problems that arrive with the equinox, and not the least of them is how to get a wasp nest off your house. My wasps have a tendency to homestead in unapproachable niches on high outside eaves and there's no practicable way of evicting them. I've tried several tactics.

(1) Sneak up on them with a can of Raid. This is a stupid thing to do when you do your sneaking via a fifteen-foot stepladder. The hard part is deciding what to do when a couple of their sentries crawl down under your shirtcollar with dishonorable intentions.

(2) Take a wild swat at the nest with a long fishing pole and then run for your life. More often than not, you'll fail to knock the nest down. But you will succeed in putting the wasps in a foul mood, whereupon they'll make it a point of honor to chase you down and put you in one.

(3) Tying a newspaper on the pole, setting it afire, and burning them out. This entails some risks. If you have a neighbor who bears a grudge, you can figure he'll call the police and report that you're trying to burn down your house for the insurance. You will inevitably leave a big black smoke stain on the eave, blister all the paint in the vicinity of the nest, ruin a good fishing pole, and have to greet the Fire Department with excuses and a drink.

(4) Removing to a safe distance and shooting the nest down with a twelve-gauge shotgun. This is a pretty good desperation approach but recommended only if getting rid of the wasps is worth the considerable damage to your house and the lawsuit resulting from the death by ricochet of your next door neighbor's dog.

I thought of these and several other seasonal complaints the other afternoon during an excursion in the Saline River bottoms. It seems to me that any country that can overcome bathtub ring, dandruff and refrigerator frost should be able to solve such perplexing and disquieting aggravations.

Effects of Elevator Riding

Arkadelphia—I was sitting with several college teachers around a faculty coffee urn here the other day, discussing the monkeyshines of the state legislature, when one of their colleagues came in. He seemed preoccupied and mildly agitated.

"Why is it," he said as he filled his mug, "that I begin to hate and resent people when I get on an elevator?"

"The common word for it is paranoia," one of them replied.

"Claustrophobia," another said.

"Nothing of the sort," he said, shaking his head. "It's not me. I think everybody feels the same way. There's just something unnatural about riding an elevator with a lot of other people on it."

This problem had been preying on his mind for several days, he said. He had been to Little Rock the previous weekend, and because of an elevator in an office building there, had come home a nervous wreck.

He had boarded it at ground level with a horde of other people one afternoon and was feeling fine until the thing stopped at the second floor and two more men squeezed on. They obviously had been talking and joking about something while waiting, and they continued the conversation when they got on. He happened to be sandwiched between them—a short fellow between two six-footers conversing over his head.

As the elevator ascended, he noticed a certain uneasy tone entering their repartee, and he knew somehow that they were resenting him for eavesdropping on a discussion that was none of his business.

At the same time, he was resenting having to listen to them. He was being forced into overhearing a private exchange that he didn't care a damn about. But what could he do? He couldn't not listen. And he had no inclination to join in, contributing some such peacemaker comment as: "Is that so?" or "You don't say?" Even if he had, he figured their reply would consist of an icy stare that meant: "Butt out, fella. This doesn't concern you."

He decided the prudent thing would be to hum a tune. That would distract his own attention and would show them that he wasn't inclined to nosiness. He started humming the first thing that came into his mind. That turned out to be "I Enjoy Being a Girl."

When he realized it, he was embarrassed and more self-conscious than ever. In his nervousness, had he hummed it loud enough for them to hear it? And were they now thinking to themselves that this guy was some kind of fairy or something?

To compensate, he turned to a passenger behind him—one who was minding his own business—and said something like: "Think it'll rain again today?" The passenger's response was a polite, suspicious smile that he interpreted to mean: "I don't know you. Let's keep it that way."

This increased his anxiety and discomfort and he found himself wondering: "Maybe I've got bad breath or something."

"This thing sure is slow," he said aloud to nobody in particular, just to break the tension.

Nobody offered a reply. The two men who had been talking had lapsed into a hostile silence, and in the uneasy quiet everyone stared at the lighted panel indicating which floor the elevator was now approaching.

When he got off, he uttered a quick wordless prayer that he'd never have to see any of these people again as long as he lived.

One of his fellow academics, having listened to all of this, offered an analysis: "It's just a symptom of overcrowding," he said. "There's been studies, you know, showing that rats in an overcrowded situation like that turn to crime and homosexuality and a lot of them go insane."

"It's not overcrowding per se," one of the others said. "It's the territorial principle. You know what that is. The theory that people instinctively feel that a certain minimum amount of space around them is private property. It acts up when somebody violates it. Like when somebody reads over your shoulder when you've got a newspaper. Or when you're sitting at a lunch counter with a lot of empty stools all around you and somebody comes up and sits in the one right next to you."

"I think that's the secret of the flight to the suburbs," the rat expert said. "People aren't wanting to get away from blacks or crime or pollution or stuff like that. It's just that a house with yards and fences—tangible borders, you know—represents a tangible and adequate square of territory that nobody's likely to violate."

"Some people think this territory thing is why we lost the Vietnam war," the territory expert said.

"Hell, I don't care about that," the man who hates elevators said.

"A throwback to our primitive forebears," the rat expert said. "You know why people in a restaurant will glance around nervously from time to time to see if anyone is watching them eat? The old fear of predators. Try something some time: When you're in a restaurant, start staring at somebody who's eating on the other side of the room. Pretty soon, they'll notice you, no matter how preoccupied they are or how far away you are. Conditioned reflex. A holdover from when we were savages on the savannah and had to guard and fight for our food."

"You know another one," the territory expert said. "The coffee pot there. It represents the primeval waterhole . . ."

"Why don't you just start using the stairs?" I said to the man who hates elevators.

He said he believed he would. Then, brightening, he said: "While we're on the subject of evolutionary quirks, I wanted to ask you something about the state Senate . . ."

Hot Lull Before Football

Someone just told me about a conversation he overheard at a Little Rock bar.

Two guys were discussing the Razorbacks' prospects for the upcoming football season, and one of them, a scrawny little fellow, probably a native Texan, took the opportunity to say:

"You know, Fayetteville is the crummiest town I ever saw. It's never turned out anything but good football players and ugly women."

The other guy, who looked like an all-conference tight end, only bigger, glared at him and said, "You don't say? My wife is from Fayetteville."

"Oh, is that right?" the little guy said, squirming. "What position did she play?"

Maybe it's the heat, I don't know. But for whatever reason, here in the lurch between the political primaries and the start of football season, not much is going on in Arkansas.

Things have been so slow in El Dorado, for example, that a major controversy has developed down there over a rooster.

Last week, some malcontent complained to the police that the thing woke him up at an unreasonable hour every morning with a lot of obnoxious, cheerful crowing. He wanted to press disturbing-the-peace charges.

The police chickened out on the case (no foul play involved, they said)—sorry, the heat's getting to me, too—so Grouch wrote the daily newspaper, suggesting that someone provide the bird with a one-way ticket to Norphlet, which is just out of earshot up the highway.

Norphlet residents responded by saying sure, send him on. One said the concrete jungle of metropolitan El Dorado was no place for a self-respecting rooster anyway. Another suggested that if El Dorado weren't such a Gomorrah, where people stay up all hours playing cards and drinking sody-water, it wouldn't mind having a rooster around to greet the rosy-fingered dawn.

Another, who really got his feathers ruffled (no more, I promise), said he'd never heard of anybody complaining about a rooster crowing except St. Peter, "and he had a guilty conscience."

The mayor of Norphlet issued a formal invitation to the rooster and its owner to move on out. The El Dorado paper devoted a substantial portion of its front page to what it alleged was an interview with the rooster, although there was some question of authenticity. There were a couple of developments, but this is getting absurd.

I checked all this out with a member of the Chamber of Commerce, who assured me that the controversy would blow over as soon as something interesting happened. "Things ought to be picking up soon," he said. "Maybe this week we'll have a wedding or a burglary or something."

The only town where there seems no lack of excitement is over at Benton. Burt Reynolds had been over there filming the movie *McKlusky*, and the women of Saline County, clutching their copies of *Cosmopolitan*, have been getting long-sought revenge for all the hours their pot-bellied husbands have spent slobbering over *Playboy* centerfolds.

Ron Meyer, general manager of the *Benton Courier*, reports that he's never seen anything like it.

"Beds are unmade, dishes unwashed, little children have been left running in the streets," he writes.

"Bra and dress sales have hit the skids. Hot pants have been whacked off an additional two inches and body shirts have been shrunk down to size. . . . Shorts have been rolled up at the bottom, down at the top. Our courthouse lawn has become a showplace for a milky way of belly buttons."

Meyer says he's heard only one woman complain that she never did care much for Burt Reynolds anyway and couldn't understand what all the fuss was about. "But then one of the station wagons from the State Hospital honked," he says, "and she had to go."

People Will Eat Anything

On the assumption that some people will pay good money to eat anything, the Hamburg Kiwanis Club cooked up the First Annual Hamburg Armadillo Barbecue last night.

Something came up—pardon that—and I didn't get down there, but earlier, I talked to Bill Johnson, a Hamburg attorney and Armadillo Day publicity chairman, about it.

"The armadillo isn't native to this area," he said, "but in the last ten or fifteen years, we've had a sort of armadillo-in down here. You can't drive down the road without running over a couple of the things."

A while back, he said, some of the club members were talking about the armadillo invasion, and it seemed a shame to them that while their area had been unexpectedly blessed with this new natural resource, it apparently wasn't good for anything except making a mess of Highway 82.

Some of the older members remembered that in harder times folks used to eat armadillos, and that inspired School Superintendent Bob Turner to suggest the community armadillo barbecue.

No one had the courage, apparently, to object. No one brought out the fact that 90 percent of an armadillo's diet is worms. No one said, "Bob, have you ever tried skinning one of them things?"

Turner had a couple of points in his favor, though. One was that eating them was the best proposal yet for keeping armadillos off the streets. Another was that Gillett already had an annual coon supper, Grady had an annual fish fry, Gould had an annual turtle derby, Warren had an annual tomato festival, and 'possums taste bad. The armadillo was about the only thing left that was both edible and unappropriated.

So the barbecue was on, and for several weeks, members of the Kiwanis Club have been prowling around the country roads of Ashley County at all hours, bagging armadillos, and bringing them back to town to be skinned, dressed and salted away for the barbecue. They accumulated nearly 80 by the first of this week.

The Extension Service helpfully sent over some ghastly recipes on the lost art of barbecuing armadillos, but Chief Cook

W. T. Higginbotham, who's also the Ashley County judge, had some ideas of his own about that. Probably his best idea was to supplement the menu with 750 barbecued chickens.

I was curious how they went about skinning and cleaning an armadillo, but all I could get out of Johnson was a weak and somewhat pained response: "It's hard," he said. "They tend to stink pretty bad."

Had he ever actually partaken of an armadillo filet?

Well, no.

Did he plan to?

Well . . .

I called up George Purvis of the state Game and Fish Commission and told him some crazy people down at Hamburg were actually going to barbecue some armadillos with the intention of eating them.

"I've had barbecued armadillo," he said.

"It's not bad. It's mild-tasting meat—not gamey. . . . It's probably closer to rabbit than any taste I can think of."

"Okay, George," I said. "I'll see you around sometime."

Later, after having given the matter much thought, I devised a recipe for barbecued armadillo that I thought I could live with:

> Get someone else to catch, kill, skin and dress armadillo for you. Cut up armadillo meat any way that suits you, or not at all if you don't feel like it. Place armadillo meat on two-foot pine plank. Season and place in oven. Bake for several hours or until tender. Remove from oven. Take armadillo meat off plank. Throw away armadillo meat. Eat plank.

The Great Armadillo Barbecue

People who would pay good money to eat an armadillo have something fundamentally wrong with them. Either they were not brought up right, or they are so guileless that they let fast-talking members of the Hamburg Kiwanis Club bamboozle them into believing that eating an armadillo is OK. Some people will swallow anything, so to speak.

And not just a few people, either. Last summer, the Kiwanis Club of Hamburg enticed 2,500 people to its first annual Armadillo Barbecue, and this summer they're expecting 5,000 for the encore. The madness is spreading, like rabies.

One of the television stations heard about the upcoming Second Annual Armadillo Festival the other day, and, laboring under the misconception that I am some sort of authority on armadillo cuisine, solicited my opinions about this insanity.

This is a transcript, only slightly embellished, of our interview.

TV Interviewer: Why do you think 5,000 people would turn out for an armadillo

barbecue?

Me: I can't think of any rational explanation. Maybe they're desperate over the high cost of meat at the supermarket.

TV Interviewer: Our information is that members of the Kiwanis Club of Hamburg are already out collecting armadillos, bagging them, skinning them, salting them away. The news release we received from them doesn't explain, however, how they go about this task. Do they shoot the armadillos, or trap them, or what?

Me: My understanding is that they collect them off the highways after they've been run over by automobiles. That way, the club not only gets meat for its barbecue, it also performs a public service at the same time.

TV Interviewer: All kidding aside now . . .

Me: You think I'm kidding? What do you think is the cause of the great famine among the Ashley county roadside crow population?

TV Interviewer: What do you have against eating armadillos, anyway?

Me: I have just about anything you can

think of against it.

TV Interviewer: Many people eat 'possum. I can't see the difference, really . . .

Me: Nobody who'd ever amounted to anything would eat 'possum or armadillo either one. You have never heard of Beethoven eating armadillo. Or George Washington, except maybe during the worst days at Valley Forge when the only alternatives were shoe leather and saddle soap. If Frank Broyles ever ate any armadillo, I've never seen it written up in Orville Henry's column.

TV Interviewer: I can think of people like Daniel Boone and Davy Crockett—who might have . . .

Me: Davy Crockett did a lot of damfool things. He even ran for Congress.

TV Interviewer: Well, getting back to the Hamburg event. I understand they're going to have a new feature at the barbecue this year—an armadillo beauty contest. Is that for armadillos or girls?

Me: It's for armadillos. You have to feel a measure of sympathy for the judges.

TV Interviewer: Well, I suppose you *could* have a Miss Armadillo Contest for girls. I mean, a girl would just as soon be Miss Armadillo as Miss Pink Tomato, wouldn't you think?

Me: I think any girl who aspired to be Miss Armadillo would deserve to be Miss Armadillo.

The Possum as Alternative

S ome notes on alternatives to high-priced meals:

Possum: "You see," writes the self-described leader of the Eat More Possum movement in Arkansas County, "we had the answer to high meat prices all along. Just think what a tremendous effect it would have on beef and pork prices if everybody in Arkansas would eat possum for just a week."

Yeah. And it wouldn't hurt the highway beautification program any, either.

Fish: There was an editorial in the paper the other day that said: "Bring down the price of meat by going fishing!" It went on enthusiastically to recommend Lake Conway as the logical site to start this crusade.

Well, that's not a bad idea, but in all candor it's not a very practical one, either. That kind of romanticism can be costlier than roast beef. I know, because for years I inaugurated every fishing season with a trip to Lake Conway, and I finally had to give it up for economic reasons.

I'd have to have a new fly rod to replace the one that the kids used all winter as a practice javelin. That's $15.98. And a new fly reel (automatic), that's $6.95 more. And since the old tackle box was appropriated

for the kids' rock collection, I'd have to have a new one, and a small one runs about $4.98.

The fishing license is $3.50. A life jacket (now mandatory in a boat) would be around $4.98. Boat rental would be $2, and a couple of boxes of bait would be $2 more. For hooks, lines, sinkers and corks, I could get by for no more than $1.70.

All that comes to $42.09.

All right, now, the last time I went to Lake Conway, I went with a certain Steinmetz, and the two of us managed to catch, in a day's time, two fish. I estimated the total weight of the two fish at a half-pound, and I figured that if we had dressed them out and taken them home, instead of throwing them back in embarrassment and disgust, we might have brought home four ounces of edible meat. A quarter of a pound. Half of that—two ounces—would have been my portion.

Suppose, now, that I sally forth to the lake tomorrow, having spent my $42.09 in the name of fighting high meat prices and have the same luck I had on my last trip. Two ounces of meat for $42.09.

That is $336.72 a pound.

And I doubt if even Earl Butz would consider that a bargain, although you can never tell about that guy.

I could dispense with all the fancy gear,

of course—cut my own pole, hitchhike to the lake and fish from the bank. Figuring expenses that way, my two ounces of fish would cost only $3.70—or about $30 a pound.

It wouldn't cost me much more than that to stay home and eat beef.

Blackbird: Jessie Lanphere of Bull Shoals offers this alternative. "Fried Blackbird: Kill and dress bird. Split dressed bird down the center. Salt and pepper and roll in flour. Fry in fat until brown. Add water and cover. Let simmer until tender."

According to Miz Jessie's recipe, one blackbird makes two servings, which means that Pine Bluff could raid its one big downtown roost for enough eats to serve the entire population of Arkansas, with enough left over for Louisiana, Mississippi, Alabama and much of Georgia.

Horses: In the mail is this note from Hot Springs: "For what it's worth, the same day your paper had the story about the soaring popularity of horse meat, the longshots started coming in at Oaklawn for the first time."

Curbing Flesh Fantasies

I intend no implication of sinfulness or vulgarity when I say it, but Hot Springs is a city that always turns my mind to matters of the flesh.

There are healing waters to soak it in, and massage rooms where you can get it soothed and pounded, and stuffed chairs on hotel verandahs where you can relax it, and night clubs and restaurants that invite you in to indulge and multiply it.

As a result, after a few indolent days around Central Avenue, you find that you've become preoccupied with the neglected and decrepit condition of your torso. And you notice that you're suddenly bothered by a vague sense of remorse and self-reproach.

You walk past the mirror in your hotel room and notice suddenly that your reflection is coming more and more to resemble a pear. You stop and try to discern, hidden somewhere in that Humpty Dumpty residue of a thousand second helpings, the lithe form that once ran the low hurdles and the high school football end-around.

The reflection taunts you. It dares you to stand up straight and see if you can any longer see your feet over the abdominal overhang. It asks why you don't get a second job, moonlighting as a bowling ball. It suggests that if you took a deep breath you might float away.

That's a dangerous state of mind. Because, as you're driving back home, you're likely to resolve to launch another physical fitness campaign and to stick with it this time until you look like Charles Atlas or Dick Butkus.

Such campaigns end, I've found, in grief, humiliation or disappointment. This particular one ended in humiliation— when, after several assiduous nights of sweat and strain, I challenged my nine-year-old to a bicycle race around the block and lost by 200 yards, pedaling frantically to keep apace while she coasted along, turning occasionally to offer a word of pitying encouragement.

Another one ended in disillusionment and pain after an over-the-hill-gang basketball game in which my ambition told me there was no reason I shouldn't be Jerry West, but after which my muscular system went on strike and kept me at home, in bed, paralyzed, for three full days. That was a tough one to explain to the boss.

And I recall being inspired once—by a newspaper statistic concerning Joe Frazier's proficiency at rope-skipping—to run out to the sporting goods store and buy a championship metal-handled jump rope with which I managed, during my first training session, to trip myself on my concrete driveway, raspberrying both knees and pinching a nerve in the back of my neck—the latter an injury that still bothers me from time to time.

Those were exceptions, though. Ordinarily, I can bridle my fantasies at least to the extent to avoid physiological disaster. I can delude myself with the old Keep It Sensible, All Things In Moderation, Rome Wasn't Built In A Day approach.

That means twenty sit-ups, ten pushups, and fifty side-straddle-hops the first night, and adding five of each every night, and promising myself that come hell or high water I'll stick to the schedule until I look like Jungle Jim.

It also means a willingness to ignore the snickers of the kids as they stand over in the corner observing this pathetic and elephantine ritual. It means defying the years-long traditions of after-dinner sloth and Dagwood-style dozings. It means mastering the inherent and historic resistance to forced labor that shows no immediate profit.

All that's easier than it sounds—when old roly-poly reflection's jibes and insults are fresh in your mind. I've worked up to glorious plateaus before—as high as 35 situps—before I came to my senses and found a plausible excuse to sink back into the customary degeneracy.

When Hot Springs begins to aggravate my conscience, I try to keep in mind A. J. Liebling's maxim that a pot gut is only in the eye of the beholder.

The Goggle-eyed Pestilence

There were only a few of them early last year, but by fall their name was legion. And now, with the coming of spring, they're back, roaring through the neighborhood at dusk every night like a helmeted and goggle-eyed pestilence.

I know how it happened. One kid, maybe twelve or thirteen years old, got a motorcycle, and every afternoon after school he'd wheel it around the neighborhood, showing off. The other kids were eaten up with envy and admiration.

They went to the old man and said, "Listen, I'm eleven and three-fourths years old and all my friends are riding around on motorcycles and you won't let me have one. All my friends laugh at me and make fun of me and say I'm a baby because I still have to ride around on a crummy old bicycle. I'm embarrassed and humiliated and if you don't get me a motorcycle I'm going to kill myself."

They kept on until the old man said, "All right, already, if it means that much to you; now go on and let me watch this ballgame."

So there are maybe 50 of them now, maybe 75, roaring down the street in squadrons. These are no Hell's Angels or Cocaine Katies because many of them are so young they can hardly reach the handlebars. They're so young they can't stray far from home; and they have no desire to go very far, anyway. They just want everyone to see that they have their machine and know how to ride that dude.

That's all right for them, but it's driving me crazy.

You see, since they're not really going anywhere, and since motorcycles cover ground pretty fast, their only option is to ride up and down the street a lot. No, I don't mean a lot: I mean constantly. From the time they get out of school in the afternoon until "The Partridge Family" comes on TV at night.

And since this is essentially some sort of adolescent status ritual, there is competition to see who can be the most conspicuous. And since their range is limited to the street that runs in front of my house, that means seeing who can make the most noise with his machine.

It is at this point that I lose all sympathy for the little rascals.

I believe that human suburban existence would be a real bummer if it weren't for the subtle little pleasures that render it tolerable. And I number among the most important of those little pleasures being able to sit in the yard on warm afternoons and enjoy the quiet of the spring outdoors.

Reading a book, maybe. Or grilling some hamburgers. Or watching the cardinals that come to the feeder at dusk. Or waiting to see if the squirrels will come up from the woods to eat the peanuts that my neighbor Mr. King left for them. Or just pulling a weed to chew on and watching the constellations climb up over the eave of the house next door.

That stuff is important to me, even if my nine-year-old daughter thinks it's a drag and wishes I'd come on in the house so her friends won't see me out there and think old Laura has some kind of peculiar old man. (At least I could take a transistor radio out there with me, she says, and turn it up real loud.)

The point is that the yard ceases to be a refuge of peace and tranquility when this junior Panzer division cranks up and starts the daily maneuvers. The squirrels retreat to the woods, barking piteously. The only birds that come around are starlings, who are immune to provocation and indecency. You might as well try to relax in a stampede or at a women's shoe sale.

One of the neighbors says I exaggerate—that the whole matter is sound and fury,

signifying nothing, with the kids providing the sound and me providing the fury. But it signifies a whole lot to me. I worry when I feel myself becoming a sort of Walter Mitty's Mr. Hyde, with visions of stringing an invisible wire across the street and pulling it tight as they approach.

The other afternoon I went out to the garage and painted a big sign. This is what it says:

> If you saw The Godfather you know terrible things can happen to people who get on the bad side of a man who talks funny and appreciates peace and quiet around his house. A man of that description lives here and nothing gets on his bad side quite so much as people coming down this street on motorcycles making a lot of unnecessary noise.

If nothing else works, I'm going to plant that message at some prominent spot in the front yard.

Smiley's Camelot to End

Sheridan —It will sadden many people here to learn that this is Smiley's last week of freedom. He will be chained up, along with the rest of the city's dogs, when a new voter-approved leash law goes into effect February 8.

For three years, Smiley has provided something of a community bond for many of Sheridan's townspeople. Every day, he poked around the city, covering an extensive territory, relentlessly investigating every activity he ran across with indiscriminate diligence.

His relaxed pace and comprehensive curiosity were something of a symbol of life in a small town, and his adventures were something everyone knew about, talked about, laughed about, took for granted, and cherished in an unspoken way.

Whether you were one of the children he dutifully followed to school in the morning, or one of the merchants whose counters he occasionally napped on, his

daily visit got to be as much a part of your daily routine as the arrival of the postman or the morning tenor of the mill whistle announcing reveille.

A measure of the sentimentality attached to Smiley was a resolution introduced in the state legislature earlier this week by Senator Harold King of Sheridan. It asked that the dog be made an honorary citizen of Sheridan, "and thereby exempt from the leash law."

The senator and the dog cross paths mostly at football games. Hence, this passage from the resolution:

"Smiley attends the various football games . . . and is an enthusiastic supporter of competitive sports and demonstrates his interest and approval by running onto the football field after each touchdown is scored and makes a couple of victorious circles around the field . . ."

Now, Smiley is a low-slung and sad-eyed basset hound, five years old, and people who know mature basset hounds know that they seldom get enthusiastic about anything. The only enthusiasm I've ever seen in Smiley is for romance. What the senator is mistaking for athletic fervor is really no more than simple curiosity.

Smiley just wants to be where the action is, and activity at a football game is no more interesting to him than the construction of a new house on the Leola highway or a shift change down at the flooring mill. He has to check these things out, and make notes.

Insofar as a free spirit like Smiley can be owned, he is owned by the Clinton Graves family. But hundreds of persons feel a proprietary interest in him, and afford him diplomatic immunity when he's in their neighborhood.

Larry Jordan, the postman, says even the meanest dogs around town acknowledge Smiley's prerogative—with never a protest or a challenge—to come into their yards, investigate whatever mysteries have lured him there, stay as long as he likes; and take whatever action he deems necessary and appropriate.

The same is true with most of the townspeople.

Hershel Koon rushed over one night and locked the front door of the First Baptist Church during a storm, and, next morning, when the janitor opened the church, he found Smiley, who'd had some business to attend to during the storm, snoozing comfortably on one of the velvet-covered front pews. When Bruce Gartman opened his furniture store one morning, he discovered that Smiley had sacked out for the night on one of the new sofas he had on display.

Such accommodations are part of the price you pay for having a town dog who performs his duties as faithfully as Smiley does. He doesn't have to ask.

But, Camelot will end for Smiley next week. Graves, a grocer, didn't know beforehand about King's attempt to vouchsafe Smiley's role by legislative fiat, and he doesn't necessarily approve of it.

Smiley, he says, will obey the law the same as other dogs. "It wouldn't be right if they made an exception for him." Graves said. "It wouldn't be fair to the other kids in town who own dogs."

So Smiley will go on the chain. And nobody, probably, will hate it any more than Smiley will.

On the Horns of a Dilemma

A call came in the other day (collect) from a man up in Stone County who offered to give me a goat if I'd drive up there and pick it up.

There was nothing wrong with the goat, he hastened to point out. It just didn't get along well with his wife's dog. And while he was hesitant to get rid of the goat, his wife was just a little more hesitant to get rid of the dog.

The offer seemed momentarily attractive because it had just been announced that milk prices were about to take another great leap forward. But it turned out that this was a billy goat, not a dairy goat. It had horns, and a disposition that was nothing to speak of.

There was a time, I suppose, when it was advantageous to have a goat around your place. Enumerating those advantages, Governor Jeff Davis once said:

"Did you folks know that goats was one of the finest things a farmer ever raised? The sheriff don't get after them. The tax assessor don't put them on the books, and you don't have to feed them anything, only just throw them a copy of the *Gazette* or *Democrat* once a week. The beauty of it is, if one of them dies, you don't lose anything—only a stink."

But times have changed.

I knew a man in Pine Bluff a few years ago whose family gave him a goat for Christmas. They put a ribbon around its neck, put it under the tree, and surprised him with it on Christmas morning.

His first surprise was that his gift ate the wrapping off several of the other gifts, as well as some of the other gifts themselves, and a considerable portion of the tree. But he made a big fuss over it to please the children, and then quietly gave it to some of his wife's relatives' children as a Lincoln's Birthday present.

They, in turn, after expressing their appreciation in a few well-chosen words, managed to get it included on the menu at a civic club's beer-and-barbecued-goat cookout—with almost total emphasis, it turned out, on the beer.

That in mind, I told him I appreciated his offer but guessed I would have to decline.

I figured that would be that, but he persisted.

"Listen," he said, "if you don't want this goat, do you have any suggestions about what I can do with it? I've got sort of fond of him and I hate to just shoot him."

"I can understand that," I told him. And I could. It would be immoral to execute a goat that wasn't bothering anybody for no better reason than that he had a personality clash with some woman's dog.

But no solution occurred to me. There are several people on whom I would wish a goat, but not to the extent of driving up to Stone County, bulldogging the thing, and making a personal delivery. Did he have a vet up in that area he might consult? No. A zoo? No.

I gave him the names of some people he might take the problem up with—politicians, advertising men, and people who are always writing me nasty, critical letters—and told him to let me know how it turned out.

Why should I worry about a goat that I've never even met? I asked myself. But the thought troubled me all afternoon—the idea of that poor guy having to shoot his goat just to accommodate some damned dog. Probably a French poodle.

At home that night, Martha said: "You sure seemed preoccupied tonight. What's on your mind?"

"A goat," I told her.

But the man called back the next morning. "Listen," he said, "I'm afraid I'm not going to be able to let you have that goat after all."

"But I never said . . . ," I started to say before he interrupted.

"No," he said, "you know I was telling you about my wife's dog?"

"Yeah?"

"Well, the Lord rest his bones, the most terrible thing happened to that dog last night. You'd never guess in a million years . . ."

First Grade, or, Rousseau Revisited

Because of the rain and a flat bicycle tire, I had to take the kids to school the other morning. We got there a bit late, and were hurrying down a hallway when a woman came tiptoeing out of one of the first-grade classrooms just ahead of us.

She put a finger to her lips as a sign for us to be quiet, and there seemed something urgent—almost desperate—in the gesture.

She hadn't got five paces from the door, though, before a little boy dashed out of it and fell into step behind her. She was his mother and it was his thinking that whenever she left, so would he.

They apparently had been performing this ritual continuously since the first day of school during the previous week.

The boy had not yet accommodated to the new order and its appalling demands and restrictions. The new arrangement obviously terrified him; and if he had begun to suspect that it was inevitable, he seemed determined to hold out against it as long as he could.

The boy's new teacher came to the door momentarily; and while the mother stood helplessly by, did her best to coax the kid back into the classroom. He was silent and resolute. He knew that they knew his conditions.

I wondered if this impasse didn't represent one of the most complex sociological situations that exists in this day and time. It was, in a sense, a dramatization of the biblical Fall—a translation of Rousseau's grandiose philosophical abstractions into grade-school situation comedy.

Up to this point, the poor kid had been relatively free and unfettered. He had lived comfortably with the presumption that he could tricycle his life away if he felt like it. He was unburdened by responsibilities and obligations. He was happily ignorant of the fact that life requires a series of brutal and irresistible transitions.

Now, suddenly, he was being apprenticed out. He was being bridled into a complicated bureaucratic scheme that he instinctively wanted no part of. He was required to do strange new things by strange new people he didn't even know. And the people he did know—in particular the one person he had relied on to keep his world functioning smoothly—not only insisted that he submit to this cruel insanity but also proposed to up and abandon him.

I knew from experience that there was no way to handle the matter logically and reasonably. I knew because I had been through it earlier with my own two kids, and had been pretty much traumatized myself at the age of five by a first-grade teacher whom I still suspect moonlighted as a Marine Drill Instructor.

There's simply no way a child of six can understand the rationale for this jolting departure from routine. With my kids, I tried reason, rewards and bribes before resorting finally to threats.

I also tried a series of pathetic metaphors, but kids somehow just can't get a handle on such proverbs as "A journey of a thousand miles begins with a single step."

Mainly, I used the Road of Life thing, with the road beginning there in the first grade and proceeding on through modeling clay, scissors and paste, recess, spitwads, bullies, the New Math and cafeteria food, then on past algebra, book reports, blackheads, Chaucer and going steady.

This figurative road got all tangled up in the end, full of U-turns and blind alleys, with the destination turning out to be the glory of adulthood personified by me. They had no idea what I was talking about, and generally took the position that it was all spinach and the hell with it.

I wanted to tell the lady there in the hall that the best solution might be to offer the child some tangible symbol of security. In my own case, that turned out to be a pacifier. I was as attached to that thing as Linus is to his blanket, as CBS is to Lassie. I became self-conscious about it in short order, and took elaborate precautions to camouflage it; but its mere presence gave me all the reassurance of a shield.

These dilemmas have to be handled individually, though, so I didn't butt in. I got the kids on to class, and as I walked back past the first-grade classroom, the poor woman was sitting dejectedly at a table circled by six-year-olds, and she was the only one who seemed to mind.

Woozy—With Nostalgia

Football season starts Friday night at high schools across Arkansas, and already I'm woozy with nostalgia. You couldn't tell it by looking, but I, too, was once one of those helmeted gladiators who take to the turf every Friday night each fall to bring honor and glory to the old alma mater.

I just got out the old high school yearbook, reeking of mothballs and cedar, and found a picture of myself, all suited up and carefully poised to make it appear that I was making a spectacular Otis Taylor-style catch of a long pass, the unshaven face of Yellowjacket No. 80 aglow with what the coaches call, with wistful admiration, "desire."

I remembered the thrill of running onto the field while the band struck up "On Wisconsin" and that great night I grabbed two over-the-shoulder passes in our game against the conference champions.

With each passing year, it's easier to recall those good things, and easier to repress the other side of the story. You tend to forget that there were more raspberried knees and strained ligaments than there was honor and glory.

You forget that in that same game against the conference bosses the final score was them 64, us 0; that after a few more heartless stabs at fight songs, the band, like the rest of the fans in the stadium, got up and went home in disgust before the end of the third quarter.

No, you don't forget that, either. You try to forget. You try valiantly to forget. But the shame, the humiliation, the regret, the pain—they persist. The truth is that we had a lousy football team that year. Lousy is too kind a word for it, really. When people talked about our offensive team, they meant all of us.

We were so bad that the old Aggie joke almost literally applied to us: Our opponents could've gone home at the half leading, 7 to 0, and we still would've lost, missing a field goal in the final seconds. We were so bad that the opposing teams always scheduled us for their homecoming games, even when the game was played on our field. Off the field, our coach wore a dis-

guise.

Our pep squad consisted of one guy with a bugle, and he resigned in dismay after the first game. "I felt ridiculous," he said. Our cheerleaders weren't elected; they were drafted.

We hated to see Friday night roll around. The coach always had to wait until just before game time to select his starting lineup because the players with any pride or self-respect seldom showed up. They called in sick. Our best player used to chase rats around his uncle's garage on weekday afternoons hoping to catch a good case of bubonic plague. On Fridays, he'd go down and try to join the Army.

In truth, that "desire" on No. 80's visage was merely a desire to get the season the hell over with. Ten Fridays, as a member of that team, was an eternity.

But we didn't dread Friday nights nearly so much as our fans did. The alumni association said it was an insult to the teams of former years for us to call ourselves the Sheridan Yellowjackets. They suggested the Sheridan Chickens, the Sheridan Slugs, the Sheridan Incompetents.

But that wouldn't do, either. They didn't want the name of the town associated with us. They proposed that we rename ourselves the Texas Longhorns. "Then we could be happy when you got stomped every week," they said.

My parents went to see one of our games. Some friends saw them there and they were so embarrassed that they lied and said they'd only gone to see the band perform at halftime.

We had a tackle who once actually threw a block and the coach was so excited he ran onto the field and kissed the guy. That tackle was the only player on our team who got a varsity letter. Nobody cared that the player he blocked on that immortal play was our other tackle.

Our defensive line was so bad that our only effective defensive game plan was to threaten the opposing teams with a collective lawsuit for whiplash. We got the ball so infrequently that one of our backs didn't record a single carry all year. He was the only one who didn't end the year with a net loss in yardage gained.

I could go on but I won't. We never won a game but we did achieve one meager triumph. The local oddsmaker at the pool hall offered ten to one that we wouldn't score six points during the year. So

faithless were our followers that he couldn't find any takers.

We showed 'em, though. We got a touchdown in the final game. The sweetness of that achievement was diminished only slightly by the fact that the coach made us run laps afterward for getting his hopes up.

Showers Serenaders

Someone sent a news clipping yesterday announcing that a community in Vermont was sponsoring a singing-in-the-shower contest. Attached to the clipping was this note, "Would it be a good idea to have such a contest in Arkansas?"

It would not be a good idea. It would be a bad idea. It would be a dreadful idea, in fact, and I will tell you why.

Singing in the shower is among the happiest and most valuable activities I know, but it would become pointless and probably harmful if it went commercial. That is because the essential ingredient in shower-singing is privacy.

People who really give the old larynx a workout in the shower do so precisely because no one is listening. There's no one to grimace when they hit a sour note or forget the words. There's no one to snicker when they come to the two-octave drop in "Old Man River" and, choosing the better part of valor, switch abruptly to "The Tennessee Waltz."

Since there are no critics in the shower, they not only can sing however they please but whatever they please. The integrity of the repertory doesn't matter a whole lot in the shower. When I'm in the shower, for instance, I'll sometimes suddenly launch into the chorus of "I'm the Happiest Girl in the Whole U.S.A." I would think twice about that if a bunch of judges were eavesdropping.

And what about my whiskey-tenor friend who's so modest and self-conscious and considerate of others that he's never in his life sung a cantorial prayer in public? "In the shower," he confessed, "I'm a free man. I sound like Yossele Rosenblatt."

"Yossele who?" I asked him.

"Rosenblatt," he said. "God, he was great."

Do you think he would sound like Yossele Rosenblatt with a bunch of strangers on the other side of the shower curtain, grading him on such qualities as "lyric expression" and "blend of water and voice"? I don't think he would. I think he would get squeaky and embarrassed, and maybe tickled. I think he would sound more like Truman Capote than Yossele Rosenblatt.

Besides, the important thing about singing in the shower is not how well you sound to other people. The important thing is how you sound to yourself. My guess is that even in the shower this guy doesn't really sound like Yossele Rosenblatt. My guess is that he couldn't touch old Yossele with a ten-foot pole. But when he's in the shower, he thinks he sounds like Yossele Rosenblatt. He is sure of it. And that gives him a big lift.

He may have a lot of crummy chores to do today, but he has had his nice leisurely morning shower and he leaves the house feeling all right because he's thinking, "Well, I can sing cantorial prayers like Yossele Rosenblatt, so things could be worse."

Or take another guy I know who's a Methodist and who used to sing in the church choir until the day his little boy told him he sounded like a circus seal barking. That hurt this guy tremendously. He knew he wasn't any candidate for the Mormon Tabernacle Choir but he didn't think he was that bad.

He hasn't sung in public since (or been to church much, either, come to think of it), but he still goes into the shower in the morning and bellows "When the Roll Is

Called Up Yonder" to his heart's content and believes, with no one around to contradict him, that Tennessee Ernie Ford couldn't do it any better.

Both of those guys are championship-caliber shower singers in my opinion, but neither of them would ever enter a stupid contest to prove it. The very idea of such a Watergate-style contest is inimical to the spirit of legitimate, uncorrupted shower singing.

If I had to guess, I would say that the No. 1 favorite selection of the real shower singers is "Figaro." You can get rid of a lot of hostility and tension singing "Figaro" in the shower. It is a good one because you can let out all the stops and sing it as loud and as pompous and as Wagnerian as you feel like. You might be the most inhibited person in the world, but you'll never go crazy if you yell your way through "Figaro" in the shower every morning.

But the kind of people who'd enter a shower-singing contest would never sing "Figaro." They would put on the dog trying to impress the judges with their best Andy Williams or Roberta Flack. They would get so wrapped up in their performance that they would probably slip on the soap and fall and break something.

In my opinion, that would serve them right.

With a Song in Your Heart

A University of Arkansas student is involved in a personal crisis, and no one has been able to offer him any relief or assistance.

"Noting that you claim some authority on singing in the shower," he wrote to this column the other day, "I thought you might be able to help. I hope to God that you can because I think I am on the verge of losing my mind."

This is the problem. A few weeks ago he woke up in the middle of the night with a song on his mind. It was a pleasant song with a nice melody. He knew it by heart from the first note to the last.

But it occurred to him, as he hummed it quietly to himself there in the darkness of his dormitory room, that he couldn't remember the name of it. And he couldn't remember any of the words that would give him a clue as to the name of it.

Over and over, he hummed it, sure that the title would come to him presently. Occasionally it would seem that he was just on the verge of it, but then it would disappear again. He tried sneaking up on it—that is, he would pretend that he had forgotten the thing, that he was thinking about a passage from Immanuel Kant or *Playboy*, and then would abruptly snap his attention back to the song, thinking the title would pop into his head. But that strategy didn't work, either.

So he decided to just go to sleep and forget about it. That was impossible, of course. The more he tried not to think about the song the louder the aggravatingly familiar melody strummed in his mind. He finally realized that if he didn't remember the name of that song he would go insane.

So he woke his roommate and said, "You've got to tell me the name of a song that goes *dum-dum-de-dum-dum, dum-de-dum-dum-dum*."

His roommate, struggling into consciousness, said, "Listen, I don't mind you getting drunk but . . ."

"No," he said, "I'm serious about this. You got to tell me the name of this song."

He went through all the dums again. And then again. He kept it up until his roommate, finally convinced that this guy had lost his grip, took up his pillow and went to another student's room and sacked out on the floor.

He spent the rest of the night pacing and humming. He sat through his classes the next day, but he did so absent-mindedly, his lips moving constantly. By nightfall, his roommates were convinced of the earnestness and legitimacy of his dilemma. So they got several guys together—the dorm experts on classical music, pop music, rock music, even Merle Haggard's greatest hits—and had him hum the melody over and over while they essayed guesses as to what the title of the song might be.

They made no headway.

To try to get his mind off the song, they put the 1812 Overture on the stereo and turned the volume to high and strapped the earphones on him. Even with that mighty diversion roaring through his head, though, he continued to mumble that same *Dum-dum-de-dum-dum, dum-de-dum-dum-dum*.

It was the next day that he appealed to me.

"If you can't tell me the title of the song," he wrote, "maybe you can give me some advice on how to stop thinking about it. This may sound like a joke to you, but believe me I need help."

I worried with all those dums for several days. First, I decided it was the theme from Schubert's Unfinished Symphony but there was one too many dums. Later, I thought it might be Glen Campbell's "Wichita Lineman" but that came up one dum short. Ultimately, I settled on "Hush, Hush, Sweet Charlotte," the movie theme, sung by Patti Page. The dums are right but I doubt if it's the one. A college student in this day and time being bugged by Patti Page is just too incongruous, if not inconceivable.

Insofar as the second question, I have no advice. A song that isn't deterred by the 1812 Overture is too potent for the remedies I know. If it is any consolation, I had something of a similar problem not long ago when I got Helen Reddy's song "I Am Woman" on my mind. It stayed with me for several days, like a pepperoni heartburn. You have to convince yourself that you can live with these things, although they did give me a pretty hard time about it down at the pool hall.

Whipping Okra With a Stick

Anna Benham, who grew up at Marianna, came in the other day with a question: can you get a reluctant okra plant to bear fruit by whipping it with a stick?

I've tried to keep up with the recent investigations into the psychology of plants, and I knew it had been pretty well established that you can keep most plants healthier and happier by sweet-talking them and offering an occasional word of praise and encouragement.

So I had a hunch the opposite might be true, too—that you might be able to frighten a reluctant and unproductive plant into line by beating the sap out of it. As the maxim goes: spare the rod and spoil the okra.

I consulted with the best plant psychologists I know and learned that the answer to Anna's question is yes, if your okra isn't producing, whip the dickens out of it. If it survives, you're likely to get a crop.

The reason has something to do with the plant's basic reproductive urge. If it feels threatened, the plant will hasten—even redouble—its reproductive efforts in order to fulfill the obligation to posterity that is the inheritance of all living things.

Cotton farmers know the phenomenon well: the cotton stalks at the end of a row—the stalks inadvertently abused and punished by the cultivator—invariably are the first to produce bolls. It's probably the same imperative that makes a fruit tree or vine more prolific just after it has been pruned.

Further testimony from Jim Malone of Lonoke, who says the legendary Catfish Murphy of Oklahoma, one of the pioneers of fish farming in this region, used to whip his mother-to-be channel catfish in order to get them to spawn. If the fish was hesitant to lay eggs, Old Catfish would seine her out, give her a good flogging with a willow switch and a good talking-to, and then put her back. Whereupon, so the story goes, she'd start laying eggs like they were going out of style.

Another Malone observation is that

plants will hardly grow in insane asylums. They pick up the bad vibes, or something.

I keep wondering if this sort of thing might not precipitate a moral crisis among vegetarians.

There's a difference, of course, between disciplining a creature and torturing it, and the *Gazette*'s resident guru offers a case in point.

He knows this slightly irregular fellow who owns a pet raccoon and who decided recently to test its frustration quotient. He did so by putting a tray of water in the coon's cage, along with a box of sugar cubes.

You know how impeccable a raccoon's manners are, and how it wouldn't think of eating anything without washing it first. Well, this was a typical raccoon, and naturally it began lugging sugar cubes over to the water tray, proceeding to wash them, and watching them promptly disappear. He tried it again and again, always with the same result.

And at last report, the poor thing was hanging from the top of his cage—baffled, glassy-eyed and near catatonic.

It's bad enough to hunt the gentle raccoon with dogs and shoot him for sport; but this experiment is a new low as far as I'm concerned, and I hope the SPCA gets wind of it.

While I was busy researching that business of flogging catfish and okra, John A. Moore, who grew up at Hardin, delivered up another query. John wanted to know why kids don't build toad-frog houses any more.

I guess it's because, in the phrase of Aristophanes or somebody, Whirl is king, and each generation of children devises its own pastimes.

My older sister once drew up a list of activities that made her happy when she was a child, and toad-frog-house building was at the top of the list.

Also on the list were watching the old men of our neighborhood pitch washers, sending a paper message up the string of a home-made kite, sneaking into a neighbor's barn loft and picking peanuts off the dried peanut vines stored there, selling Cloverine salve on commission, tearing the mail-order catalogue pages off the back of her mother's new quilt-top, collecting enough Blue Horse notebook paper coupons to get a Blue Horse beanie, eating icicles off the edge of the roof of the smokehouse, and getting a new rubber gun with an old inner tube.

I went over that list with my own children recently and it mystified them completely. Their idea of satisfactory leisure-time activity is a Ken and Barbie fashion show or watching "The Secret Storm" on television. I didn't bother explaining to them the art and pleasure of frog-house architecture for the same reason that I wouldn't bother explaining to them why I think the Appassionata Sonata has more to recommend it than, say, the latest best-selling ballad by Donny Osmond.

Mike Trimble

With the shortest tenure of all the Arkansas Travelers, Mike Trimble filled the gap with his unique, offbeat style of humor.

A native of Bauxite, Trimble was described by outgoing Traveler Bob Lancaster as "a young man with a sense of humor and a lively interest in matters pertaining to the real world." Though Lancaster penned that description in 1973, it still holds true today.

After eleven months as the Traveler, Trimble returned to the *Gazette*'s State Desk, where he labored until he went to work for the *Arkansas Times* in 1984.

Now an Associate Editor with the *Arkansas Times*, where he works under Lancaster, Trimble is still demonstrating his ability to make us laugh; at the same time, however, he still expresses that "lively interest in matters pertaining to the real world."

I Left My Heart in Bodcaw

I guess everyone knows by now that the Chamber of Commerce over at Pine Bluff shelled out a thousand smackers for an official song, and I endorse the concept, even if their particular tune didn't turn out so hot. (Love may have built their river town, but I bet it wasn't what prompted the Grand Jury investigation of the police department.)

A Little Rock TV station has followed Pine Bluff's lead, signing off each night with a ditty extolling the civilizing influences of Central Arkansas. Alas, it, too, is a pretty crummy song, containing such lyrics as "Looking down on the Arkansas River, what a beautiful sight" (???!) and failing entirely to mention the city's main industry, orthopedic surgery and subsequent medical testimony in whiplash lawsuits.

But, as I said, it's a good idea, and it's to be hoped that every Arkansas town eventually will have its own song. The only problem is that few of the smaller towns can spare a thousand smokes to pay a song-writing team, and that is too bad.

But did you think I'd point out the problem without providing a solution? You know me better than that! I come from a small town myself. With a little imagination, any self-respecting Chamber secretary can write his own song and save a pile of cash. There are just a few basic guidelines to follow.

First of all, try to pick a theme that fits the town, such as this:

Polish, kosher, sweet or dill,
Atkins folks can fill the bill.
You've not lived until you've tried
hunks of gherkin deep-fat fried.
City life becoming hellish?
Come and try our pickle relish.
Try them once, for them you'll yearn.
Come to Atkins, get heartburn!

Here's another example.

Looking for a spot that's fun?
Come on down to Morrilton.
Join right in our frequent purges:
Throw some rocks at ol' Gene Wirges.

Morrilton is where it's at,
if you are a Democrat.

If you don't have an interesting industry or political machine, advertise the joys of living in the country, like this:

If you're tired of playing bridge,
come and live at Vimy Ridge.
Air so pure and grass so green
in the county of Saline.
Leave that city life so grimy.
Come and see our ridge that's vimy.

Or this.

If it's cities you're despisin',
come on down and live at Rison.
We will share our ample bounty;
nicest town in Cleveland County.

As you can see, I'm strictly a lyric man and will leave the composing of melodies to someone else. There is, however, one possible town song that has a built-in melody, and I'm happy to pass it along for what it's worth.

Some go to Lockesburg and some go to Bright
* Star.*
But I know a place they'll adore ya.
I'll bet you a bundle you'll want to put your
* dough*
in the bonnie, bonnie bank at Ben Lomond.

Some towns, being small, feel that they have a negative image to overcome and would prefer not to be so boastful early in the game. Here's one that's not so pushy.

It's just a place where the road gets wida.
But to us, it's fair Mount Ida.
Stop and have your gas tank filled;
we're not as dull as we are billed.

All these ideas will work for towns that are trying to attract new residents and businesses, but the truth is, some towns like themselves just the way they are, and want little to do with so-called progress. There's a way to write a song for them, too.

Welcome to Ivan.
Keep drivin'.

Chateau Ripple, 1973

Benton—You may have noticed that this newspaper has been running a series on wine. It is being written by a Little Rock fellow, Kenneth J. Forrester, who is a member of Les Amis du Vin, an international society of wine lovers.

It's a pretty good series, debunking as it does a lot of the fancy notions about wine guzzling. Don't worry about what people will think, says Kenneth J. Forrester; buy something that tastes good, slop some of it in a jelly glass and heave to.

As democratic as Mr. Forrester is, however, he hasn't quite reached the socioeconomic level of Arvin the Wino, of Benton, who seems to exist fairly well on wine, salted peanuts and a monthly VA disability check.

Arvin admits that, strictly speaking, he'd have to be classed as a wino, but he's a little mad about it, saying that if he had a lot of dough, people would think up a nicer name for him. I didn't mention Les Amis du Vin to him; it probably would have made him madder.

Arvin is a good man to talk to about the lower echelons of wine drinking, because, living as he does in a dry county, it takes a high degree of dedication to indulge his passions.

"I try to get out to the county line about twice a week," he says. Sometimes that isn't too hard, for Arvin has a buddy who possesses a pickup truck and a thirst similar to Arvin's. "He's got a wife, though, and she makes him dry out every now and again."

At such times, Arvin says, he will hitch rides up the interstate to the county line, or sometimes borrow a car.

That latter practice has gotten him in trouble a couple of times, for, according to the police, the owners of the cars didn't know they were being borrowed. Arvin replies in his defense that he would have notified the owners if he had known who they were.

Once his transportation problem is solved, Arvin doesn't waste much time shopping around. He sticks generally to a simple concord grape wine of Arkansas manufacture, though he isn't necessarily motivated by state pride.

"It's cheap," he says.

He has had his flings with Strawberry Hill and Zapple Apple and Cold Bear, but he always has returned to his Arkansas wine, with an occasional departure into Tiger 186.

"That stuff is too sweet," Arvin says. "Makes your chin sticky."

Serious students of wine know that different shapes of wine bottles indicate different types of wine, and Arvin takes note of bottle shapes, too, although for different reasons.

"You get more in a fifth," he says, "but I generally get me a bunch of pints and half-pints. You can roll over on a flat bottle and it won't bust as easy as a round one. I had to have six stitches in my belly once."

Arvin says he prefers wine to beer or the hard stuff because there's no refrigeration problem and you get more for your money. "Hard whiskey makes me sick," he says, "and I can get me some wine and have plenty left to get me some peanuts or crackers."

Trying to somehow bridge the gap between Kenneth J. Forrester's world and Arvin's, I asked if he had ever had any fancy wine. He said he had—once—and that he'd never wanted to try it again.

He had come into a little extra money once, he recalled, and he also had a pretty good little buzz on from some afternoon celebrating, so when he and his pickup-driving buddy arrived at the county line, they asked for a bottle of the best French wine in the place.

It was too sour, Arvin said, and besides, he had a devil of a time getting into the thing.

"Damn bottle had a cork in it," he said. "We like to never got it pushed down in there."

Fame Comes to Arvin the Wino

Benton—Some people just can't handle fame, and I fear that Arvin the Wino is one of them.

Arvin, who lives here and commutes regularly to the Pulaski County line to dispose of his veteran's disability check, was interviewed in this space awhile back, in what amounted to a poor man's guide to wine drinking.

The problem is that Arvin, who probably hadn't used a newspaper for anything except a blanket in the last 10 years, squandered a dime of his VA money to read the account, and now is so enamored of seeing his own words in print that he envisions a series of articles, maybe even a book, possibly even a movie of his life, in which he would play the title role (and not incidentally, would be flown to California, the home of Ernest and Julio Gallo).

My mistake was dropping in a few days ago to see if Arvin had read the article. Oh, my, yes, he certainly had.

"Listen," he said, "I forgot to tell you about that time when me and Jack was driving back from the Line and he had a rubber tube stuck down under his shirt down to a jug on the floorboard and he was stopped by the State Police."

Arvin was off and running, bubbling over with accounts of his bleary-eyed misadventures, and he stopped only to register a complaint about the original article and to suggest a remedy.

The problem was the "Arvin" business, he said. Since I had chosen not to use his real name in the paper, he had been unable to convince any of his friends that the article was really about him. "We got to use my real name in the next one," he said.

Overlooking for a moment my intention that there never be a "next one," I began to explain to Arvin that the libel laws prevented the use of his real name. It was tricky going, the object being to get across to Arvin that his real name couldn't be used while hiding from him the fact that he would be the benefactor in any libel judgment. I didn't care how hungry Arvin was for fame, the prospect of him interpolating a fat libel judgment into X number of cases of wine did not appeal to me.

The explanation, as it finally came out, was something along the line that if Arvin's real name appeared in the newspaper the price of wine would skyrocket, the Razorbacks would be kicked out of the Southwest Conference and Justice Jim Johnson would never be allowed to run for public office again.

Arvin accepted that logic, but was rather sullen about it and a little defiant.

"What if I just change my name to Arvin?" he asked, and I went through the whole tortured lie again. Arvin was still adamant. He had heard some guys down at the filling station talking about how funny that guy Arvin the Wino was, and he was determined that the reading public would not be denied the privilege of hearing about him again.

In desperation then, I unleashed the final argument. I say desperation because first of all, it probably would hurt Arvin's feelings, and second and more important, it would reveal the most closely-guarded secret of all newspaper columnists: that we are egotists, liars and thoroughgoing fakers.

"Arvin," I said, "you didn't even say all that stuff. You just sort of hinted at most of it. I was the one that put it all together and made it sound good."

Arvin sulled up even more. "Prove it," he said.

"Good grief, Arvin, you know you didn't say all that stuff."

"That don't prove nothing. I'm a drunk. I'm always forgetting what I said. That don't mean I didn't say it."

That's when I left in a panic, and the only reason this is appearing in the paper is that today is Sunday and while Arvin might spend a dime to read about himself, I'd stake my life that he'd never spring for 30 cents.

Santa Lives! (at Prescott)

Prescott—The following poll had its beginnings on the Interstate between Texarkana and Prescott, on a day when every tractor-trailer rig spared by the mad bomber at Widener was busy blowing me off the road as I puttered along at my patriotic 50 miles an hour. My companion in the car was the radio voice of Paul Harvey, and as much as I hate to say it, old Paul was pretty gloomy company.

Watergate tapes, energy shortages, Arabs, truck blockades: poor old Paul had to tell me about all of this over the radio and you could tell it was getting him down. Finally, he just couldn't take it any more, and after relating one last doom-filled dispatch on the gasoline shortage, he threw up his hands (Paul Harvey is the only newscaster in the world who can throw up his hands over the radio) and said, if my memory serves me right, "Just what kind of Christmas do they think the rest of us are going to have with all of this going on?" That was followed by one of old Paul's marvelous sighs, and *THAT* was followed by his trademark, the most eloquent silence in all of electronic journalism.

I have never been one to take Paul Harvey lightly, so I ruminated over his last question as the trucks continued to whoosh past me on the highway. No doubt about it, this has been a banner year for bad goings-on. Was Paul right? Were Judge Sirica and Rose Mary Woods and King Faisal and the rest of the international grinches going to swipe the holiday season from under our noses?

Well, I determined to find out, and the following responses, gathered at the Interstate Exxon Station, Harvey's Kwik Sak and the Wolves' Drive Inn, constitute the fruits of about 45 minutes of painstaking research. No names were taken, no breakdown on socio-economic or racial groups was recorded, and no population projections were made. This means that my poll is probably as accurate as any Louis Harris ever conducted.

The question was this: "Will Watergate and the energy crisis and all other bad news have any effect on the way you feel this Christmas?" The first and most telling result of the poll is that everyone thought it was a pretty dumb question. Everyone was nice enough to take a crack at answering it more or less seriously. It was the look that gave the real feeling about the question, a look that said: "I will answer this weirdo's question, and speak very slowly so as not to upset him and then I will walk slowly to my car and lock the door before taking down his license number."

But the presence of a notebook and a tape recorder lends a probably unjustified air of legitimacy to an undertaking of this sort, so I am able to report that I got responses of one sort or another from every subject.

The unanimous results of the poll show that ten folks in Prescott, at least, are not about to let Walter Cronkite spoil their Christmas. One gentleman at the filling station allowed as how there was a possibility that the never-ending flow of crummy news could conceivably affect his holiday, but that he was simply going to unplug the tube on Christmas Eve and not plug it in again until the first bowl game came on.

Another man said that with all the bad stuff going down lately, he needed his holiday spirit more than ever, and he was going to feel good at Christmas if it killed him.

Only down at the Kwik Sak was there a hint that somebody's holiday might turn out a little sour, and I don't think that counts. The lady there said that no one at her place was going to let Watergate or the energy crisis enter into their holiday, but that there was an unassembled ten-speed bicycle hidden in the garage that might indeed spoil Christmas, New Year's and George Washington's birthday if it wasn't put together properly by Monday night.

I don't think the lady needs to worry about her Christmas being spoiled just because her husband doesn't know pea-turkey about putting a bicycle together, for that is the kind of problem Christmas thrives on. On Tuesday morning, and on every Christmas morning from here on, everyone in the family is going to have a good laugh remembering how old so-and-so over there stayed up all night and skint his knuckles all up trying to put together some furriner bicycle.

Mgwphwuglug!

"Well," beams the lady in the front of the dentist's office. "How are we this morning?"

"We are afraid," I reply.

The lady picks up a sinister-looking instrument, and I figure the ordeal has begun. "What are you going to do with that thing?" I ask apprehensively.

"I am going to write on this card with it," she says taking what indeed turns out to be a pencil and scribbling on an index-sized card.

I sneak a look. The card has my name on it, and the lady has written, "Sweaty Palms," across the bottom.

I take a seat beside a fish bowl with no fish in it. Pretty soon, one of the dentists comes in with a bag of fish. He empties them into the bowl. Maybe he has been checking their teeth. They seem to have pretty good choppers. Then again, maybe he locks them up at night in the office safe. Maybe they have been on vacation. Maybe they have been away to school (heah, heah).

"Mr. Trimble."

It can't be my turn already. I haven't even got halfway through the little folder where Johnny Whitetooth clobbers mean old Mr. Tooth D-K with a toothbrush and administers the coup de grace with a wad of dental floss.

It is my turn. Another nice lady takes my hand and puts me in the recline-o-chair. She goes over to my card and underlines the words, "Sweaty Palms."

"Dr. Cloud will be with you in a moment," she says, and splits.

I check around to see if the coast is clear. Might as well go ahead; it's the only chance I ever have to have any fun in this place. I grab the water squirter and speak into it: "Mission Control, this is Apollo 7. Pitch and yaw increasing, and manual override is negative function, repeat, negative function."

I peer into the little round basin where the water is shooshing around in a circle. "Houston, the gyros can't compensate. It's the thrusters. I'm going to have to go EVA. I don't care what von Braun says! I'm going EVA. End of transmission."

"What about the ADA?"

It is Dr. Cloud, and the mission is scrubbed. The water squirter goes back into the instrument panel.

Dr. Cloud is my favorite dentist. That means I fear him slightly less than I do the Boogie Man or nuclear war. He always says, "See you in six months," but upbraids me only mildly when I show up four years later with my teeth covered with a green, sticky substance and with a filling gone from having bit too hard into a Willy Wonka Goo-Goo Cluster. He is very reassuring, eschewing those antiseptic-looking green coats. He wears civvies and a welder's mask.

He picks up The Needle, and I whimper. He puts it down, goes over to my card and draws another line under "Sweaty Palms." This time, he discreetly turns his back as he prepares The Needle.

"This will hurt a little bit," he says. Dr. Cloud certainly knows his business. He has called it right on the button. He's nice enough to say nothing about the tears running down my cheeks and fouling up his equipment.

Proceeding apace, now. Thank God, the drilling's over. Wait a minute! What's that he's putting on the drill bit? *THE SANDPAPER DISC!! NO, DOC, NOT THE SANDPAPER DISC!*

It's too late. *BZZZZZRAP BZZZZZRAP* My toenails claw their way past the socks and into the shoe leather. Why does he always have to use the sandpaper disc?

"All done," he says triumphantly, and whips out a mirror. "Take a look. Got a little surprise for you."

Great Scott! What's he done to my busted front tooth? That tooth has been sliding off at a 45-degree angle since I whacked it on the monkey bars in the second grade. I'm used to it, and now it's gone. Dr. Cloud has put a whole tooth in there without so much as a by-your-leave. The man has taken liberties!

"It was so shot through with decay that that was the simplest way to repair it," he explains. "Besides, see how much nicer that smile is?" I am not aware that I am smiling, or that I will ever smile again.

That's it. I am helped from the recline-o and presented with an orange card by the lady in front.

"See you in six months," says Dr. Cloud.

Fat chance, Doc. Four years, soonest.

Freeway, Moon and Holy Ghost

Having been enlisted as a teamster last week end to deliver a dog to my attorney in Indiana, I got the chance to re-experience an old sensation: Screaming down the interstate in the dead of night, belly and brain arumble with truck stop coffee, while great bugs smash into the windshield and radio evangelists show the Way and the Light over WWL, the voice of New Orleans.

As far as I know, no research group has ever investigated just what combination of fatigue, caffeine, diesel smoke and Holy Writ produces this strange euphoria, and it's probably just as well. They'd probably make it illegal, create a national commission on nocturnal highway abuse, and publish pamphlets on how alert parents can spot the tell-tale signs of late-night cruising around on the interstate.

I haven't done much serious thinking about the phenomenon either, except to note that it seems to manifest itself more readily in the warmer months, when the car windows are rolled down and an occasional hard-shelled bug whaps you on the elbow with the force of a Benjamin BB rifle.

It is certainly not the cheapest high in the world, what with the gasoline and oil, and it may not be the safest since you're constantly dodging armadillos and being buffeted around in the wake of big Kenworths and Peterbilts, whose drivers are just as high as you are on the heady drug of the night-time freeway. But it's one of the most exhilarating, and when your radiator hose finally busts at Marion about 2 in the morning, you've got to stalk around the car for a while in order to come down to earth enough to go into the truck stop and order the coffee that will start the whole process all over again.

A good clear channel radio station is a necessary ingredient, and WWL usually provides just the combination of raucous disc jockeys, country music and fire-and-brimstone preaching needed to get the juices flowing and set you to squirming around in the car seat. Last weekend, however, some station functionary was apparently asleep at the wheel, for Billy Graham gave the same sermon three times in a row before someone replaced the tape cartridge with the Mull Family Singing Convention.

Now, Billy is still a whale of a preacher, despite the old sourpusses who think he's gotten too fancy with his visit to the White House and all, but the same sermon three times over is a little hard to take, no matter who's delivering it. You start getting hypercritical the third time around, challenging Billy to describe in detail the "immorality that has been reported taking place in the very church sanctuary during young people's services." You also feel a little uneasy when Billy talks for 15 minutes about the nation's obsession with material wealth and then offers at the end of the program to take some of it off your hands.

Finally—and I hesitate to take a stand here, because it's purely subjective judgment and I know it's going to make a lot of folks mad—George Beverly Shea can't sing for beans. I don't care what anybody says to the contrary. He might be all right for funerals, but for making a joyful noise, I'll take the Chuckwagon Gang or the Happy Goodman Family every time.

That's why I greeted Brother Mull and his wife with a whoop of relief. Plenty of hand-clapping gospel music and no lectures about materialism; just send in your dough and receive the Mull Family Bible, a red-letter edition complete with subject index, scriptural interpretations and genuine photographs of the 6-day Arab-Israeli war in the Holy Land.

The hands itch for the wheel just thinking about it.

Testing the Thoroughbreds

Hot Springs—If horse racing is indeed the sport of kings, a lot of snooty people might be inclined to assign Orville Terrell, Vernon Myers and Jerry Magie the social status generally reserved for the Spook, that hairy unfortunate who spends much of his time suspended upside down in the comic-strip dungeons of Id.

But they are wrong. Orville, Vernon and Jerry are at the very least dukes of the sport of kings, possibly even princes, and they constitute as agreeable a trio as ever second-guessed a horse race.

Orville, Vernon and Jerry work for the state Racing Commission in its Oaklawn Park testing barn, a brisk walk from the amenities of the Park's betting windows and beer concessions. The Commission is there to see that there's no hanky-panky such as doping up the horses and to that end, the winner of each race—and often an extra "spot check" horse—is subjected to urine tests just after it runs. That is where our three friends come in, for it is they—armed with a long-handled cup and the patience of Job—who accompany the horses into a private stall to collect the goods.

The idea of talking to the fellows at the test barn came from a friend of mine who writes newspaper editorials for a living. Not only did he think it would make an interesting piece, he said, but he had always felt there was a certain spiritual kinship between his job and theirs, and he'd like to know a little more about them—compare professional notes, so to speak.

So there I was at the test barn, where Orville, Vernon and Jerry were swapping yarns with Dr. Don Burrows, the Racing Commission's vet for that day's activities. Vernon, who lives at Perryville, and Jerry, who comes from Bigelow, were expounding at length on the past grandeur of Little Italy, a community near the Pulaski–Perry County line. Jerry had got just about halfway through a colorful account of an Italian wedding when word came that the two horses from the seventh race—No Advance, the winner, and To the Rescue, the "spot check" horse—had been washed down, walked and watered, and it was time for the team to spring into action.

Vernon took the winner, and not wanting to be associated with an also-ran, I went with him. As No Advance was being led into the stall, Vernon explained the tricks of the trade. There weren't many.

" 'Bout the only thing you got to make sure of," he said, "is whether you got a filly or a gelding. It makes a difference. You'd be surprised at how many folks would forget to check."

Other than that, he said, the only other requirement for the job is patience. "It's all pretty much up to the horse," he said. "They're supposed to be trained to go when you whistle at 'em after a workout, but sometimes they do and sometimes they don't."

We went in the stall, and the door was closed behind us, and No Advance, a beautiful gelding with Arkansas Derby hopes, proceeded to prove Vernon's theory that you can lead a horse to drink, but you can't make him water.

Vernon began the short, low whistles designed to produce results, and from the next stall, we could hear the same technique being applied to To the Rescue. In a matter of moments, we heard the door to the next stall open and To the Rescue was led out.

"See there?" Vernon said. "Sometimes you're in and out in a minute. Looks like this is gonna be a bad 'un."

Vernon continued his patient whistling as horses from subsequent races came and went. The pattern was the same. The stall next door would open, there would be a few short whistles, and the door would open again to let the horse out. Jerry and Orville began to rag Vernon a little.

"Hey, Vernon, you gonna get chapped lips, all that whistlin'."

Vernon remained patient, but he was beginning to frown through his pucker.

Another horse went in and out next door. "Just got to have that touch, Vernon. Heh, heh."

"Phooey," said Vernon. "Let's walk him around some more." No Advance was taken from the stall.

While the horse was being walked and watered some more, Vernon's colleagues commiserated. "Now, we kid him and everything," said Orville, "but it happens to all of us. You should have been here last year. Remember Jovial John? We'd have to stay up with him pretty near all night some times. That rascal was hard to catch."

The additional walk was apparently just what No Advance needed. Back in the stall, a few short whistles, and then: "Bingo," Vernon said quietly, quickly leaning forward with his cup, not unlike a fencer thrusting at a very small opponent.

We emerged from the stall, Vernon proudly bearing the fruits of his labor, accepting the accolades of his fellow workers.

The wait with No Advance had consumed the rest of the racing day, so Vernon had some time to relax. He is a welder by trade, but he takes off each year to work for the Racing Commission for the full season.

Why?

"Well," Vernon said, slowly shifting a chew of tobacco about the size of a golf ball, "the money ain't all that great, and it's not real exciting. I guess I just love racing."

Standing Up for Bowie's Knife

The State Supreme Court has ruled that a butcher knife is not a Bowie knife, and I, for one, can't see how anyone could ever have contended differently.

The case at bar, as they say, was that of Roy Rowland, who happened to have a couple of butcher knives in his truck when stopped by Little Rock policemen in 1972. Rowland, who said he was carrying the weapons as a symbolic protest, was charged under an 1881 law that prohibits the carrying of "any dirk or Bowie knife, or sword or spear in a cane, brass or metal knucks, razor, blackjack, billie or sap, ice pick or any pistol of any kind whatever."

Some prosecutor had the temerity to say that Rowland's two butcher knives were the same as Bowie knives, a base calumny on the memory of James Black, the Arkansas smith who forged the first legendary blade for Col. James Bowie, the hero of both the Alamo and a long-running TV series.

It took Associate Justice George Rose Smith of the Supreme Court to set the notion right, and I say to the judge: hurrah!

Butcher knife the same as a Bowie knife, indeed! Is Don Knotts the same as John Wayne? Is the Daisy Red Ryder model the same as the Benjamin Pump? Is Maxie's Reliable like Tiffany's?

"A new country and a new generation," writes Raymond W. Thorp, the chronicler of the weapon, "were dominated by James Bowie's knife." Furthermore, he says, the weapon "held the center of the American scene for more than two generations."

Try to imagine, if you will, any old butcher knife holding the attention of anyone's scene for a second longer than it takes to slice enough baloney for a sandwich. You can't do it, can you? Well, neither could George Rose Smith!

It was 1830 when James Bowie rode into the Hempstead County town of Washington in search of James Black, whose reputation as a master craftsman of knives had spread far beyond the reaches of the Arkansas frontier. Bowie already had achieved some fame as a knife-wielder, having dispatched a number of his enemies with a conventional model in a donnybrook that began as a duel on a Mississippi River sandbar. Bowie had something special in mind for a fighting knife, however, and he knew James Black was the only man to make it.

He took Black a carved wooden model of the knife he had in mind, and Black copied the knife in steel and submitted it for Bowie's approval. He also, however, submitted another knife, which was based on Bowie's design but unlike Bowie's single-edged model was double-edged along the curved portion near the tip of the blade.

Bowie liked Black's design better than his own, so he took the double-edged weapon and headed back for Texas.

No sooner had he arrived than he was set upon by three brigands hired for the express purpose of doing him in. Bowie decapitated one of the attackers with a single stroke of his new blade, disemboweled the second with an upward stroke. The third thug was picking them up and laying them down by this time, but Bowie overtook him and neatly bisected his skull clear down to the shoulders.

The rest, as they say, is history.

Black made other knives in different shapes, and almost all of them became known as Bowie knives, particularly the stiletto-like *Arkansas Toothpick* much favored by mountain men for its accuracy in flight. But Black's original design remains the one that fires the imagination, the weapon that accompanied Jim Bowie to the Alamo and was cremated along with him.

Now really, can you truthfully equate a knife like that with that thing the lady at Franke's holds as she says, "Natural gravy on your roast beef, sir?" No, Mr. Prosecutor, it just won't wash!

No, a butcher knife is most definitely not a Bowie knife, Mr. Prosecutor, and in waging this lonely struggle, Roy Rowland's name has joined those of Miranda and Escabido in the annals of American jurisprudence.

Only thing wrong is, Mr. Rowland also had a .38-caliber boomer in his possession when he was arrested, and Justice Smith says there ain't no way in the world he can get out of that one.

A Disgusting Habit

They lurk back there in the darkest recesses of the mind, then dart out unexpectedly, taking control of your conscious actions, sometimes for only a moment, and then they slink away, leaving only that feeling of self-loathing, that realization that you have once again succumbed.

Probably everyone is possessed of these demons, these dark, dirty little habits that we keep secret at all costs. In extreme cases, they may involve narcotics or alcohol, but major or minor, they are alike in their sinister nature, alike in that we are shamed by them and at the same time powerless to break free from the hold they have on us.

I am no exception. For years, I have recognized the vile habit for what it is, but only to myself, never indicating to anyone else the sordid details of my degrading obsession. It has finally reached the point where the soul must be cleansed, where I must shout out the truth to the world at large in hope of starting on the long road back, and possibly even encouraging others suffering from the same addiction.

I read *Nancy*.

There! I've said it! I read the stupidest, most asinine, unfunniest comic strip in the nation and read it every day. It is not so bad when I am alone; then I am spared the furtive page-flipping, the pretense that I am really looking through the want ads for a used car. So far, I have never been caught, although there have been some close calls. It is the prospect of discovery as much as anything else that prompts me to bring the whole thing out in the open. It is not so bad, somehow, to voluntarily admit to reading *Nancy*, but the prospect of being discovered in the act, of being publicly branded by my peers as a *Nancy* reader, is just too much to bear.

I can't really remember when it began, or if, like most addictions, there was any pleasure in it at first. I don't think so. For as long as I can remember, *Nancy* has been a crumbum strip. It has never elicited so much as a faint smile, only groans, and not the kind of admiring groans that follow a clever pun, but *real* groans, indicative of genuine pain, pain and indignation that a man can make a good living turning out such tripe.

But, like a moth to a flame, I am drawn to the want ad section every day. Usually, I lie to myself along the way. "Just going to check on what Tracy's doing," I say under my breath. But I always end up at the same place, without really knowing how I got there, and there is Sluggo, with spaghetti all over his head.

There are days when I vow that it's over; I'm going cold turkey starting with the morning paper. The knot begins to form as I peruse the front page, and the fist in the gut tightens as I move back through the sports section.

By the time I get to the lost-and-founds, my hands are shaking, and there is a thin film of sweat on my upper lip. It is getting close, now. I have checked out *The Family Circus* and *Belvedere*; I'm almost through. I can see it over there, over on the corner of the page, but I'm not going to look. I'm not going to . . .

Aaaaaaagh! Sluggo's bought a bag of peanuts and he's waited until he sees a sign saying "Loading Zone" before pouring them all down his throat!!!

It is on days such as that that the guilt is the worst, and I stumble, unseeing, through the day, going home to bed only to be tormented by nightmares peopled by Fritzi Ritz, Irma and Rollo the Rich Kid.

It has been a long way down, but with no way to go but up, the day seems a little brighter somehow, the air a little clearer, now that I've made the admission.

All I can do now is urge the rest of you out there to do the same. I know you're out there; I can tell by the empty stares I see every morning downtown. Come out of the closet. Together, we can lick this thing. When you get back in the classified ads and feel that knot in your stomach, give me a call. We'll talk it over. Maybe I'll come over and we can have some coffee.

The important thing to remember is that no one can be expected to kick the habit on his own, and we're just going to have to take it one day at a time.

Dolls Still Need a Momma

Hot Springs—Bettie Sharp's corporeal world is not beautiful to look at, much less to live in, consisting as it does of a ramshackle house beset by building inspectors and a standard of living closely regulated by an 84-year-old widow's Social Security check.

How much more pleasant, then, to spend as much time as possible in a world of crisp starched crinoline and little top hats, where miniature ladies and gentlemen stand in proper poses and wait for the children to come and pay their respects. That was Bettie Sharp's world once, and it is one she dreams of inhabiting again.

Mrs. A. Bettie Sharp has been making dolls since she was a young girl at Weatherford, Texas, and until recently, she had been able to make a good living from showing and selling her dolls, and repairing the dolls of others.

She once ran a doll museum on Whittington Avenue here, and then she moved it to Central Avenue over the Mayflower Restaurant. Her business was good, and she still has clippings of newspaper articles about her exhibit.

"Oh, I was written up a lot," she said. "And everyone just loved my museum. The little children 'specially loved it. I charged 75 cents for everyone else, but the little children got in for a quarter, and they'd just stay and stay."

She closed her museum in 1969, and in 1972 she moved to Dallas and set up a little doll hospital, where—at first—she seemed to be doing all right.

"The newspapers used to give me free advertisements over in Dallas," she said, "because I'd go down there and show them my dolls."

But it didn't work out. Last year she was injured when a freezer door hit her sharply on the head, and she says the doctors told her the injury probably wouldn't ever heal completely. Then in November, she got word that there was a problem with a house she thought she had sold at Hot Springs, so she bought a bus ticket with the last of her money and came back to see what the trouble was.

It turned out that the person to whom she had sold the house had defaulted on the payments, so it still belonged to her. The house had been vacant for a time, and vandals had all but ripped it to pieces. Having no place else to go, she moved into the place and cleaned it up as best she could.

But some things were impossible for her to fix, such as the ripped-out ceiling and the broken windows, and a water bill run up by the former tenants had caused the water to be shut off. She was told that the building was condemned, and that she couldn't live there.

An article in the Hot Springs paper chronicled Bettie Sharp's troubles, and city officials, who really didn't relish much the role of Scrooge in the first place, turned on her water and more or less decided to let the condemnation notice get lost in the bureaucratic shuffle.

Thanks to that newspaper article, Bettie Sharp's present world is safe for the moment, but it's one she never wanted, and she'd rather talk to a visitor about her museum, or about the exhibit of dolls she had at the 1946 Texas State Fair, or about what she might do now if she had the opportunity.

"I've still got a lot of dolls I could show," she told her visitor. "And I could start a little doll hospital. Do you know of a little place in Little Rock where I could start a doll hospital?"

She also remembers what a nice time she had a few years ago when she visited some friends at an apartment complex for retired persons. "Oh, they loved me there," she said. "I got everybody down in the gameroom to sing, and I put on a party like you've never seen. They wanted me to stay there all the time."

She thinks she might like to do that, but she has no money, and it is hard for her to recall the name and address of the place. "So many things have happened: there's too many things to remember."

She can't afford materials, but there is a hickory tree in her yard, and she showed the visitor how she was painting faces on the nuts and gluing them to pencils to make little dolls.

"Now look at this," she showed her visitor, picking up a foam plastic egg carton and laboriously tearing off a section. "Most people would just throw this away, and I was about to, too, but just look."

She picked up one of the pencils with the little hickory-nut face glued to the end and placed the piece of egg carton on the nut.

"See? It's a bonnet," she said. "A bonnet for a doll."

The Mailman Cometh

One of the unexpected benefits of this new job has been the mail I get from friendly folks out in the state who are eager to help me out or straighten me out or both.

I used to get a few letters at the office, most of them mimeographed jobs from the Army Engineers saying that someone wanted to build a boat dock in the river and asking if I had any objections. It's nice to be consulted by the Engineers about boat docks, but there's nothing quite so heart-warming as receiving a hand-written communication that begins: "Dear Mister Smart Guy . . . ," and goes on to relate that anyone who's too dumb to know when the White County Fair opens up shouldn't be entrusted with an automobile and a type-writer and thrust upon an unsuspecting public.

Other mail has been of a more gentle nature, and has offered both encouragement and suggestions as to where to go skulking around for subjects with which to fill up this space four times a week.

H. E. Harvey of Clarksville, a regular adviser of the previous Arkansas Traveler, has been nice enough to take me under his wing, warning me about the pinkos, fellow travelers and nattering nabobs of negativism who lurk about in the editorial offices of the newspaper.

Probably the most valuable communications have come from James M. Oliver Jr., who writes from Block 20, Corning, on a fairly regular basis. Mr. Oliver checked in even before I began the enterprise, expressing his best wishes and letting me know that he wasn't expecting too much. Subsequent letters have indicated that his expectations have not necessarily been exceeded, but the kind encouragement is still there, along with gentle warnings about the dangers of verbosity. He involuntarily traded his WWI rifle for a desk job at old Camp Pike after three days on the firing range produced a target that was as devoid of bullet holes as the day it left the factory.

I have received one short note from my mother, an English teacher, correcting my grammar in one particular passage and commenting that I should know better.

Friends have been very helpful in submitting ideas for columns, although some of them are best taken lightly. Those scamps on the *Gazette* copy desk, for example, have supplied me with a list of "leads" that includes such gems as "There's a guy at Mountain Home who's raised a turnip in the shape of a Sherman tank," and "What about the rumor that the movie *White Lightning* was actually filmed at Tarrytown, N.Y.?"

Willard Stewart of Des Arc thinks his wife's speeding ticket is about the funniest thing that's happened around those parts in a long time, and he recommends a piece about that. Mrs. Stewart, on the other hand, says if I really wanted a story, I'd write about the woman who used to dress all in black and climb over the roofs of Des Arc businesses at night, and who later shot her husband in the toe and ran off to join a carnival.

The telephone also has brought messages of encouragement and greeting, many of them from folks I hadn't seen or even thought of in years. The most surprising of these came from Gerald Magby, whom I haven't laid eyes on, I guess, since he used to smoke up the neighborhood on the back of an old Harley-Davidson in his role as Bauxite's first authentic motorcycle outlaw. When he called the other day to wish me well, I just about fainted dead away.

Gerald was the majordomo of the Norton Town Nightmares, a local sandlot football team of which I was the youngest and least effective member. He also had a literary bent, having taught me, at the age of six or so, a bit of doggerel about a Hermit Named Dave that I proudly performed at the dinner table to the accompaniment of dropped forks and shocked expressions. It was Gerald who penned those immortal words on the barrel-launching pad of the neighborhood bag swing: "Don't jump unless you can make it, or you will be setting on the ground!"

Gerald also fell out of our tree once and busted his head.

It was good to hear from old Gerald.

A Note to Mr. Fleming

Jonesboro—Well, Flem, you went and died on us, and I'll bet you're pretty amused right now about how all of us at the paper are carrying on about it, seeing as how you were the office's most eloquent exponent of joyous, hell-raising wakes.

As for me, I was stuck up here in a motel room when I got the news, and the sense of loss, coupled with the fact of being in a town full of strangers, set off a string of long distance telephone calls to friends. Not necessarily to talk about you, but to talk about anything—politics, football, anything—in a desperate, pitiful little affirmation of life.

You might have snickered a little at conduct like that if you were talking about being guilty of it yourself, but I suspect that you would have understood it, and probably even approved.

For, quite frankly, John, for all your friendly doom-saying and cheerful pessimism at the office, for all your reputation as the paper's jolly cynic, well, you just never quite brought it off.

Not that you didn't play the role well. Since you had worked on just about every paper, great and lousy, that anyone had ever heard of, you could spin off a never-ending stream of hair-raising yarns and, with just a slight arch of one of those magnificent bushy eyebrows, assume the role of the detached but slightly bemused observer.

Who else but a certified hard-boiled egg could laugh—and make us laugh—about a near fatal tumble down an elevator shaft? Or about the bad boozing days, and when you lumbered aboard the wagon for good? (I still have a letter in which you described that event as "A shotgun wedding, where under the threat of death I promised to love, honor and obey my liver.")

But there were just too many things that gave you away, John. There was that column of yours for one thing. Being something of a pragmatist where conservation was concerned, you took some flack from hard-core environmentalists but you kept on plugging for what you thought was possible, and you didn't quit yelling until something got done. Yours was also the only outdoor column I ever saw that could be read with pleasure by someone who hated the outdoors, filled as it was with those oddball world records, the adventures of Clyde and periodic references to your two favorite Indians, Low and Falling Rock.

Then there were all those loans. I think where you made your mistake there, John, was in being a natty dresser. Maybe we somehow got the impression in the newsroom that you were more prosperous than the rest of us. I wonder how much of that money you ever got back, John, and I wonder how many of us knew that you sometimes had to borrow yourself in order to make those loans.

And the other stuff. The shepherding of the drunks, the listening to the problems, the encouragement of the young ones who were just starting out and needed it badly.

There was one other thing, John, that would have given you away even if you had managed to keep all the other stuff a deep, dark secret. It was the laugh.

It would start out softly and then get

higher and louder until it was an ear-splitting, eye-watering, table-pounding laugh. It was no cynic's laugh. It cut through the years and the pain and got to the substance, and it grabbed cynicism by the lapels and shook it senseless. It sang of love and friends and good times, and it fairly trembled with the vibrance of life itself.

I was about to say that I would miss that laugh, and I'm sure I will in time. But not right now, John. Right now I can hear it plain as everything.

No Muse Is Good Muse

Mr. Jim Oliver, my friend and advisor at Corning, had written cryptically of a project he had in mind for me, revealing none of the details, but adding that it would require "poetic license."

Mr. Jim's comments and suggestions have been right on the money so far, and I was anxious to tackle his unnamed project, but I discovered on checking my wallet that I was not licensed poetically, that indeed, I never had been, and that I might at this very moment be a fugitive from forces of justice sworn to protect an unwary public from the unpredictable ravings of uncertified scribblers. With that in mind, I set about yesterday to achieve some degree of literary legitimacy, a task already deemed impossible by a number of my more vociferous correspondents.

There being no Poetic Licensing Board listed in the telephone book under State Offices, I turned for aid to those friendly folks at the state Revenue Department, operating on the theory that if they can license folks to commit mayhem on the highways, they can license them to do the same thing on the pages of a newspaper. Also, the Revenue Department engages in a little poetic license of its own, parading as it does under the fancy nom de plume of State Finance and Administration Department, so I figured they'd also be in charge of such matters for everyone else.

The Information Lady at FAD was encouraging. No sooner had I asked, "Is this where I apply for a poetic license?" than she replied, "Yes sir, we handle that. Let me connect you with Revenue."

A click and a ring, and the Revenue Lady came on, whereupon I repeated my request.

"Would this be in a professional capacity?" she asked, and I said yes ma'am, it would.

"I think we handle that here," the Revenue Lady said, "but let me switch you to the man who'd know for sure."

Another click and another ring, and a man came on the horn: "Could I help you, sir?"

"Yes, I need to know who to see about getting a poetic license."

"Very well, sir. That's 'poetic'?"

"Yes," I said.

The Revenue Man asked to be excused for a moment, but soon returned apparently with a big book, for I could hear him leafing through pages.

"Just what type of business are you engaged in?" he asked.

"Well," I said, "I've got a line on this job, but they said I'd need a poetic license."

"Oh," he said. More pages turning.

"Is this like a writer?" he asked.

I replied that I hoped so.

"Oh, well," he said, sounding relieved, "I imagine your best bet would be the state Contract Licensing Board. Companies that build bridges and like that, under contract, they go to that Board. Would you contract to have something written by a certain date?"

"Sort of," I said.

"Well, sure then, that's where you need to go. Three seven two four six six one."

The people at the Contract Licensing Board were nice, too, but I ended up being advised to call the Little Rock City Hall.

"It sounds like some sort of privilege tax to me," the lady said. I gave up there. I don't want a poetic license that isn't any good beyond the corporate limits; I need a state-wide permit. I do some of my best stuff beyond the civilizing influence of Central Arkansas.

I guess the only thing left to do now is to appeal direct to Lily Peter.

Bang the Drum Swiftly

Monticello—At the tender age of 20, Bill King of Pickens is a busy man. He is studying to be an elementary school teacher, fretting about missing meals and playing the hell out of the bass drum for the University of Arkansas at Monticello's marching Boll Weevil Band.

The first activity probably doesn't interest too many people other than those who know that Bill King loves kids, and is good with them, and the second is pretty self-evident, seeing as how he is now in fighting trim at 278 pounds, down from an off-season high of 299. It's his role as the bellwether of UAM's marching band that has earned him an appreciative following and a spread in the UAM football brochure as impressive as that devoted to any of the school's grid stars.

Saying that King "plays" the bass drum is a little like saying that Julia Child whips up an occasional light lunch. Starting with the drumstick twirls that are the bread and butter of your basic marching band bass drummer, King has developed a routine that includes over-the-head drumming, behind-the-back drumming, under-the-leg drumming and drumming while the drum is flung around his head and shoulders. All this to a rhythm bearing only a passing resemblance to the old familiar street beat of yore.

The Boll Weevil band was practicing last week for their first show of the season, so a reporter drove down to take a look at Bill King. Band director James Dunlap, into whose life King lumbered three years ago, said that the group hadn't had much time to work up a half-time show, so the performance would consist mainly of marching on the field, putting Bill King in front of the band and letting him do his stuff.

Dunlap takes no credit for King's flamboyant style, which was apparently developed during King's days as a drummer for Dumas High School. "My direction of Bill consists of me telling him to get it on," Dunlap said.

The band was gathering at the practice field to go through their routine, and King soon made his appearance, driving a beat-up white Chevy equipped with a bass drum in the front seat and a definite list to port. He emerged from the driver's side, munching potato chips and finishing off a huge root beer.

"Drinkin' while drivin'," he whooped as he pulled the green bass drum from the other side of the car.

There were a few important things King had to attend to before getting down to music. First of all, he complained piteously to Dunlap, those noon band practice sessions were playing hob with his lunch schedule, and he'd sure appreciate it if Dunlap would allow him to skip the next day's session in order that he might catch up on his eating. Dunlap was skeptical, so King moved on to another topic—well, not really another topic—opining that it sure seemed to him that it was about time for a band picnic. That lunchroom fare was starving him to death, he said. Dunlap was more hopeful about this, saying that next Tuesday might be a good time.

The important stuff taken care of, King had time to chat with the reporter for awhile before the marching began. He began playing the drums in the seventh grade at Dumas, he said, and although he's an all-round percussionist, his size dictated early on that he'd tote the bass drum in the marching band.

"I started out just twirling the sticks like all the other guys do," he said. "The rest of the stuff sort of grew out of that. I expect I've done just about everything except stand on my head, and I'm going to figure out a way to do that this year."

Broken drum heads haven't been much of a problem, he said, but he admitted to being hell on drumsticks. "Mr. Dunlap keeps buyin' 'em and I keep bustin' 'em," he said.

The band was forming up now, so King harnessed himself to his drum and went to take his place on the field. One quick pass down the field to the strains of the UAM fight song, and the group amassed facing the home side with King smack-dab in front on the 50-yard line.

The song was "Black Magic Woman," a frantic arrangement that includes what probably is the only bass drum solo in the AIC. *BAM!* King struck the drum, reaching under a high-kicking right leg. *WHAM!* He struck the drum reaching under a high-kicking left leg. *WHAPADITTY!* He executed a fine paradiddle while flinging the drum in the air.

Then, the solo: Whapaditty *BAM*, bam *BAM* whapa*DITTY* bam, whapaditty *BAM* whapaditty *BAM BAM!*

Three times through the routine, and Bill King was steaming with sweat, but still able to improvise a snappy exciting street beat with the rest of the drum section while the band moved off the field.

Dunlap dismissed the group for the day, and said everything was ready for Saturday's halftime show, except they still hadn't found a hat big enough for Bill King.

That might be just as well, if he ever figures out a way to stand on his head.

The Scene of the Crime

Fayetteville—I have always been a little wary of people who reminisce fondly about their college days. My own brief stint at the University of Arkansas here was so filled with misadventures, both academic and social, that I find it hard to believe anyone else could contemplate his own experiences in the world of higher education without coming down with acute depression and a severe case of the hives.

For several years, anytime one circumstance or another would bring me here, I would avoid at any costs setting foot on the college campus, fearful perhaps that some long-memoried campus cop would spot me and pull out a fistful of parking citations, or worse, that I might be seen by an old professor, who would then proceed to collapse into fits of sarcastic laughter.

As time wore on, however, curiosity began to chip away at that layer of terrible memories. They were doing such remarkable things up there. They were occupying buildings, marching for peace, smoking strange plants and illegally cohabitating. Now that was my idea of higher education!

So, here I am, returned at last to the scene of the crime, ready to soak in a little of this campus revolution, only to find out that I'd missed the whole thing. At some time or another, all the fun stuff stopped, and after two days of wandering around and asking impertinent questions of total strangers, I have concluded that college life here today is about the same as when I rather shakily wore the classification of student.

Examine with me, then, some facets of campus life, comparing things as they are now with things as they were in the dim mists of the early '60s.

Campus Politics: When I was in school, the big flap among campus politicos was the reorganization of student government. Now, the big flap is over reorganizing student government back to the way it was before it was reorganized. It is all good fun, especially for the two percent of the student population who are aware that there is such a thing as the student government.

Registration: When I attended school here registration consisted of herding everyone into the men's gym, locking the doors and letting the law of the jungle prevail. After several years of experimenting with computers and preregistration techniques the administration has come up with a new system this semester whereby they herd everyone into the men's gym, lock the doors and let the law of the jungle prevail.

Activism: The only thing that stirred the student body to a demonstration of public indignation in 1963 was a shortage of student tickets for the Texas game. There were also a few tense moments when one frat got another frat's time-honored section in the Greek Theater for a pep rally. I have searched in vain the last couple of days for something to top those stirring examples of commitment to the public good but so far have come up empty-handed. I thought for a moment I had found a pamphleteer outside the Student

Union, but the cards he was handing out turned out to be good for one free taco at some local dispenser of excess stomach acidity.

Messing Around: Discreet inquiries over a two-day period seem to indicate that male students here today try about as hard and succeed about as seldom as they did in the early '60s. About the only concession to the sexual revolution seems to be that an outfit called the Sensitive Products Corporation now advertises each day in the student newspaper. As for the time-honored college custom of getting one's head high, booze seems to have made a comeback. Parents are apparently so relieved that their children might be drinking their kicks instead of smoking them that students who are of age can now partake of the grape in their dormitory rooms, a practice that was pretty generally followed in my day, rule or no rule.

All in all, it's a pretty dreary assessment. Here I'd come, ready to be overwhelmed by all this daring conduct, and the most exciting thing I've seen so far is a fair-to-middling dogfight in front of the Student Union.

It is bad enough having time pass you by, but it is depressing indeed to have it lap you.

Charles Allbright

Sitting ever so silently, facing the large double-paned windows of that historic building at the corner of Third and Louisiana Streets, Charles Allbright begins his day as the current Arkansas Traveler.

The telephone rings. He scratches a few notes. Soon the daily stack of mail arrives. He types. He re-types. The pecking of an ancient manual typewriter filters around a newsroom where the constant hum of the computer fills the air.

He walks. He frets.

This is the Arkansas Traveler of the last twelve years, the one who says of his work that he is "just taking notes."

A native of McGehee and son of a school superintendent, Allbright is one of the funniest writers in the Mid-South today. Behind his success is an insight, an empathy, an ability to see things in perspective.

He cares. That is, perhaps, his strongest suit. He can make us cry. He can make us laugh. Why? Because he loves people. He loves our state. And he loves being the Traveler.

He is "just taking notes" and doing it beautifully every day.

A Lesson in Silence and Song

A funeral procession crept by Lindsey's Gro. and Sta. on Highway 70 between Hot Springs and Glenwood the other day, multiplying the confusions of a Chicago man who said he had lost himself en route to the Crater of Diamonds.

The out-of-stater had just started asking directions of two men taking in the shade in front of Lindsey's when the hearse brought the procession by. The two men quit listening, stood erect and faced the road.

His eyes following theirs, the visitors pointed at the hearse with half a cold cigar. "Who is that?" he said. One of the men, holding a cold drink bottle loosely by its neck at his side, shook his head. He was a stranger there himself. "Who died?" the Chicago man said, turning aggressively on the other. The second man had removed a wide-brimmed straw hat and was watching the procession with his feet close together. He said nothing.

The visitor was seized by growing agitation. Here something of apparent large significance was going on before his eyes, and he wasn't being allowed to grasp it—after driving all that far! Making matters worse, a pickup truck had stopped on the near shoulder of the highway and its occupants, an elderly man and woman, sat there expressionless, angling glances into the faces going by.

As the last of the cars edged by, the Chicago man was making rumbling sounds and looking like he could use some Gatorade. The pickup clumped back onto the highway. The second man got back into his straw hat and went into the Gro. and Sta. The man with the cold drink returned to it, although not swigging as before. It was he who explained the old-time custom.

At last, the visitor said, "Well, I'll be damned. You mean; it's no matter who you are—when the time comes it's like you was Roosevelt or somebody."

He was shaking his head, a mixture of mirth and sympathy. Where he came from nobody would get away with that kind of business. Life was too full, too fast.

"What you'd get," he said proudly, "is run over—and by a wagon going maybe 70 miles an hour."

Noise came from a rear window of his big car, idling nearby—a child hollering, "Daddy, what is it?" From the front seat a woman was turned, hollering at the girl to roll up the window. He went toward them, hollering at both to shut up hollering. Then they were back on the highway, roaring off toward the Crater of Diamonds. In the wrong direction.

We had gone looking for the songbird of Glenwood, perhaps the last of the troubadours, a retired farmer removed by age from his land, but not from living.

So at 70 or so he had come to town, and the word was that with his fiddle and his guitar and his harmonica, often played in combinations, he had become a delight to the children on the streets of Glenwood, and maybe a distraction to some of their parents.

Yes, that was all so, said Ray Ross at the Glenwood *Herald*. Or it had been. From a shelf he took down a broken-handled coffee cup on which was stenciled the name "Earl Nicholson."

"He came in once a week from the street to visit. We didn't always have time, understand. But the point is, what Earl was doing was important to him."

The *Herald* files show that the songbird was silenced on a Saturday night, walking to the nursing home to give his weekly volunteer concert of hymns, which meant that he was dressed for Sunday a day early, in clothes too dark to be separated from the night. The account said the driver was distraught but helpless; that it happened near the home of a doctor who was there in a half minute, but whose help was not needed.

Earl Nicholson was 81. They keep his coffee cup like he was Roosevelt or somebody.

And Miles to Go Before They Sleep

You could read this better with a road map.

George Andres is 85, and has lived all his life in the Sutton community, which is 13 miles south of Prescott in Nevada County.

Worth Andres, 50, is George Andres' son. He has lived all his life at Sutton, too, commuting to work at the Ivory Handle Company at Hope.

Together, father and son have combined 135 years of not traveling around much, although in 1919 George Andres did ride in a buggy to a basketball tournament at Hot Springs. Worth Andres once went to Baton Rouge in a car. Who needs travel?

Recently, the occasion arose for the Andres men to take a drive to Little Rock, that being to put Del Collins on an airplane. Collins, who is George Andres' son-in-law, had been visiting from Kansas City.

At about 7:30 p.m., at Adams Field, the Andreses said goodbye to Del and headed back home to Sutton.

"To get out of town, you just go back across the freeway and turn left," Del Collins had told them.

Between the airport and the freeway, the Andreses stopped for gasoline, then proceeded as instructed.

Something went slightly wrong. They missed the turnoff, which necessitated doubling back. The second time they crossed the freeway from the opposite direction, the Andreses turned left.

After a pleasant drive of two hours—it was well after dark then—the men picked up a sign in the headlights:

WEST MEMPHIS
13 Miles

You can get farther away from Sutton than West Memphis, but you have to go to Kentucky to do it.

(Much later, someone would ask, "Well, didn't you see a sign that said Brinkley or something?"

(And George Andres would say, as a matter of fact he had seen a sign that said Brinkley. "I thought that was down around Gurdon.")

Unable to cross the median, the men drove on to West Memphis, turned around and headed for Little Rock.

It was getting on midnight when they arrived back. Somewhere off the freeway they gassed up again, gathered fresh information about getting to Sutton, and telephoned George Andres' wife, Mattie.

"Don't worry, we'll be home shortly," he assured her.

Again they were back on the interstate, this time without difficulty, and with night settled in around them they watched the freeway flatten out ahead.

Only it didn't flatten out as much as you'd think, heading south like that. When they had driven about two hours, the hills turned into mountains. That's when they spotted the sign that said:

FORT SMITH
43 Miles

By freeway, Fort Smith is something more than 250 miles from Sutton, a point of progress achieved six hours after the men had left the airport. They turned around and headed back for Little Rock.

Which is when a state trooper flashed them down.

"You're going in the right direction," he said helpfully, "but you're on the wrong side of the median."

So at about 4:30 a.m the Andreses arrived at Little Rock for the third time. They filled up with gasoline for the third time, checked the oil and tires, and gathered fresh information about the best way to get to Sutton.

What went wrong is not clear. Shortly before dawn the two pulled up in front of the State Capitol building. Being there, they went ahead and made an educational tour of the darkened grounds. No arrests were made.

It was a fellow happening on foot along West Seventh Street who told the Andreses how to get to the freeway that would take them south and home.

So, 15 hours after leaving, having driven 813 miles, George and Worth Andres made it back home—at about the same time Del Collins, after a good night's sleep, was leaving for work at Kansas City.

George Andres fed his cows and hit the sack.

Worth Andres said, "Since I'd never traveled around Arkansas, I enjoyed the trip. It would have been better, though, if it hadn't been night and I could have seen something."

And then he hit the sack.

A Lurch Forward

The old year lurched out on a wistful note for an acquaintance of ours. He was recounting Tuesday, in the countdown hours, an experience he had just undergone at a record shop.

"It's hard to describe," said the man, a fellow in his early forties. "You see, I went to the shopping center for something else. I just happened to drop in to inquire about this record I'd heard on the radio."

You could tell he was kicking himself.

In the store, he was going through the single records when an attractive young girl appeared on the other side of the counter. She had long hair and was wearing a fashionably rotten denim outfit.

"Tell me the title and I'll help you find it," she said.

"It's called, 'My Eyes Adored Ya'," he said.

"Your what?"

The man swallowed. He felt his face flush.

" 'My Eyes Adored Ya'," he said. "I think that's the name of the song."

He also thought something flickered in the sales clerk's eyes. Quickly, she ruffled her forehead and let her fingers walk across some of the titles.

"I don't know," she said. "I've never heard of that. Like, I guess it's an old song, isn't it? And maybe out of print, huh?"

Our man tensed. He said like, no, it wasn't an old song, like maybe three weeks ago when he first heard it and like it had been all over the radio since then.

"At any rate, it certainly isn't important," he said. "Let's just forget it."

He moved to leave, but she stopped him with a hand on his forearm.

"Marsha," she said, calling out to a carbon copy associate who was waiting on another customer two aisles away. "Marsha, this gentleman is looking for a song called—what did you say the name was again?"

Our man felt a massive tic develop beneath his left eye. He heard himself saying, in a voice that carried throughout the store, stopping all transactions, " 'My Eyes Adored Ya'."

Marsha's customer was seized by a sudden fit of coughing and turned away.

Marsha herself said, gee, she didn't know.

"Like maybe if it's on the old charts, sir, we could order it for you—if it doesn't go too far back."

Our man opened his mouth. Nothing came out, and he closed it. He turned and made along the aisle for the open door. Eyes were on him, he knew that, and in the background he heard Marsha ask the other young lady, "Did he ever say who the artist was?"

He said he wanted to turn and say, "It wasn't by any damned artist, it was by some damn singer!"

But very quickly it wasn't mattering all that much.

"It doesn't matter, either," he was saying in the countdown, "that I know I'm right. That song is a new one, and if they're all that young and cool they ought to know the songs better than I do."

The only thing that mattered, he said, and that not very much, was starting out a new year, feeling out of print and everything.

From A Ditch To Zent, List Has 'Em All

The United States Geological Survey has put Arkansas into a computer.

All the other states are in there, too.

What this means is that by merely pushing a button, or maybe two or three buttons, any location anywhere can be turned up—presto!

The latitude and longitude co-ordinates are shown immediately, along with county name and elevation where applicable.

Take A Ditch. This location, A Ditch, is the first Arkansas place identified in the know-everything computer. A Ditch is in Mississippi County. We do not know the elevation. Probably it is not applicable except to crawdads.

At the other end of the list is Zent. Zent can be found in Monroe County. The Geological Survey should make that fact known to the state Highway Department because Zent cannot be found on our Highway Department map.

Between A Ditch and Zent are listed 22,000 Arkansas places with names.

You would think there wouldn't be that many names, 22,000, to go around. It is achieved by doubling up.

For example, the list includes 329 place names beginning with Little—as in Little Rock, a town approximately in the middle of the state, and about halfway between A Ditch and Zent.

Little is big in Arkansas. Big, on the other hand, begins the names of only 204 places, as in Big Flat and Big Fork and Big Piney. Only in Biggers is Big bigger. Biggers is in Randolph County.

Push the computer buttons and see what comes up in Arkansas.

The Geological Survey lists Accident School in Benton County. An unlikely place to matriculate.

In White County flows Bad Luck Creek.

Okay is in Howard County.

These Arkansas locations have become part of what is known as a nationwide Geographic Names Information System. Everybody can get at them—governments, industries, schools, the public, anybody trying to put a finger on something geographically.

Looking for a cemetery?

Jaybird Cemetery is in Marion County. Faulkner County has a Republican Cemetery, and things have gone that way in most elections. Carroll County, more favorable to Republicans, offers Democrat Hollow.

There is a Three Brothers Cemetery in Baxter County (and a Three Sisters Landing in Garland County).

Other places listed by the survey: Happy Home Cemetery in Jefferson County, Aunt Dilley Cemetery in Perry County, Captain Smiths Cemetery in Madison County, Smart Cemetery in Cleburne County, Bills Cemetery in Crawford County and Rough and Ready Cemetery in Drew County.

Strangers playing with the Arkansas computer might begin to wonder about our preoccupations: Dead Man Point in Monroe County, Dead Mule Bend in Jackson County, Dead Timber Lake in Mississippi County.

In Arkansas 354 names start with Mount, as in Mount Judea, Mount Olive, Mount Pleasant and Mount Pleasant—there are two of those.

We have 60 Mount Zion churches.

There are 25 Antioch churches and eight Antioch cemeteries.

Thirty-seven Bear Creeks.

Fifty Cedar Creeks.

Punch the computer for an Arkansas place beginning with West, as in West Memphis, and 104 names come up. Eighty-two place names begin with East.

North, as in North Little Rock, outscores South, 77 to 72.

Yell County, the computer says, has both a Sunrise Point and a Sunset Point. That's because it has one of those 354 Mounts—Mount Nebo. The sun comes up at one end and goes down at the other.

It is easier to list names of presidents *not* used. All are here, as Arkansas place names, except Fillmore, Arthur, Taft, Coolidge, Truman, Eisenhower and Reagan.

Folks living in Trumann might say that the man from Missouri didn't know how to spell his name.

M and M's for the Buck

With any luck this first story in from the deerwoods will be the worst. It is difficult to imagine that things would go downhill.

Details are incomplete, but the report involves a central Arkansas doctor who was set up on a deer stand down in Chicot Country.

What happened was that thing that is always happening to deer hunters. Something or other calls them a few feet away from the stand, and in that very instant the biggest buck of all time appears.

This has happened thousand of times in the Arkansas deerwoods. At this very moment it is happening to probably 500 hunters.

As smart as they are, you would think that Arkansas deer hunters would learn better. But no. Every year huge bucks keep appearing between them and their rifles, which are propped against trees "not 30 feet away."

Invariably, the hunter and the buck stare at each other for a long time. After that, details vary with the men bringing them back to camp.

What makes the report of the doctor's hunt notable is that he did not try the customary things, i.e., knocking the buck senseless with a fist, only to have it get up and run away, or holding the buck with a half-nelson until help comes, which it never does in time.

The doctor said neither of these. What he did was reach inside his hunting jacket and pull out some M and M's—the candy that won't mess up your hands—and started throwing them at the buck.

"He doesn't know why," our source reports. "It was the only thing he could think of."

But throwing M and M's? How did that sound back in camp? Was he trying to knock the buck out, or maybe lure him into staying around, eating candy, until he could get the gun and shoot him?

"He doesn't know," our source insisted. "The thing is, you don't just stand there staring at a big buck and not do something about it. He had three M and M's, so he started throwing them."

The buck, like all the rest, got away. The haunting thing about it is that anybody who will come back to camp and tell a story like that probably has just seen the biggest buck of all time.

Delmar Runyan of Crossett took his 13-year-old son, Tim, to deer camp for the first time.

"Nobody got a deer, but you couldn't say there wasn't any action," Runyan says.

In his first hour in camp, making up for lost years, Tim Runyan swallowed half a pouch of Red Man chewing tobacco.

"He wouldn't have known a buck if he'd seen one," said the elder Runyan.

The thought persists that if Tim had had the M and M's, and the doctor the pouch of Red Man—well.

Hounded by the Bailiff

About a month ago our man Leland DuVall finished up his duty as a civil court juror, having served the allotted 12 days for one term of court. They paid him off and dismissed him.

A few days after that the bailiff telephoned DuVall and told him to appear in court the next morning for jury duty.

DuVall pointed out what the situation was—that he already had served the limit.

"Is that so?" the bailiff said. "All right, I'll take your name off the list."

A few days later DuVall got another call from the bailiff, who advised him to show up in court the next morning.

DuVall went back through the explanation. The bailiff said, oh, yes—he'd take DuVall's name off the list.

Nothing more happened for four days, at the end of which time the bailiff called DuVall and told him to appear for jury duty the next morning.

"Don't you remember?" DuVall said hopefully, "We've discussed this. My name isn't supposed to be on the list any more."

"Oh, yes," the bailiff said. "I'll take it off." This kept happening until, after the fifth time, DuVall initiated a call of his own to the court. He got the clerk, who listened to the story and then assured him that from that moment forward his name was stricken from the list.

Thirty minutes later DuVall got a call from the bailiff.

"About jury duty in the morning—forget it," the bailiff said.

"Thank you very much," DuVall said, relieved at last."

"Yeah," the bailiff said, "they've settled that case out of court."

Shortness of Cash Comes From Waiting in Line

It was Sunday evening. In Fayetteville, Katherine Shurlds made one of those impromptu dashes to the grocery store.

"With my three items in hand, I surveyed the checkout stands and found only one open."

Only one customer was in that line. But what a customer!

"A young woman was overseeing the totaling of what looked like her annual shopping spree."

Katherine Shurlds sighed and dug in for a wait.

Eventually all things do come to an end. The clerk reached into the cart for the last item.

The customer shrieked, "Oh! I need some diapers!"

She scurried away.

The checkout clerk certainly did not waste time.

In the diaper customer's absence she started getting the mountain of items into paper bags.

And ran afoul of nasty luck.

"As she was sacking groceries," says Katherine Shurlds, "the clerk dropped an item on the lady's eggs, breaking half a dozen or so. The lady returned with her diapers just as the clerk took off to get another dozen eggs."

In this supermarket in Fayetteville, on a Sunday evening, people were coming and going with urgency.

Something about the situation inspired the store manager to decide that another checkout line should be opened.

That is how you get to be store manager.

Katherine Shurlds made her move toward the new line, opened by a young man.

But no!

"Two teen-aged boys behind me darted around me to be first in the new line."

Katherine fell in behind them.

"Their purchases were totaled and one cried, 'We don't have enough money!' So one of the lads headed to the car for more change."

On her quickie trip to the grocery store, the three-item customer found herself embarking on a new career.

"Now our line had grown. We waited and waited and waited."

The teen-ager returned from the car. He conferred with his friend, the young man who had anchored their spot in the new line.

Their conference was long and intense. And disappointing.

"They finally admitted, 'We still don't have enough money.' "

Katherine Shurlds knew what to do about that.

"Hearing that they were only 20 cents short, I volunteered, 'I'll pay it!' Anything to get that line moving!"

By plunking down 20 cents, Katherine bought her freedom.

Or you would have thought so.

"The boys thanked me profusely and left.

"The checker began totaling my purchases. As I opened my change purse again, a wave of embarrassment swept over me."

A really big wave.

"I wasn't going to have enough money now!"

It was heads down and mumbling time.

"I quietly said to the checker, 'I don't have enough now. Just take this off.' "

Katherine Shurlds set aside one of her items.

But the checker would not hear it.

"He insisted that I tell him how much I was short."

It set off a new round of conversations.

Katherine sensed the onset of a commotion behind her.

This man behind her, like Katherine Shurlds, apparently had made an impromptu Sunday evening dash to the grocery store.

Now he was well into a new career of his own.

The man declared, "I'll pay it!"

Katherine Shurlds laughed. The checkout clerk laughed. The man with the new money laughed.

She accepted the generous offer.

"As I thanked the man, he looked behind him. 'With my luck,' he said, 'I'll be short and there won't be anybody behind me!' "

Hunt, Fly a Smash at News Conference

Ray L. Hunt, of the Texas oil Hunts, was in Little Rock recently to talk about why he and his brothers spent $68 million to acquire Union Life Insurance Company.

That was not a hip-pocket transaction, even for the Hunts, and the visitor went through a round of interviews with Arkansas newspaper and broadcast representatives.

During a television interview taped at The Little Rock Club, Hunt was set upon by a persistent fly.

That of itself was worthy of news coverage. One would no more expect to see a fly in The Little Rock Club than a mouse in Pleasant Valley.

But there the fly was, buzzing in and out of the bright television lights, making nose dives at the millionaire and being ignored to the best of everybody's ablity.

Millie Ward was there, a copywriter for Combs-Resneck and Associates, advertising and marketing representatives for the life insurance company.

"It finally got so bad that the television girl said, look, we've got to stop this and get that fly."

Ray Hunt took the interruption in good humor. The fly took it as an opportunity to disappear.

All parties got settled again and the interview was resumed.

The fly came back, looking for Hunt.

Millie Ward couldn't just sit there.

"The fly was doing nose-dives, buzzing in and out, landing on the man's arm and then on his head. Nobody was doing anything."

The copywriter grabbed a newspaper from a coffeetable, rolled it up and took a swing at the fly. She missed and hit the millionaire on the arm.

"Then the fly landed on his head again. I had the newspaper drawn back but I couldn't bring myself to do it."

The fly buzzed in and out, nose-diving the oil man, being pursued by Millie Ward in the manner of a batter homing in on a curve ball.

In a moment of fatal judgement, the fly veered away, landed on a window and got smashed.

The interview proceeded without further thrash.

Combs-Resneck and Associates does not offer fly-killing as a service, but if it comes to that the job will be done with class.

"That rolled-up newspaper was a *Wall Street Journal*," the heroine said later. "It gave dignity to the occasion."

Lost Son's Call From N.Y. Leaves Mother Shrieking

On a Friday morning, Ryan Allen flew up to New York to get a weekend of culture and hang out at the Hard Rock Cafe.

Ryan Allen, 15, is a student at Little Rock Central High School.

His main man, not counting rock musicians, is Vincent van Gogh.

Here was life at its fullest. A van Gogh exhibit at the Metropolitan Museum. Then hanging out at the Hard Rock Cafe.

It helps when you have an aunt living in the Big Apple.

On Friday morning, Ryan Allen flew up there to meet his Aunt Lin and do it all.

At 5 p.m. Friday, Sally Allen answered the telephone in Little Rock.

On the line was her son, Ryan. He was standing more or less in the middle of Grand Central Station.

For the last 30 minutes Ryan had been separated from his Aunt Lin Campbell, she having lost herself in the rush hour crowd that was herding toward a subway.

Ryan Allen had no key to his aunt's apartment. Even if he managed to find it, he'd have to wait outside on the steps. In the cold. In Brooklyn Heights. Stay there until Aunt Lin found herself and returned home.

Almost choking, but not quite, Sally Allen instructed her son to go nowhere. Stay right by the telephone. She took the number.

"I'll call you back right away."

A mother's nightmare began to unfold.

"I called Aunt Lin's apartment repeatedly and got no answer."

Sally Allen's husband, Ryan's father, is Willie Allen, the well known photographer.

Sally says, "I called everyone we know in New York. No one is at home on Friday evening in New York City."

Over and over she called back to the pay phone in Grand Central Station.

"I wanted Ryan to know what progress was being made. None."

It was during one of those handwringing morale builders that Sally Allen heard her son yell, "Wright! Wright Anderson!"

She could not believe her ears.

"In the middle of Grand Central Station at the rush hour on Friday amid thousands of commuters, Ryan had spied a young man who had grown up a couple of blocks away from us and who now lives in New York."

Wright Anderson went up there to attend Columbia. He stayed on, in insurance.

Only a mother's shrieks broke up the reunion, and brought Wright Anderson to the telephone.

"Wright promised to stay with Ryan while I worked something out."

Working things out, Sally Allen called the Brooklyn Heights number of her sister, Lin Campbell, several more times. She called the other New York numbers again.

Nobody was anywhere.

Thank the good Lord for Wright Anderson!

Visualizing a telephone bill in the thousands, Mrs. Allen called back to the Grand Central Station pay phone to touch base.

"A man answered who apparently could not talk but only grunt."

Ryan Allen's mother quickly hung up, wild-eyed.

"I called the number again. A woman answered who could talk a lot. But it was all in Chinese.

"I hung up and called again. Screaming teen-aged girls answered. I asked if they could spot nearby a well dressed good looking young man [Wright Anderson] who was with a good looking young man with spiked hair, several earrings and heavy into black leather."

The girls said, oh, wow, that last part described several thousand persons in the station.

It is gratifying to be able to report that as she approached what is generally called hysteria, Sally Allen finally did get her sister to answer in Brooklyn Heights, which was not good because Lin Campbell was sobbing when she picked up the telephone.

But almost at that same moment, in walked Ryan and Wright Anderson.

A large celebration began up there, which Sally Allen did not get in on, although she was shrieking into the telephone.

She was still shrieking when the New York bunch, running late for the museum yelled goodby and hurried out of there.

Ridiculous Phone Call Reinforces Faith in Good Will

On their way to a national convention for secretaries of state in North Dakota, Paul and Carolyn Riviere and their two daughers pulled in for lunch at the Burger King in Bentonville.

Becky Riviere, age 4, traveled with chicken pox, a gift from her older sister. Six-year-old Cathy Riviere got rid of the spots in time for the trip.

Their mother is a teacher of nursing. Pulling into the Burger King, Carolyn Riviere decided that everybody would eat outside, on picnic benches, rather than go in and give chicken pox to Bentonville.

Lunch was eaten and the family pushed on, reaching Kansas City for the first night's stop.

When Carolyn Riviere first missed her purse, she was not alarmed.

"I supposed that I'd put it in the trunk of the car, with the games and books, the travel things."

But the purse was not in the trunk. And then it came to the secretary of state's wife. In her mind's eye, her purse was back in Bentonville, beneath a bench at Burger King.

"My credit cards, travelers checks—they were all gone."

Carolyn Riviere didn't know what to head off first.

In the Kansas City hotel room, she formulated emergency plans, then paused just long enough to make one ridiculous call.

"I knew it was a waste of time, but it had to be done. I got Information and the number of the Burger King in Bentonville."

The manager at Burger King is Tom Franklin. What Franklin related might sound ridiculous to most folks out of Arkansas.

Yes, Mrs. Riviere's purse was at Burger King. A customer found it under the bench and turned it in. Yes, the purse would be there waiting for her until she came to get it.

The victim says, "How does it go? O ye of little faith!"

The rest of the trip, with no purse and chicken pox, went splendidly.

"I'd do it again!"

The only problem was that Mom, along with her daughters, had to go around asking the secretary of state for money.

Tom O'Neal, also of the Bentonville Burger King, says that having purses in the office is not all that unusual.

"We get purses all the time."

Well, not all the time. Sometimes they don't get purses.

"But we have some purses here now," O'Neal said. He offered to go get the purses to see whether any of them was ours.

People turn things in, and then sooner or later somebody comes to pick the item up.

It is not always sooner.

"We have some car keys here now," Tom O'Neal said. He offered to go get the car keys to see whether they were ours.

Those car keys have been at the Burger King more than a year.

The Ways of the Big Apple, the Native of McGehee

Hot Springs—YWCA business took Carolyn Poff up to New York recently. Mrs. Poff is executive director of the YWCA in Hot Springs. Franklin Poff went along. While his wife was in the meetings, Frank turned himself out on the Manhattan streets.

In front of a Broadway theater, the visitor from Arkansas was fallen upon by good fortune.

A young man confronted Frank Poff with two tickets to *The King and I.*

These were special tickets.

They cost $45 each. Poff was in luck because the young man's wife was gravely ill. His children were gravely starving. Bills were mounting. Cruel winter was moving in.

The Hot Springs man was told he could have these great tickets, practically steal them, for halfprice, both tickets for $45.

Frank Poff looked at the date on the tickets: January 11, 1985.

"No deal," he said. "We won't be in town then."

The sidewalk ticket seller observed that obviously Frank Poff was not familiar with the ways of New York.

He was good enough to explain those ways.

"You see," the young man with the tickets said, "when it says January 11, that means these tickets are good to see *The King and I* any time up until that date. That's what the January 11 stands for."

Frank Poff is a real-estate executive. That's one thing. He is also a native of McGehee. In other words, the man has a quick mind.

"You're conning me," Poff told the hustler in front of the Manhattan theater.

The young man was scandalized. But for Christmas around the corner, the wolf at the door, body all achin' and wracked with pain—but for the fell clutch of circumstance he would never part with these tickets.

As it was, if Frank Poff couldn't see the $45, how about 20 bucks for the pair? Franklin Poff was too quick not to go for that.

Back at their hotel, the man from Arkansas explained the ripoff to his wife.

"After I bought the tickets, I waited for this ticket window to open. Then I showed the tickets to the guy in there."

And?

"He said of course the tickets were good only for the date printed on them, January 11. I knew that all along."

That part didn't matter, anyway.

It turned out that *The King and I* didn't even open until the day after Christmas. By then Frank and Carolyn Poff would be long gone back to God's country.

Frank told Mrs. Poff, "So I sold the tickets to this guy on the street. Let him have both of them for $45."

The ripee from Arkansas had pocketed a cool $25 profit.

The Big Apple was not through with Franklin A. Poff.

"I told Frank," Carolyn Poff says, "since he had $25 he didn't think he'd have, why didn't he invest in the lottery."

Everybody else seemed to be doing that.

What you do is, you go to a newsstand and buy a set of numbers, and then if those numbers come up in the lottery the investment pays off.

But when you buy numbers, you have to fill out a card.

"Frank got tired of filling out the cards. By the time he'd filled out $8 worth, he quit."

Frank Poff won $60 in the lottery.

That's $60, minus $8 for lottery tickets—a profit of $52.

That's $52, plus $25 profit on theater tickets—a total of $77 profit.

Carolyn Poff says, "On the way to the airport the cab driver just got hysterical with laughter. He said all he ever heard was people from the South crying about how they had been conned and ripped off and mugged.

"It thrilled him to hear that a man from Arkansas had taken the big city."

Her Ambition Realized, and There Was No Dyeing

Bentonville—On Mother's Day, after they had been to church and to the cemetery, C. L. (Charlie) McNelly drove his wife, Lois, to the rent house out by the fairgrounds.

For the honoree, this was not a sparkling celebration. Her children all had reached their teens, a heavy gift on Mother's Day. Being "about 39" was better when you didn't have to look back to say it.

Then decorating at the cemetery, the grave of her husband's mother—melancholy rode with Lois McNelly on her way to the rent house.

Why go there, anyway?

Getting out of the car, Lois saw a new sign—"Not For Rent."

That made no sense. Charlie McNelly's hobbies are old cars and old houses.

"He can fix up a house and put a sign on it," his wife says, "and the house will be rented practically overnight."

So in the early afternoon on Mother's Day, they went up on the porch of Charlie's rent house near the county fairgrounds, and he let her inside.

You need to go back a ways.

Go all the way back to high school: *"Her life's ambition is to be a hair stylist."* That's the way it went in the senior class summary.

She married C. L. McNelly, and was on her way with that ambition.

"I enrolled in beauty school and got pregnant. Then I enrolled again and got pregnant again. Three times I enrolled in beauty school, and every time I got pregnant."

You are not going to style a lot of hair pulling your own.

But children do reach school age. When Lois McNelly's youngest got there, spare hours gathered around her.

It was time again. At last.

"There is no way you can do this."

The doctor was giving his verdict about Lois McNelly's back.

When her first child was six months old, the young mother slipped and fell down a flight of stairs. She damaged a disc.

Years later she was hearing, "You will not be able to work long hours, standing on your feet."

The doctor hadn't read the high school yearbook.

She had surgery. From surgery she went to therapy. From therapy she went to beauty school. She got a job.

At last, Lois McNelly had her ambition in her own hands.

"I worked eight months, building up clientele, and then one Friday night I got called into the back room and was told I was being let go. I asked for a reason, but there was no reason. It just about crushed me."

On Mother's Day afternoon, Charlie and Lois McNelly stood in the main part of the rent house near the fairgrounds, and he said, "What do you think about having shampoo bowls along this wall?"

She said, "What are you talking about?"

He said of the house not for rent, "By the end of the summer, you're going to have your own beauty salon here."

She stood there in the room and bawled.

"But I'm not ready."

"Oh, yes, I've been watching you. You're ready."

It opens today, the Old Main Salon. The owner explains that name.

"It's in one of the oldest houses in Bentonville. It's on Main Street. And we're giving it an antique look inside and out, like the old building on the campus at Fayetteville."

For one hilarious moment, during the summer's remodeling, Lois McNelly wasn't certain.

"I drove up and saw this beautiful new sign in front. Black Old English letters on a yellow background: KURL UP AND DYE."

The work of Charlie McNelly.

"That nut!" she exclaimed. "He did it!"

Today it's the Old Main Salon. Getting ready, the owner has been to too many schools, too many conventions, too many times to the therapist, to open her door as anything but a professional.

But she will not forget what her husband did on Mother's Day.

And if you drive around back, you'll see the sign that says what he wouldn't let her do. Kurl Up and Dye.

Rotating Rotation

With her husband handling the heavy stuff, like world energy questions and how to get St. Louis in the World Series, Mrs. Greg Powell of West Memphis is free to piddle with household matters, which includes keeping two family cars running.

That's why Sunday afternoon Mrs. Powell wrote a note to herself on her kitchen bulletin board:

"Get tires rotated on sta. wagon!"

Her husband saw that note Monday morning. With some time off, Greg Powell took the station wagon down to the service sation—not a total waste of his time because Joe Gillis, at the station, has special insights into the deficiencies of the Cardinal bullpen.

Powell was back home by lunchtime, after which he went to work without bothering to take the note from the bulletin board.

So early afternoon Mrs. Powell drove to the service station—it was Joe Gillis's afternoon off—and had the tires rotated on the station wagon.

Monday evening the Powells were sitting out on the patio, visiting with neighbors, when Greg Powell alertly remembered what he had done.

"By the way," he told Martha Powell, "you can take your note down because I had the tires rotated on the station wagon this morning."

Everybody was still laughing about the foulup, the way people laugh about throwing away $5, when Greg Powell Jr., who is 18, appeared on the patio.

"I wish you hadn't told me about this," Greg Jr. said, a sick expression coming to his face. "I rotated the tires myself last night, and I was coming out here to collect my $3 fee."

Mrs. Powell paid off and fired both her helpers.

"I'm still drawing diagrams," she says, "and trying to figure out, after three rotations and the expenditure of $13, whether the tires are back where they started in the first place."

Here's something else to figure out.

A North Little Rock man went into one of those super big shopping center stores—the many-departmented kind at which you can get everything from hanging plants to instant waffles—and stood waiting for a young lady to get off the telephone and approve his check so he could go about some shopping.

She talked agitatedly into the phone, changing facial colors, and then crashed the receiver back to its cradle.

"Don't bring your car to this place!" she gritted.

The man, who had not planned to, counterfeited sizable interest, mostly in the interest of getting his check approved.

"Why not?" he said.

"Because I let them have my car to balance the tires and they still haven't got the carburetor back on!"

The man's interest turned genuine.

"Carburetor? I didn't know. . . ."

"Don't ask me," the employee shot back. "But if you get your tires balanced here, it takes them all day to get the carburetor back on!"

Time Doesn't Fly in Doctor's Office

Our friend Spurling was not looking well. We suggested that he might think about a checkup. "Not until I get my nerves in order," Spurling said.

Nerves?

"I'm not up to seeing a doctor just now."

Spurling said the last time he saw his doctor he went in and rang the bell and the receptionist pulled the glass back.

"Spurling," he said.

"How's that?" the woman said.

"Spurling. I have an appointment at 1:30."

The receptionist said of course. She consulted a book, biting a pencil with teeth that looked like a xylophone. "Have a seat, Mr. Spur"—the glass panel closed on his name.

Spurling turned and saw no seats. He saw lots of laps. In some laps hands were folded. In others handkerchiefs were twisted. A man of 45 made pyramids with an Etch-A-Sketch. A woman about twice that age read a magazine called *Momentous Pharmacy*.

Spurling felt his awkwardness.

A patient wearing a John Deere baseball cap stood, sighing, and said, "You can sit here. I'm going outside."

Spurling sat down beneath a picture of "Grouse in Autumn."

"Did you say 1:30?"—this was a woman sitting on Spurling's right. She had fat elbows, allowing no room for his own on the chair arm.

Spurling begged the woman's pardon.

She said, disapprovingly, "Your appointment? Did I hear you say it's for 1:30?"

"Yes, 1:30."

The woman harrumphed—"*My* appointment is for 1:30."

On Spurling's left a man recrossed his legs and said, "My appointment is for 1:30 too."

Our friend got red-faced remembering it.

"Can you imagine that? Everybody in that waiting room had an appointment for 1:30!"

For 30 minutes Spurling sat and read the sign on the coffee table: "Thank You for Not Smoking." He read that and listened to "Mighty Lak a Rose."

At 2 p.m. the man on Spurling's left was motioned for. In the empty chair he left *The Bible Story Book*. Spurling read this until 2:30, at which time he traded for the Etch-A-Sketch, by then in the hands of the patient in the John Deere Cap.

At 3:15, with nobody else getting a crack at *Momentous Pharmacy*, Spurling got up to wrench the magazine from the elderly woman. His knees buckled under him, having gone to sleep, and he narrowly avoided a nasty fall.

The memory of that really steamed him.

"What is it—unconsciousness? Arrogance? What rationale allows any doctor to tell a dozen patients they all have an appointment at the same time? These people lose time from work. They feel rotten enough already. Half of them have to drive all the way back to Botkinburg!"

Spurling said he would tell us one thing.

"I'll tell you one thing. The next time I get a statement saying my bill is payable immediately, you know what I'm going to do? I'm going to"—we stopped him right there.

Our friend Spurling doesn't know the first thing about medicine. Doctors work so hard, during their med school years, they forget what time it is. Then they get busy, and the whole time-telling process never gets straightened out.

At 4:15 Spurling got motioned back for his 1:30 appointment.

"They put me in this little room where there weren't any magazines or games or anything. Nothing to do but sit and feel terrible."

At 4:30 a nurse came in and told him to take off his shirt.

"What for?" Spurling said.

The nurse appeared puzzled. "Didn't you want doctor to look at you?"

Spurling felt like a fool.

"Of course I wanted doctor to look at me. But now I can't remember what for."

He got up and left.

Cured! And not even touched by a stethoscope!

People like Spurling will complain about anything.

The Answer in Life Is in Geometry, Centenarian Says

Warren—On the occasion of his 100th birthday, C. E. Englehart had some dinner tickets made up.

An orderly man, Englehart explained the tickets.

"Several times I have been to things at which tickets were given to the guests. It seemed to me this was a good way to handle the dinner."

So on Sunday after church the birthday group went to the Mill Pond Restaurant, which opened privately for the occasion, and 34 persons filed in, presented their tickets and enjoyed a fine meal.

The ticket idea conceived by C. E. Englehart worked without a hitch.

All 34 ticket holders were relatives of the honoree.

At age 100 he lives alone, C. E. Englehart does, in the house that he and his wife Della Mae built on Martin Street.

He gets up when he wants to, usually some time after 5 a.m.

"I get out of bed when I decide I'm not going back to sleep."

Englehart cooks for himself, whatever he wants to eat. He moves easily in the kitchen, having helped when his wife was there. Della Mae has been gone since his 80s.

His fig preserves won first prize at the county fair. His Irish potatoes, too. Until retirement at age 76, his working life was wood. Building and creating with wood, and supervising others doing the same thing.

"I came to Arkansas from Missouri in 1908, not knowing a thing."

So he taught himself.

"The answer is not in algebra. The answer is in geometry."

That's not only in wood, but in life. Things have a definite shape.

Once on a visit to Little Rock, Englehart was stopped by a policeman.

"You can't turn left here," the policeman said.

C. E. Englehart told him, "If you'll get out of the way, I think I can."

"My wife always warned me, anytime we saved a little money, got $300 or $400 ahead—be careful! It's going to be time for somebody to get an operation. She was so right."

In one of Englehart's operations the surgeon took his right leg below the knee. There is a replacement.

"I'd be all right if it wasn't for this," says the man who in his 100th spring still was all right enough to mow his yard.

Waiting four months, impatiently, for he artificial limb, Englehart built his own peg leg so he could get out to his garden.

"He didn't like it," says C. E. Englehart Jr. "He threw the leg out of the garden and crawled around."

In his living room on the Sunday afternoon of his 100th birthday, C. E. Englehart wears a white shirt, under suspenders, and looks like a young George Burns.

He is badgered for advice.

"Don't steal and don't lie," he says, forced to come up with something. "I might stretch the truth if I got in a tight."

On coping with a faltering memory: "My wife used to tell me two dozen things to get at the grocery store, and I never wrote any of them down."

This afternoon he could not remember what the morning's sermon was about.

"It's no disgrace to do without dinner, but it makes a hard job of it."

Englehart says be a church member.

On work relationships: "Don't take any nonsense from the man you work for. Some boss will say jump into the fire, and the worker will say, 'Fine,' and into the fire he'll go. That's damn foolishness."

C. E. Englehart had 50 men working under him. He never told one of them to jump into a fire.

On a wall in his living room is this saying.

"All Our Visitors Bring Happiness. Some by Coming. Others by Going."

City Connection Helps Thaw Pipes

Atkins—Tom Gillespie has pulled together the details of how John Manning, back during the coldest weather, solved the problem of frozen house pipes.

What you do is go under the house with a blow torch.

In the case of John Manning's pipes you go under the house twice, taking directions from muffled wifely shouts up above.

Gillespie tells it:

"Edith had him under the floor thawing out water pipes. He squirmed, slithered and crawled for about an hour with a blow torch until Edith gave him the okay. She had water running out of every faucet."

A man can be proud of something like that.

Except that 30 minutes later Edith Manning turned on a tap and no water came out. Two turns around and still nothing.

So John Manning went back under the house armed with his blow torch.

After considerable torching he hollered up, "Any water yet?"

"Nope" (muffled).

More squirming and slithering and torching.

"Any water yet?"

(Muffled) "Nope. I'll let you know when you get the job done."

That went on for almost an hour. It might have gone all day except the telephone rang. It was James Whittenburg, Edith's son.

Eventually the two got around to the man down there freezing under the floor.

"John says he's got every pipe under the house red hot and I still can't get a drop of water out of any faucet."

You could have heard her son's laughter clear under the house.

"Mom, nobody in town's got water. The city's had it cut off while they tie in that new line in the east part of town."

This kind of storytelling makes Tom Gillespie one of America's more successful newspapermen. His paper, the *Atkins Chronicle*, now has more subscribers at Chicago than the *Chicago Daily News*. Gillespie took a wry look at this recently.

"We've done it again. Another bigtime struggling daily has died a natural death while thriving little weeklies like this one continue to grow and expand. The *Chronicle* is sailing right along toward its 85th birthday and whizzed past the *Chicago Daily News* which died last week at the age of 102. We'll do our part to take up the slack and broaden our coverage so Paul and Pettie Simons, Roy Duvall and our other subscribers in the Chicago area can keep abreast of the more important happenings in the world.

"It was reported that the *Daily News* had lost about 300,000 readers. That might can happen in Chicago but it can't happen in Atkins. We're still teaching reading in our schools, maybe not as well as in the past but good enough to where we ain't turned out 300,000 people who can't read.

"Also, they said the struggling daily had lost about $11 million last year. That ain't gonna happen here at this thriving little weekly either. Annette keeps a good enough eye on our petty cash fund in that old cigar box never to let that happen."

Better Never Than Late for Styx Concert

Texarkana—Through a great stroke of luck, Chris Loveall and Scott Stuart got four last-minute tickets to a sold-out Styx concert down at Shreveport, Louisiana.

Styx is a musical group that young folks will pay $7.50 apiece to see, even if it means driving 75 miles on a moment's notice.

The situation called for a masterpiece of planning and coordination.

At 5 p.m. Saturday, with the concert to start at 7:30 p.m., 75 miles to the south, Scott Stuart left Texarkana heading north in his new car. He would pick up his girl friend, Alonna Jefferies, at Ashdown, and get back to Texarkana by 6 p.m. There Chris Loveall and his fiancée, Tracy Allbright, would be picked up.

The four would have an hour and a half to make it to Shreveport.

Everything went as planned.

Although not quite.

Six o'clock came but the folks from Ashdown didn't.

Then 6:15 p.m.

And 6:30 p.m.

At 6:45 p.m., Scott Stuart roared up to Loveall's house in a large state of agitation. Alonna Jefferies remained out in the car.

It seems that somehow Miss Jefferies had misplaced the keys to Stuart's house up at Ashdown. When they got back to Texarkana he had to break into his house to change clothes.

No time to argue about that. (Time for accusations and pouting, all right.) But the show had to get on the road.

Which it finally did at 7 p.m.

Although not quite. Scott Stuart's car was out of gasoline.

At 7:10 p.m. the foursome pulled out of the service station, heading for the 7:30 p.m. concert, 75 miles away.

"You don't have any taillights."

This was the Texarkana city policeman who pulled the young folks over on the outskirts of town.

Now they headed back through Texarkana, retracing five miles of city traffic, with Scott Stuart muttering something about miswiring some stereo speakers. Apparently the music was going out the taillights.

Down at Shreveport the big concert was just starting when the young folks got transferred to another car and finally pulled out of Texarkana.

Although not immediately. The second car was out of gasoline, too.

Actually, nobody knows what time it was when they finally left town for the third or fourth time.

Certain things are better left unsaid.

One of those things—Scott Stuart could not leave it unsaid—was how could a girl friend in her right mind be so forgetful as to leave a person's house keys somewhere. If it hadn't been for that!

Chris Loveall drove determinedly, while his fiancée consoled Miss Jefferies and Scott Stuart cursed fate.

Sometime after 9 p.m. the couples arrived at Hirsch Memorial Coliseum at Shreveport. Searching for a parking place, they heard Styx flailing away inside.

Outside, they hurried across the huge parking area, darting among cars, sickeningly late but knowing that what was left was going to be worth it.

Now they were at the ticket window at last and Chris Loveall had his tickets out. Inside Styx was flailing away.

"I can't find my other ticket!" This was Scott Stuart, frantically searching his pockets. "I couldn't have left it on the dresser!"

His girl friend, Alonna Jefferies, smiled a strange smile. Tracy Allbright looked off in another direction. Chris Loveall stood there, holding his tickets, looking at Scott Stuart as though—some things are better left unsaid.

In fact, the whole masterpiece should be brought to an end. At going on 10 p.m. Loveall sold a ticket to Stuart, who disappeared into the coliseum with the smiling Miss Jefferies. Loveall and his fiancée drove off somewhere and ate fried chicken.

There is nothing quite like enjoying a good concert with friends on a Saturday night.

That Must've Been Some Other "Mutt"

It is gratifying to be able to report that state Senator John F. (Mutt) Gibson of Dermott was not the person who back in the 1920s terrified two young school teachers by wiring up their rooming house in the Southeast Arkansas town of Boydell and producing awful noises with a countryboy scaring device.

That had to have been some other John F. (Mutt) Gibson.

The specter of possibility is raised in a letter from Caroline Horan of Bull Shoals:

"During the mid-Twenties I was teaching school at the little town of Boydell, just south of Dermott. Another teacher and I boarded in a private home near the center of town. One night we abruptly came awake to the most blood-curdling sounds either of us had ever heard. When people tell you that they have been so scared they've lost their voices—believe them! Three times I opened my mouth trying to call Mrs. Stinson, our wonderful landlady. Three times I couldn't even croak."

Caroline Horan's terrified roommate managed one week, quavery "M-m-m-rs. St-i-n-s-o-nnn!" just as the door was opened by the laughing landlady herself.

Mrs. Horan says:

"We never knew who the culprits were, but there was a mischievous young Gibson boy in town. I may be wrong but I think they called him 'Mutt.' I have often wondered if Arkansas Senator Mutt Gibson of Dermott ever lived in Boydell."

We have talked with Senator Gibson about this matter. By his own description, he was too small and sickly to have got into any such thing.

"That was called tick tacking," says Senator Gibson, whose birthplace is Boydell, Arkansas. "What you did—what the bigger boys did—was tie a string to the house. Or a piece of wire would have been better, I guess. Then you back off some distance and rub the wire with a corncob."

Gibson was pleased not to be able to recall having ever terrified anybody in that fashion. Especially not two schoolteachers. Living there at what he fondly called "Mrs. Stinson's corner."

Other Boydell boys were capable of that. They tumped over dog pens and outhouses. Mostly on Halloween.

"My name gets connected with such things because Mutt is easier to remember than some other names."

To hear Gibson, at age 63, describe his own boyhood, it's a wonder he didn't grow up to become Senator John F. (Chicken) Gibson.

"I remember one Halloween these big boys were trying to scare me. I ran down the street and came upon some girls wearing sheets. I jumped under those girl's sheets and stood there about shaking myself to death. Those girls hid me until the big boys left."

The senator said being sickly had its advantages.

Otherwise he almost surely would have been in on turning a goat loose in the Iron Mountain Restaurant.

"We had this Chinese restaurant, the Iron Mountain, around by the railroad. One Halloween night a goat got turned loose in the restaurant."

The goat had a sheet thrown over him and couldn't see where he was going.

The restaurant almost came apart.

"People were running around, hollering. That goat jumped up on the tables and started knocking off salt and sugar bowls. It's hard enough to drive a goat straight under normal circumstances."

Gibson said the owner of the Iron Mountain came tearing out of the kitchen with a butcher knife. People heard Chinese words they never had heard before.

"The boys who turned that goat loose took off running up the railroad track toward McGehee. They got a long ways out of town before they stopped running."

And hid out how long?

"We came back in an hour and a half."

Only One Possible Source For Such Piercing Eyes

There is no telling how many times Gayle Windsor stopped at that old photographic portrait.

Or how long he stood there each time.

Beholding those piercing eyes.

The man in the portrait looks out from a paneled courtroom wall.

Gayle Windsor's work—he is a lawyer—takes him into courtrooms.

"The circuit courtrooms in Saline and Grant Counties have portraits of former circuit judges displayed on the walls, along with other prominent public officials."

This man with the eyes is identified as Judge James M. Smith.

More than once he almost made lawyer Windsor late for work.

"He served as judge from 1874 through the mid-'80s," Windsor says.

The years are given there beneath the portrait. It was not merely the eyes that brought the Little Rock lawyer back to the wall.

Judge Smith had it all.

"Piercing eyes. A neat beard. Erect carriage."

That's not "neat" as in hip talk. Judge Smith's beard is closecropped, an extension of his facial contours, not an adornment on them.

Erect carriage? It's something Gayle Windsor just *knew*, even though in the portrait you can't see much below the judge's shoulders, and there on the wall he is not carrying himself anywhere.

Something became strangely clear to Windsor.

This man had to have been a colonel in the army of the Confederacy.

"For 50 years after hostilities ended, almost every Southern lawyer was called either 'Judge' or 'Colonel.' From his looks alone, if Judge Smith had *not* been a Confederate colonel, he certainly *should* have been."

Every time lawyer Windsor left that courthouse, Judge Smith's eyes followed him.

It got to be too much.

"Finally, I wrote to Dr. John Ferguson, our state historian, and told him of my suspicions."

Windsor put his money where his mouth was.

He told Historian Ferguson that if James M. Smith was not, prior to his judgeship, a Confederate colonel, then he, Gayle Windsor, would stand up and sing one stanza of "Dixie."

Dr. Ferguson has done much for history in Arkansas.

It is fitting that in his hour of peril history could turn and spare him.

"You can keep the stanza to 'Dixie,' " the reply to Gayle Windsor began, "for you win the bet."

Colonel Smith? Was he ever!

"Circuit Judge J. M. Smith of Saline County was not only the colonel of the 11th Arkansas Infantry (CSA), but he was also elected delegate to the Secession Convention of 1861 which voted Arkansas out of the Union."

It was Smith who raised the 11th Infantry, bringing in recruits from Yell and Sebastian Counties, to go with his men of Saline.

"Most of their service was in Tennessee, Louisiana and Mississippi, including the battles at Island No. 10, Tennessee, and Port Hudson, Louisiana."

The state historian concluded his confirmation to the beaming Gayle Windsor:

"Late in the war the regiment was mounted and transferred to the command of Gen. Nathan Bedford Forrest. Colonel Smith surrendered with General Forrest at Citronelle, Alabama, May 4, 1865. Theirs was the last major Confederate command to surrender east of the Mississippi River."

Those eyes tell you there was some sort of mistake at Citronelle.

Like the confusion at Appomattox.

"My wife, Betty, is from Savanah, Georgia," Gayle Windsor said. "She denies that Lee surrendered to Grant at Appomattox. General Lee thought he was handing his sword to the butler."

Recalling Peach Seed Deal by the Jot 'Em Down

Pine Ridge—They are getting ready for another Lum and Abner Sunday in Pine Ridge.

Lum and Abner Sunday will last the better part of two days, beginning Saturday and then running into the next day, June 16, when this place will be proclaimed officially a National Historic Site.

"Jot 'Em Down Store, Lum Eddards speakin.' "

Did that really happen? You'd never convince 1930s America otherwise.

In one week, Chester Lauck and Norris Goff, two young men from Mena, got 1.5 million pieces of fan mail.

Their radio sponsors? Merely Ford and General Motors, Quaker Oats, Horlick's Malted Milk and Alka Seltzer.

Grannies, that was a long time ago.

Tuffy Goff died in June 1978, Chet Lauck in February 1980.

Now it will all become historical.

Red Langston went back to Pine Ridge this spring, to poke around in the ashes of his memory.

After the Navy and World War II, W. J. Langston barbered at Glenwood. Barbered and carried a rural mail route.

In retirement, this spring, he made the 45-mile drive to Pine Ridge.

Outside the Jot 'Em Down Store, Langston observed to another man, "I've thrown many a newspaper on this porch."

The man said, "You did what?"

Langston explained that as a young man he ran the *Arkansas Gazette* motor route from Amity to Mena.

"I threw the *Gazette* on the porch of this store."

The other man said well he'd swan.

The other man asked "Did you ever happen to trade the *Gazette* to a woman for a half a bushel of peach seeds?"

It was Red Langston's turn to swan. "Yes, I did exactly that."

The other man swanned again. He said, "Miss Nancy never got anybody to believe that story."

It was a day in summer. Miss Nancy Chambers and her sister, Miss Willie, sat with other neighbor ladies under the shade of a tree in the front yard, peeling peaches.

This was 100 yards from the Jot 'Em Down. The year was 1939.

Young Red Langston, working to extend his newspaper route from Mount Ida west to Mena, approached the ladies under the tree.

The ladies peeled and listened while Langston explained why they should become subscribers to the newspaper, an opportunity he would afford free of charge for a period of 30 days.

And after that?

"Eighty-five cents a month."

The ladies were shocked and dismayed.

"Realizing I had lost a sale, I was about to move on toward the next house when my eyes fell on half a bushel of peach seeds setting beside a big bucket of peelings."

Red Langston said to a lost customer, "Miss Chambers, what are you going to do with the peach seeds?"

She laughed at him. "Why, Mr. Langston, I'm feeding them to the hogs, of course, along with the peels."

The hard-working route man said, "I'll trade you the *Gazette* for one month for the seeds."

She said, "Well, sir, you have just bought you some peach seeds."

On the porch of the Jot 'Em Down, in the spring of 1985, W. J. Langston and another man swanned at each other. Langston wondered, "Miss Nancy, is she still around?"

The other man said, oh, yes, she lives right over there.

So about half a century later, having long since outgrown his nickname, Red Langston went up to that house and knocked, and when the door opened he said, "Do you remember me?"

Grannies.

"At that very moment," Langston says, "Miss Nancy had been in there reading the *Gazette*, without her glasses, still being a subscriber after 46 years."

He brought her up to date on their deal.

"I sold your peach seeds to East Nursery at Amity. Ten cents a pound for $3. Your seeds were used in the grafting of Elberta peaches."

Pillow of the Community

Mrs. Harold A. Chalmers of Arkadelphia takes issue with a statement that appeared here recently in which a Garland County minister, preaching a man's funeral, referred to the departed as "a pillow of the community".

Mrs. Chalmers notes:

"Unless I have heard wrong all my life, what the minister meant to say was that the man was a *pillar* of the community."

It depends on what kind of community support a man has to offer.

Some men make their greatest contribution by taking a nap.

Nat Stalquist was a pillow of the community.

When we first moved to Little Rock, a lad of twelve and lacking the high degree of polish we would later acquire, Nat Stalquist was one of the first big-city residents we met.

Mr. Stalquist was a dedicated sleeper, not out of indolence but because of special physical requirements.

"Some people work better with more sleep," he always said. Then he would prepare himself by taking another nap.

He got most of his sleep, although not all of it, at Squatter's Island. Squatter's Island was down the Arkansas River bank, 100 yards or so, from where a lot of persons now stay up most of the night not getting any sleep at Cajun's Wharf.

What Nat Stalquist did at night was not clear. His name also was Mr. Stalnaker. And at times Mr. Stonnaker.

There was a giant sawdust pile at Squatter's Island. We went to the sawdust pile seeking continuity in our life. There had been a big one at McGehee, too.

That first morning we climbed up the eastern slope of the sawdust pile and without looking, jumped down the shaded western slope.

We landed on Mr. Stalquist.

He was a man accustomed to being awakened in a violent manner.

"Don't worry about it, son," Mr. Stalquist said. He clawed sawdust from the stubble on his face. Then catching his breath, he said, "Do you have any funds in your pocket?"

No, sir.

He was used to that, too.

Mr. Stalquist yawned and said he was taking the day off, to catch up on his sleep.

We went back to the sawdust pile often, to visit with this man who had not cut off our continuity when we landed on his stomach.

"My family were the bedrock of this town," he said.

Bedrock or sheetrock, he was always just waking up or dropping off.

"I was heading to work this morning but I fell in that ravine aside the viaduct."

The mishap alerted him to the need for a nap.

Not for years had Mr. Stalquist's family, a half-brother, spoken to him.

"He claimed I sold out for a mess of potash."

Mr. Stalquist traded his potash for a growing pile of small, flat wine bottles.

In late summer he did not look good and he stopped eating the peanut butter and crackers brought to him.

School took us away from the sawdust pile.

On a Saturday in October we went back. The giant pile was even larger and had been turned red by an overnight rain.

A man named Percy was pawing through the damp sawdust, looking for a covered wine bottle.

He said that Mr. Stalquist had gone into a heavy sleep at his other sleeping place, the City Jail, and didn't wake up.

CHARLES ALLBRIGHT *119*

Baby Holds Key to Enjoyable Meal With Colonel

In Bentonville, Tim and Beth Kenyon took their two sons to supper at Kentucky Fried Chicken.

At age 3, Joshua Kenyon manages a drumstick nicely.

Baby brother is something else. At 4 months, Tyler Kenyon is diverted through a family meal by playing with—well, this time it was the car keys.

When the meal was finished, Dad emptied trays into the trash receptacle and the four Kenyons went out to the car.

Of course, the car keys were nowhere to be found.

Tim Kenyon led the family back inside.

He could barely report what had happened.

One of the Colonel's young employees listened. She said those things happen. She would dig the keys out.

Tim Kenyon said no, no! He had done the dumb thing. He would dig the keys out.

But the Colonel's young employee insisted.

She approached the 55-gallon receptacle, pushed up her uniform sleeves and dug in.

It is interesting that at certain depths you seem to run mostly into baked beans.

A few gallons down from there, it's heavy on the slaw.

All the way down are chicken bones, limp boxes and biscuit parts.

At about 40 gallons down, the Colonel's young associate virtually disappeared.

That's when Beth Kenyon shifted her baby from one hip to the other.

From out of Tyler Kenyon's blanket, the car keys fell to the floor.

"What is there to say?" Tim Kenyon wondered later.

How about, "It's finger lickin' good."

When the Chips Are Down, Call for Another Bag

On the surface, it could be the smash young success story of the decade.

How could Mike Sells, age 22, graduate from Hendrix College in the morning, and mere hours later, that very evening, sit down and join friends in eating a yard full of potato chips bearing his name?

Mike Sells Potato Chips.

And he a theater arts major, knowing nothing about business.

It would appear that Hendrix has done it again.

"Actually," says Bob Sells, father of the graduate, "these Mike Sells Potato Chips take some explaining."

The explanation begins with Carol and Charles Chappell, on vacation up in Ohio.

The Chappells are neighbor friends of Mike Sells' family.

The Father of the new graduate pulls together the details.

"Dr. Chuck Chappell was one of Mike's English profs at Hendrix. Carol Chappell is a doctor, too—a medical doctor. Call up their house and ask for Dr. Chappell, and a youngster will say, 'Which one?' But that's another story."

Last year the Chappells were on vacation up in Ohio, in the Dayton area. It was Carol Chappell who spotted the sign.

MIKE SELLS POTATO CHIPS

You don't just drive away from something like that.

"Carol went into a store and found this enormous display of Mike Sells Potato Chips. It turned out that everybody in Dayton, Ohio, knew about Mike Sells Potato Chips."

The Chappells brought a bag of the potato chips back to Arkansas and turned it over to the Sells family.

Bob Sells took charge of the special bag of chips.

"I gave strict instruction that nobody was ever to eat them."

After all, only a neanderthal would eat a family treasure.

"I don't know what happened," Bob Sells says. "One night I was sitting around and, well, there they were. I picked up the Mike Sells Potato Chips and ate them myself."

It is no easy thing, being the one who ate the family treasure.

"I took the empty Mike Sells bag to work with me."

The elder Sells, an executive at Southwestern Bell, was covered with rue. To say nothing of salt and cooking oil.

There was but one thing to do.

"I got on the telephone and called the other Mike Sells, up in Dayton. The headquarters was right there on the empty bag."

The other Mike Sells listened with genuine interest. About how there was a young Mike Sells down in Little Rock. How the Chappells bought the chips and drove them home.

How the father, Bob Sells, swelling with pride, ordered everybody never to touch the potato chips. And then calmly sat down one night and ate them all himself.

"At first he didn't believe it," says Bob Sells, referring to the Mike Sells up in Ohio.

So it was that mere hours after the graduation ceremony at Hendrix College, the honoree and his family and friends sat out and ate a shipment of Mike Sells Potato Chips.

"Mike Sells up in Dayton, he sent down a whole thing of his chips for the graduation party. Big bags of potato chips. They were a gift from him."

The chips were a big surprise to the honoree.

His dad, off the hook, got together some barbecue to eat with them.

Special Assignment Was Book, Not Travelers

Back during the summer a letter poured in expressing curiosity about our special assignment. The letter also raised a vague professional question.

"If he is writing a big expose, what is he going to expose by sitting out at Travelers Field every night?"

Obviously the writer did not stay around to see the Travelers play baseball.

Whatever, the flattery was poorly concealed between the letter's two lines. Only a fool would not have been gratified.

In truth, we spent the summer writing a book of pictures. The book is to be called, *25 years of Arkansas Gazette Photography: 1950–1975.*

Friends we have not seen will scoff at this. How can it be, they will say, a person no older than Allbright writing about things that happened back in the 1950s?

It is a good point. The answer is that those behind the book wanted a fresh approach. They insisted that the photographed events of 1950–1975 be examined through youthful eyes.

Still another question arises. Somebody is going to wonder, how can a book of pictures be written? That is not so easily explained. It is, in fact, what took so long.

As the title suggests, this new book will be targeted at a selected readership. To get anything out of it, you will need to have lived some time between 1950 and 1975.

Persons older than that also will want a copy, as well as those who might have been out of town on a business trip.

Readers born since 1975 will be slow to accept what went on in Arkansas during the period.

It is our impression, having finished the project, that during the quarter-century in question photographers for this newspaper averaged taking 200 pictures a day. It could have been 2,000.

We have been privileged to go through the complete files, holding up negatives to the light, much in the same way that nonauthors hold up negatives deciding what to send off to the Foto Studios at DeSoto, Missouri.

Not all of these tens of thousands of pictures appear in the book. In this busy day and time, who wants to carry around a book weighing 330 pounds?

Also, among the many negatives we found entries for which the filing information held clues understandable only to photographers.

Holding up a negative from May 1951—the file envelope was labeled "Old Bitty"—we anticipated finding an aged chicken, perhaps the oldest chicken in Benton County that year. That is not who was on the negative.

"Don't expect us to write everything down," a photographer explained. "That's what reporters are for."

He said that whoever labeled the subject on the negative "Old Bitty" probably had not been with the newspaper for many years.

Another negative was identified by photographer's notation, unaccountably, as "Spare Ribs." It showed a man walking down the street with a balloon.

"Count Pulaski Disrobes," on the other hand, conveyed precisely the information intended. Its envelope contained a negative of the count's bust being unveiled.

So the research went, throughout the summer. Our fan club would have spent time out at Travelers Field himself.

The book is, for all this, a serious undertaking. The purchase price we have heard suggested would be called modest, if what you were buying was a houseboat.

We will get none of the money. We won't get a houseboat, either. But the journey backward was worth something.

Solid Friendship Helps Keep the Bar-B-Q Pig Running

McGehee—On U.S. Highway 65 south of McGehee, Rick and Debbie Runyan have a drive-in called the Bar-B-Q Pig. Rick is the meat smoking virtuoso. Debbie Runyan otherwise holds things together.

In the rear, the Bar-B-Q Pig is outfitted with a table and a radio and other family comforts. There is a back door through which a 10-year-old son, Erick, comes and goes in various pursuits while his parents serve their customers.

In the middle of a Saturday afternoon, young Erick reeled in through the back door, exclaiming, "Dad, I need a doctor!"

It was an understatement.

Playing on rain-slicked ground, the youngster had fallen and dealt himself a fierce-appearing head wound.

People know about the closeness of Rick Runyan and his son. This sight coming through the back door caused the father's knees almost to buckle.

"I just grabbed him up and ran out of there, heading for the hospital."

Somehow, Erick Runyan's mother gave chase.

Her husband recalls, "I think somebody on the parking lot brought her."

In the middle of a Saturday afternoon, when folks along the delta turn out in large numbers to eat barbecue—right then the Bar-B-Q Pig was abandoned.

Tom Blankenship was just driving around. He said to his wife, Maydean, "Let's stop by the Pig." At Blankenship's concrete business, up the highway from the Bar-B-Q Pig, nothing was doing on Saturday afternoon.

"We drove into Rick's and went around to the back," Blankenship says. He and Rick Runyan are best friends. "I thought we'd just visit and have a cup of coffee."

In the back room the air conditioner was on and the radio was going. Seeing nobody, Tom Blankenship went to the front.

Nobody was there, either. Not on the inside.

Standing outside at the order window was a man who had just driven up in a Louisiana car.

"I'll take a couple a pig sandwiches," the customer said.

"A couple of pig sandwiches?"

"Yeah, and a couple of large Cokes."

Tom Blankenship said, you bet—"A couple of pig sandwiches and a couple of large Cokes."

What he said, turning to his wife, was "Maydean, nobody's here!"

At the hospital, about an hour after the mishap, things were settling down. Young Erick Runyan was acquiring his stitches and old Rick Runyan was reacquiring his equilibrium.

For the first time, Rick turned to Debbie Runyan and said, "Baby, did you lock the building up?"

Debbie Runyan said, "I don't know."

Rick said, "Is the money still there?"

Debbie said, "Yes, it is."

Yes, the money was there. More money than the Runyans abandoned.

After all, what is there to making a pig sandwich?

Tom and Maydean Blankenship discovered that what you do is, you take some bread and you take some meat, and some slaw and some sauce, and you put all that together and wrap it up and say, "You bet, sir, here's your sandwich."

A cheeseburger? Blankenship, working the order window, says his wife jumped back there and started playing the grill like a Hammond organ.

"We turned out barbecue and cheeseburgers and fries and chips, every-thing including Certs. The only question was the milkshake."

The customer asked for strawberry.

"I found something red and made a milkshake out of that."

And there was the cash register.

"I didn't know how to work it. Once I got the register open, I just left it open. And, man, did I make change!"

When Rick Runyan walked back in, the Bar-B-Q Pig was humming.

Friendships. What are they worth?

One of these men says of the two of

them, "We've been drinking out of the same straw for some time."

Given the reverse, the meat smoking virtuoso would have run up the highway and stirred concrete all night.

So it turned out, because a small boy was all right.

Tom Blankenship says, "If we'd known they were in trouble at the hospital, we could never have done it."

Minnows and Briefcases

Jack Mauzer, who travels western Arkansas and eastern Oklahoma, was driving south past Clarksville on Interstate 40 the other day when a pickup truck pulled up beside him, the driver honking and waving.

Jarred from wool gathering, Mauzer honked and waved back, animatedly, in the manner of old friends meeting on an unexpected byway—only to realize they didn't know each other in the first place.

The man who wasn't Jack Mauzer's friend also wasn't waving at him.

"He was pointing at something about my car—a tire was what I supposed."

Whatever, it was urgent from the way the other man was pointing, stabbing his finger, working his mouth in large syllables.

Mauzer nodded that he understood—he understood nothing—and began slowing down to pull off. The other man sped away, departing with a smart salute.

"He was pointing to my briefcase," Mauzer says. "The briefcase was exactly where I put it, on top of the car, when I took my coat off before leaving Fort Smith."

Mauzer notes that the trip covered more than 60 miles—"which ought to be a record."

Sixty miles is a record for briefcases riding west to east. For golf shoes traveling north to south, 60 miles is nothing.

We know the fellow who claims the golf shoes record. He says he was summoned from the fairways by a telephone call at the Blytheville Country Club.

"I put my spikes on top of the car, forgot them, and drove all the way to Pulaski County in my stocking feet."

That was at least 160 miles, he said, over the course of which probably 100 motorists honked at him and grinned.

"I figured everybody was being friendly, until this guy at a filling station outside of North Little Rock handed the shoes to me."

Hearing about the golf shoes, another acquaintance was reminded of his minnow bucket.

"You're not going to believe this," he said, "but I drove a bucketful of minnows home from Lake Nimrod, all the way to Little Rock on top of my car. Not one of those suckers spilled out."

The fellow with the heavy golf shoes supposed that lots of folks had waved and smiled, seeing the minnow bucket up there.

"They would have," the fisherman said, "but it was at night."

The heavy minnows jogged yet another fellow into recalling a remarkable thing he had done, which was drive all the way from Eureka Springs to Little Rock with a key case on top of his car. He remembered the incident well—"it happened in the fall of '61.

"I unlocked the car door and put the keys up there while I took my coat off. It was the last I remembered the keys until 170 miles later when I got out of the car."

The remarkable thing he said, was that most of the highway had been "hilly and jerky"—the rest he had covered doing at least 65 miles an hour, although 75 was more like it. "Still those darn keys didn't budge an inch."

Something else seemed even more remarkable than that. How had he driven a foot without the keys?

"Heck, that's been so long ago," he said, "you can't remember all the details."

The Invisible Legislator

Some of our more callous readership have been thrown into high good spirits over the inability of a member of the Arkansas state legislature to read.

The deficiency came to light last week out of an incident at a downtown Little Rock parking lot.

What happened was, the legislator insisted on entering the parking lot through a gate that simpler people use for an exit. The lot attendant was equally insistent that everybody had to come in the same way.

It boiled down to a hollering and grinning match, with the legislator hollering and the attendant grinning.

"Now I know why I'm a legislator and you're a parking lot attendant!" the elected official hollered.

"At least I can read," the grinning attendant said.

That was a low blow, for which the attendant owes the legislator a public apology. The pressures on trying to legislate and do things like read at the same time can be enormous. Some of your really conscientious legislators have to work at throwing off their brooding, beginning every day about sundown.

Which brings up another incident.

The very night he read about the parking lot incident, James Carson was heading home from work. It was about 10:30 when Carson, driving west on Markham Street, reached the intersection at Van Buren Street, just north of War Memorial Stadium.

"The light turned red so I came to a stop," Carson says. "From about three or four lengths behind me, this car swung around and sailed on through the red light, never even slowing down."

Carson picked up the license number, two digits and the official designation of a state legislator.

"It was really depressing, learning on the same day that one of them can't read, and here was another one who was stone color blind. Or something."

Coming in to report the incident, Carson had a friend with him. The friend made a curious observation.

"Is it possible," he said, "that legislators don't see themselves as other people see them?"

He answered himself.

"I guess that's really not a fair question, since a lot of people can't see them at all."

Win Rockefeller had a reading difficulty, his eyes sometimes taking him from right to left. A lot of people thought it was something else.

Reading a teleprompter, a device that rolls words like credits passing on a screen, Governor Rockefeller would say to the television audience:

"As I told you in the Special Session of 1986—"

It was then 1968, which put the governor 18 years ahead of his time.

"Hot dog!" his opponents would cackle, cuffing each other in merriment.

"Uh-oh," temperance people would mutter.

"Never mind," associates in the studio would whisper, "they know what you mean."

If the telecast were live, Mr. Rockefeller had to plunge on, knowing he had fluffed it, but driven to keep up with the rolling words.

If it were a taping session, he would mutter something unrehearsed, back off mopping his forehead and say to the technicians, "Gentlemen, shall we try that again."

The man's greatest moment as an orator, in his own judgement, came as a distinguished lecturer at Ohio University. Because of airplane difficulties and a State Police car breakdown, the speech started about two hours late, the scholarly audience having long since slipped into an advanced state of lassitude.

What brought them to was a line that the governor should have read, saying. "The freedoms for which so many in this room fought and others died."

What he actually read was, "The freedoms for which so many in this room fought and died."

The campus newspaper ran that as its quote of the week for two weeks in a row.

Tourists: Weird, but Nice

Eureka Springs—A scholarly appearing man walks into the state-operated tourist information center at Corning, in far northeast Arkansas, looking for want he calls historic cemetery information.

"Yes sir, we'll do the best we can," the Arkansas greeter says.

"What I'm trying to find," the visitor says, "is the grave of the horse my grandfather rode down here during the Civil War."

Mark up one failure, a rare one, for the Corning tourist information center.

Down in the far southwest, a woman is jerked through the door of the Texarkana tourist center by a dog on a leash.

"Is there a place where I can water my dog?" she asks, her voice edged with urgency.

The information specialist says, "We don't have actual watering bowls, but there's a nice fountain out there where he can get a drink."

The visitor is jerked back out through the door, shouting "That's not the kind of watering I'm talking about!"

Mark one up for education at the Texarkana tourist center.

Up at Bentonville, near the Missouri line, a man strides into the tourist information center wearing a big, friendly smile and nothing else but a pair of droopy boxer shorts.

"Yes sir!" the Arkansas hostess blurts. She lurches half out of her chair, sees the shorts are held together with a giant safety pin, and locks eyes desperately with the approaching tourist.

He says something with a foreign accent.

"Sir! How's that sir?"

Now they are separated only by the counter, which is both good and bad—he's mighty close, but at least you can't see his underwear.

It turned out that the visitor couldn't have been nicer. The center hostess' explained to us:

"He was from Holland, and he just didn't understand what kind of shorts American men wear on vacation. I mean, to this man a pair of shorts was a pair of shorts."

At the Governor's Conference on Tourism here, we sat in after hours while a room full of prettily uniformed hostesses let their hair down and told about their experiences at Arkansas's border information stations.

The consensus was that most of the thousands of tourists who come to Arkansas annually couldn't be nicer; also that a few of them couldn't be weirder.

"We have this one regular visitor," one of the girls said, "who if you take your eyes off him, he'll drop down on the floor and start doing pushups, that or walking around on his hands. Except for that, he's a very nice and conservative gentleman."

Being a hostess for the State of Arkansas, the specialist is supposed to keep her cool. Especially when a visitor expresses amazement that she is wearing shoes, or asks where the hillbillies are, or wonders which way to the moonshine.

"How long did you have to practice to learn to talk like that?" a visitor asks.

But the funny folks are not the problems.

"The one you dread is the man who comes in with a map all opened up. He doesn't know where he is, where he's been, or where he's going. You're supposed to straighten him out, and the map is probably of South Carolina."

By the tourists themselves, the Arkansas centers are rated among the country's very best, meaning the friendliest and most helpful. One way or another, the greeters come up with information about farming, local taxes, day after tomorrow's temperature at Pocatello, Idaho, and New Jersey telephone exchanges.

Some things are stumpers, though, like horses' burial grounds, and the kind of telephone call that came in long distance to one of the border centers.

"How far am I from Little Rock?" a distressed female caller said.

"Where are you calling from now?" the information specialist asked.

"I don't know," the woman said.

Washing Machine Sings Blues

We set out Wednesday to track down a report that a resident of the Wrightsville area was receiving radio programs on his washing machine.

This report came to us from a man who had talked to an actual employee of the telephone company, a fellow named Tom Davis.

Davis, an expert in communication, was said to have listened personally to radio programs on the washing machine.

"Tom Davis has been around 15 years that I know of," our man said. "If he says the washing machine is playing the Top 50, or giving out the news or all of those other things, then that's exactly what the washing machine is doing."

It seemed to make no difference how much the Wrightsville resident changed stations—from WASH to RINSE or even to OFF. The programs kept coming.

"The only time he can't hear the machine broadcasting is when it's making so much noise washing something. But this man apparently doesn't have all that many dirty things."

Tom Davis was brought into this because he was in the area on other business. The Wrightsville resident saw the telephone company truck. He asked Davis to come into his storeroom, off the carport, to listen to a few numbers on the washing machine.

The victim's idea, better than no idea at all, was that maybe this telephone line, passing close to the washing machine, was giving out radio programs.

Davis told him that was not possible. Yet what Davis heard, himself, was not to be denied. As our man explained it:

"Tom Davis has been around for 20 years, and if he heard the washing machine playing songs, then that's what he heard."

Our man was wondering what would happen if the radio station—it seemed to be KAAY—should call up and offer the Wrightsville listener a prize for answering something.

"I guess he'd just have to stick his head in there, right inside the washing machine, and answer the best he knew how."

We tried to find Tom Davis Wednesday, before he aged any faster. This was not to question his veracity, which is not in doubt. Davis services the weather news wire for this newspaper. Throughout all these years—it has probably been 25—we do not recall a day without weather of some sort.

But we wanted to get an expert's slants on some other broadcasting oddities. There was, for example, the report some years back that a fellow was picking up "One Man's Family" on the fillings in his teeth. He said it wouldn't be so bad if he could get Lum and Abner.

"All I hear is Father Barber, out there in the garden. He keeps sighing and saying, 'Yes, yes'."

We knew a fellow who used to live in Levy at North Little Rock. All night long he got Radio Free Europe on his window air conditioner.

We asked him what the air conditioner was saying.

"How the *&!$ should I know," he protested. "It's all in Polish!"

Later he moved to Lakewood and carried the problem with him. It was not solved until one night an electrical storm knocked out the air conditioner. Without his broadcasts he slept poorly for weeks.

It is not talked around in the family, but we have this relative who gets Muzak on his attic fan.

"Listen to that!" It was the first night at the new place, and he sat up abruptly in bed.

"What is it?" his wife whispered, fearing burglars.

"I'm not sure," he said. "It's either Montovani on 'Tangerine' or Carmen Caveilero doing 'Brazil.' "

With his own bedroom, he does not have to share the music any more.

It Was an Automatic

Nashville—Marcus Ray Blakely is the *Arkansas Gazette* distributor here.

It was beginning to drizzle the other morning when Blakely picked up his papers. He drove to his men's clothing store on South Main Street, the Country Gent, to get some plastic wrappers kept there for rainy mornings.

With Blakely was Patrick Hamilton, a high school sophomore, who helps regularly with the newspaper rounds. Young Hamilton waited in the back of Blakely's Pinto, preparing to roll and wrap, as Blakely went into his store at 4:40 a.m.

Entering the Country Gent, Blakely heard sounds up on the roof. The frivolous thought occurred to him that it was too early for reindeer. He stood listening to the sounds, suddenly not feeling frivolous at all. Somebody was up there.

Next door to the Country Gent is the Pile Drug Building. It flashed in Blakely's mind that somebody was looking for access to drugs. Quietly, he moved through the darkness to the store telephone and called the police.

The official response was superior. No more than 30 seconds went by before Blakely heard the police car wheel into the alley out back.

He stepped back outside his store, into the early morning darkness, wondering what to do.

He hadn't decided when the silence was shattered by a horrendous clattering above his head. Somebody had jumped from the roof onto a metal awning, and now a man picked himself up from the sidewalk and was darting into the street.

"Halt!" Blakely shouted, having no time to think better of it.

So shouting, he raised a finger and pointed it at the fleeing figure.

(Recalling it for us Wednesday, Blakely said he hadn't exactly drawn his finger out of a holster; he more or less "brought it straight up at the side."

(And was the pointed finger cocked, like, with his thumb? He thought a moment and said, "It was an automatic.")

The worst thing that could have happened happened. In the middle of the street, the man stopped and slowly turned around. Blakely thought, "Oh, Lord, what do I do now?"

He did what a man of his caliber had to do. He stabbed the darkness with his finger, and commanded:

"Come over here!"

The man did as he was told. Then, still shrouded in the darkness of his storefront, or fervently hoping he was shrouded, Blakely ordered, "Get in the car!"

Resigned, the roof climber got into the Pinto with a wide-eyed Patrick Hamilton.

"What's he got you for?" the climber asked.

Patrick allowed that he was there to roll newspapers.

Out back, Officers Herbert Turley and Cecil O'Bryant were equally successful. Blakely drove around to the alley, where they were holding a second man, and turned over his prisoner.

Persons with legal interest will note that nobody has been referred to as being guilty of anything, merely suspect. In this day of evolving justice, a fellow coming out of a darkened store with the cash register on his back, pushing the safe in front of him and having a money sack in his teeth, he is a suspect. It may develop that he wasn't even there at the time of his arrest.

But on that morning, two were apprehended, to become more formally associated with other local misdeeds, and officers have described Marcus Ray Blakely to the *Nashville News* as having "the fastest finger on Main Street."

Says Blakely, "I've had more fingers pointed at me than I can count."

Are there circumstances under which he would not draw to invoke the law?

"Those same circumstances, next time."

The captured man never knew.

The Call of Duty

At Fort Smith Friday night City Administrator Ray Riley got home cold and bone weary from one of those late municipal meetings, only to be told by Mrs. Riley that his day was not done.

A couple in distress had called four times. They reported to Mrs. Riley that some city equipment had struck their gas line. The gas company had cut the supply off. It was 20 degrees outside and maybe worse inside. They were cold and their baby might get pneumonia.

Sure enough, as Mrs. Riley was telling it, the cold citizens called again. They wanted to know what the city intended doing about it.

Riley suggested a motel.

"Who's going to pay for it?" the caller asked.

If the city had wrecked the line, then the city would pay, Riley said.

"What about a reservation?" the cold citizen said.

Riley said, all right, he would try to take care of that, too. He dialed several places before getting a room, then called the victimized citizens, saying they were set for the evening.

"Sleep at last," Riley thought. But his telephone rang again.

It seems the family had this dog, a special breed, and the dog also probably would get pneumonia if it were left in the cold house. What was Riley going to do about that?

"Well, I guess we could get a room for the dog too," Riley said. "Or on second thought would it be better if you took it to a neighbor's for the night?"

The citizens agreed to that, which solved everything.

Until the next morning. Then they called from the motel room to advise Riley that they couldn't get a plumber to go to their house. What could he do about that?

In retrospect, Riley says: "I don't know how many plumbers I called, but I couldn't get one. One fellow told me it was Saturday, and besides, he didn't make anything off of a call like that anyway."

Another man told the city administrator he was employed by the government and didn't have to work on Saturdays any more.

Riley was looking up more numbers when the folks called from the motel. They had found a plumber.

Finally, Riley said with a sigh, it was all solved.

Which it wasn't. When the folks returned home from the motel they found that burglars had broken in during the night—what with the dog's being gone— and had made off with a number of the family's prized possessions. What was Riley going to do about that?

The city administrator admitted he really couldn't think of anything unless it would be to sit down and cry with them, which he was prepared to do.

There is no official record of the crying, only of a final telephone call.

It seems that when the plumber got to the house, he found that the city hadn't damaged the gas line after all. Some pipes under the house simply had fallen into bad repair, and needed "two or three days" of work before gas could be restored.

The citizens said they were sorry for involving Riley in the first place.

The city administrator says: "I've been wondering how they're doing, but I'm afraid to call. I'm scared they might tell me the dog is pregnant."

CHARLES ALLBRIGHT   *129*

Fill Now, Pay Later

Along the Campaign Trail:
A camera crew in a van pulled into the Mobil station up at Rector the other day and a spokesman asked Jerry Vangilder, who runs the station, whether it would be all right to shoot some footage there.

Vangilder said he had no objection, so long as business wasn't interfered with. He went back to work and the camera folks set about their preparations.

Some minutes later Vangilder found himself being greeted by an earnest fellow with an outstretched hand.

"My name is Jim Lindsey," the fellow said, "and I'm running for governor."

Our correspondent reports that the station manager wiped his hand, accepted the extended hand with his own, and said, "My name's Jerry Vangilder and I'm fixing this tire."

The cameras recorded the message to its conclusion, and then the visitors packed up and departed.

A few days later Vangilder got a letter from the film production people at Little Rock asking his permission in writing to use the on-site footage, a necessary disclaimer.

Vangilder wrote back that it would be all right with him. He said it would also be all right with him if somebody would send a check for $18 to cover the gasoline the folks in the van drove off with without paying for.

"I'm sure it was an oversight," Vangilder told us Tuesday. "Jim filled his car up, too, but he paid before he left."

In Western Little Rock, Mrs. Euell Slayton answered her doorbell to find a nice-looking man standing there, mid-30s, wearing a business suit and an engaging smile, and holding a handful of campaign cards.

"I won't take much of your time," the man said, "but if your family will consider my candidacy, I want you to know I'll work to get us going in the right direction."

He handed over one of his cards, said thanks, and departed.

About 45 minutes later Mrs. Slayton answered her doorbell again and found the same candidate standing there.

"I won't take much of your time," he said, "but if your family will consider my candidacy, I want you to know I'll work to get us going in the right direction."

He handed over another card, turned to leave, then paused: "Do we know each other?"

Mrs. Slayton said, well, not really.

The candidate thanked her again, and was gone for the second time.

The Slaytons are seriously considering his candidacy.

"We aren't all that sold on his sense of direction," Mrs. Slayton says, "but there is a great deal to be said for his thoroughness."

Family solidarity is an important thing in elections. At Pine Bluff a friend of Randall Baker's explained the importance of sticking together this way.

"A long time ago my wife and I promised to talk things over with each other, and then always vote for the same man. We've never gone back on that, except for the one time when she sneaked off and voted for Eisenhower instead of Stevenson. I didn't get on her too bad because I did the same thing."

"I Could Have Been . . ."

At Hot Springs, Alyce Robinson's sixth grade class at Jones Elementary School made up a list of what they called "I Could Have Beens."

Such an exercise is challenging, even for the mentally agile.

Here is an example:

"I could have been a plumber, but my plans went down the drain."

It took half an hour for us to make that up, and we happen to be fast witted.

Or here is another:

"I could have been a brain surgeon, but I went and lost my head."

That took almost 45 minutes but, as you can see, it was worth it.

Now we are working on one about an aspiring redcap whose career fails because he keeps losing his grip. It promises to be a dandy.

Alyce Robinson's sixth graders have set a hot pace for all of us. This is by a student named Jonathan Smoke:

"I could have been a zookeeper, but I kept monkeying around."

Darren Johnson countered with, "I could have been a teacher, but I didn't have the class."

To which Staci Rice said, "I could have been a nun, but I didn't have a prayer."

Denice Jeter said, "I could have been a candymaker, but I'm not that sweet."

Jimmy Schmeltz declared, "I could have been a pet store owner, but that's for the birds."

Which inspired Jonathan Smoke to come back and say, "I could have been a baker, but I didn't have the dough."

So Darren Johnson also came back and said, "I could have been the devil, but I got fired."

Libby Schnipper said, "I could have been a doctor, but I never got a shot."

Danny Beck could have, too, except, "I didn't have the patience."

Leigh Johnson said, "I could have been a puppetmaker, but there were too many strings attached."

Jamie Thornton said, "I could have been a tapemaker, but I couldn't make it stick."

Laurie Owen could have been a penmaker, "but I didn't have the flair."

To which Jonathan Smoke came back a third time and said, "I could have been a skeleton, but I didn't have the guts."

Jonathan would have a hard time proving it.

These additional "I Could Have Beens" have been inspired by the initial efforts of Alyce Robinson's sixth-grade class at Jones Elementary School at Hot Springs:

"I could have been a steamboat captain, but I went overboard."

"I could have been a dentist, but I didn't have the pull."

"I could have been a cowboy, but I didn't know the ropes."

"I could have been a pilot, but I didn't know what was up."

"I could have been a hot dog salesman, but I couldn't cut the mustard."

"I could have been my own tailor, but my wife gave me fits."

She could have been a streetcar conductor, says Rosemary Busby Smith of Little Rock, but she didn't have the desire.

"I could have been a director of Marineland, but I couldn't see the porpoise."

Why wasn't she a hematologist?

Because, "It wasn't in my blood."

Mrs. Smith reports that her family spent a weekend coming up with "I Could Have Beens." It isn't clear which family member gets credit for this:

"I could have been the manager of a girdle factory, but the bottom dropped out."

Don Baker is a sophomore at Sylvan Hills High School.

"I could have been a procrastinator," Don says, "but I kept putting it off."

He didn't become a fortuneteller because he couldn't see any future in it.

"I could have been a clockmaker, but I didn't like the hours."

Don Baker is one of Dixie Martin's journalism students at Sylvan Hills.

So is sophomore Denise Oldham.

"I could have been a weatherman," Denise says, "but I didn't have the degrees."

Classmate Dave Morris—"I could have been a farmer, but I couldn't cultivate my mind."

Annette Wood also didn't make it. "I could have been a gambler, but I wasn't playing with a full deck."

And Sara Laster stumbled her career away—"I could have been a ballet dancer, but I wasn't on my toes."

Dixie Martin, who teaches these failures, says, "Thanks for giving us an idea for a mentally challenging activity on a rainy Friday."

We readily accept thanks. All blame, on the other hand, goes to Alyce Robinson's sixth grade class at Hot Springs' Jones Elementary School. They started the whole thing.

"I could have sold concrete," says Jo Laurence at the Benton Child Development Center, "but I got all mixed up."

Indifference kept her from being a tailor—"I didn't give a darn."

Also, "I could have been an auto salesman, but I didn't have the drive."

Our associate, Ralph Patterson, confided, "I could have been a priest, but I was holy unsuited."

Patterson remained a film critic until the movies made him reel.

Billie Beal of Conway flubbed a whole series of career opportunities.

"I could have been a butcher, but I cut it too thin.

"I could have been a diver, but that went by the board.

"I could have been an internist, but I couldn't stomach it.

"I could have been a gambler, but my ante said no dice."

Then what to do?

Finally Billie Beal contemplated raising turkeys. "But I was chicken."

Sometimes the chicken are fortunate. Because see what happened to Charles A. Stuck of Jacksonville:

"I could have been a turkey raiser but they gobbled up the profits."

Hard luck dogged Stuck's footsteps. "I could have been a well digger but I went into the hole."

So he turned to the arts. "I could have been a violinist but I didn't have the guts."

Charles Stuck gave up in frustration—"I could have been a surveyor but it wasn't on the level."

At North Little Rock, G. C. Avriett ponders what might have been.

He could have been an analyst. "But I got psyched out."

Somebody left this off and then departed, unidentified except by the initials "VAF":

"I could have been right, but I was already president."

Dr. John Workman confesses, "I wanted to be a dairy farmer, but I didn't have the pull."

He stood up and reached for higher things.

Once more into the slough of despondency ("I Could Have Been, But—"), and then George Clark, communicating from the Donaghey Building postoffice, will have the last word.

Jack Graham of North Little Rock could have been a hostage.

"But Iran."

At DeQueen Middle School, the fifth period 8th English class stumbled on all counts:

"I could have been a postal clerk, but I was canceled."

"I could have been a newspaper reporter, but it was too pressing."

"I could have been an accountant, but it didn't add up."

"I could have been a plumber, but my face was flushed."

These are from somebody maintaining anonymity at Melbourne:

"I could have been a canner, but I kept blowing my lid."

"I could have been a BB target range manager, but I didn't like cheap shots."

Phillip McRae of Conway knows somebody who could have been a lawyer.

"But he couldn't pass the bar. He kept going in."

Mrs. Wiley Murrell of Fayetteville sent a list of these things to her daughter, Laura, at Bryan, Texas—"figuring why should we suffer alone?"

Now Laura Murrell and her fiancée, Mike Nelson, fire from long range—"Although not Aggies ourselves, living in Bryan–College Station for two years is bound to have affected us."

Something has:

"I could have been a masseuse, but I rub people the wrong way."

"I could have been a drummer, but I didn't stick to it."

"I could have been a pianist, but I got too keyed up at concerts."

But George Clark at the Donaghey Building postoffice has enjoyed all of this he can stand.

"I could have started all this frontiers of failure foolishness," Clark writes, "but I'm not All Bright."

Old Notes Rise to Top of Desk Clutter at Year's End

As an old year shuffles toward the exit, curious things happen in the clutter of a person's desk. Old notes work their way to the surface. Where did these notes come from? What do they mean?

Here is a reminder that says, "Check on Little Rock 10th grader's definition of *heredity*."

Below the reminder is this definition, attributed to a Little Rock high school sophomore:

"Heredity means, if your grandfather didn't have any children, your father probably wouldn't have had any either, and neither would you, probably."

Here is a telephone message taken by an office associate—we have not seen the message before:

"Your mother called. Said something about the dog's appointment with the vet, urgent before noon."

The urgent message is dated May 28.

Yes, and here is another year-end note, the source no less mysterious.

Possibly it will lead to the identity of the young scholar who defined heredity. The note instructs:

"Here's one to check with Vida.

"A Little Rock Central High student yelled from the bathroom at home that the water was too cold. Would his mother come and turn on the hot water?

"The mother yelled at him, 'Turn it on yourself!'

"The Central student shouted, 'Not on your life!'"

(Something is fishy here. In all our own years as a Central High School scholar never once did we hear anybody shout, "Not on your life!")

At any rate, the year-end note says, " 'Not on your life,' shouted the student from the bathroom. I'll turn on the C for Central, but I'll never again turn on the H for Hall!' "

The old year is dying, but not fast enough.

Unaccountably, this is attached to our desk calendar on the date August 20:

"SAN JUAN, Puerto Rico—The sad truth about passion fruit is that it probably reduces passion.

" 'It lowers your blood pressure,' says Carlos Cueves, who sells the fruit juice out of a small shop here. 'And if your blood pressure goes down, your sex drive drops.' "

Will somebody check this with Vida. Or maybe with the veterinarian, before noon.

"Check on music company in Texarkana. Owner said to be named G. Sharp."

"Lady called to say an author named Danielle Steele (believes that's correct) has written a novel called *Circles* (if she's not mistaken), and that this work is real literary trasheroo.

"Called to say that the waiting list for *Circles* at Fletcher Library, buckle of Little Rock's culture belt, has grown to 92."

Least of all is it clear where this note came from:

"Allbright, fellow without a name came into your office this morning. Walking not too steady. Said you all knew each other from somewhere.

"This fellow wanted to tell you about the big chess match. Said in the world championship chess match in Iceland between Bobby Fischer and Russian Boris Spassky, temperamental Bobby got off to a bad start and blew up.

"Fellow in your office said Fischer told hundreds of chess enthusiasts crowding around the match, 'Please leave. Go out into the foyer and watch the match on closed-circuit TV.'

"Chess enthusiasts supposed to have gone out into the foyer, which as you would understand in Iceland was ringed with radiators.

"It got very, very hot.

"In fact, this fellow who came by said you probably could say, 'There's nothing quite as hot as chess nuts roasting in an open foyer.' "

With time running out on 1984, notes of unspecified origin continue to work to the surface of an orderly person's desk.

Here is a telephone message:

"Man called after noon Christmas day.

"Said he and his mother-in-law went to Excelsior for light mid-day meal. Wife ordered shrimp and avocado sandwich. Didn't say what he and mother-in-law had.

"Waiter returned from kitchen and said, sorry, no shrimp and avocado sandwiches.

"Wife takes menu and says, 'Oh, I guess you're out of shrimp.'

"Waiter says, 'No, we have the shrimp. But the chef informs me that they are in the purchasing room.'

"Husband of wife says, 'Well, we intend to purchase the sandwich.'

"But the waiter says, no, that is not the problem. The problem is that where the shrimp are is locked up. The chef doesn't have the key.

"This man on telephone was not really sure why he was calling.

"It just seemed to him that this was an interesting thing to happen at a big outfit like the Excelsior."

This telephone message has surfaced on the desk:

"Fellow with a very thick tongue called to inquire about the origin of the word 'nog,' as in eggnog. His mother told him 'nog' was from the Greek word that gives us 'noggin'. But he confides in her present holiday condition she couldn't find her

own with either hand.

"This fellow says he 'noggonna' believe it until Allbright says so or Richard Allin says so.

"He emphasized, 'Stress that part about *nogonna believe it.* Allbright loves that sort of stuff.' "

When he finds it in his typewriter, Allin noggonna believe it either.

Here is a note beginning, "This is so silly I don't want my name signed to it.

"The question I'd like to see posed to people is: Where, between your neck and your scalp, is there a place that should be washed and doesn't get washed?"

The author of this question took a trip with a sister.

"Of course, we both left home fresh from the beauty shop with a shampoo and hair set. The next morning my sister was 'touching up' my hair and began laughing."

Why did the sister laugh?

"Because some of the hair color put on my hair had not been washed off the top rim of my ear."

The author of the question, presumably a woman, says she was shamed by her ears.

"Think about it. Do you wash the top rim?"

Telephone message of unspecified origin:

"Woman called to say she saw a man driving down the street—it was in the Heights—with a Christmas wreath around the hood ornament on his car.

"This woman said, 'I have never seen anything like that before.'

"She wondered what the driver had in mind."

Message identified as "Shrimp and Avo Sand #2":

"Fellow called back and said his wife re-ordered and got a French dip thing with fruit garnish.

"Order showed up without the fruit, which wife mentioned—'I don't see my fruit garnish.'

"Waiter explained, 'That was an orange slice. It didn't look just right, so I took it from the plate.'

"Husband said he wasn't complaining, what with Christmas and everything, but he told the waiter he couldn't understand this, a big outfit like the Excelsior, with the shrimp locked up in the purchasing room and the fruit garnish being removed from sight.

"Says the whole thing was settled more or less permanently when there was an emergency phone call and the waiter disappeared altogether."

Stroke Silences King of the Drum

Across South Arkansas the news is spreading, like a muffled drum-roll, that James Nelson King has been struck down by a massive stroke.

For friend and foe alike, the news is not easy to accept. Or even to believe.

Throughout Arkansas collegiate circles James King is known as "Big Bill," bass drummer, without peer, a young black man off the deltalands at Pickens whose skills and showmanship made him the pride of the University of Arkansas at Monticello marching Boll Weevil Band.

Topping 6 feet 3 and 285 pounds, Big Bill toyed with his drum as though it were not much more than a snare—tossing it into the air, hitting it behind his back, between his legs. Descriptions are next to impossible because those who have not seen Big Bill perform will not believe what you say he does. Those who know will say you have sold him short.

Just say Big Bill King kept both sides on the grandstands filled at halftime. And he wasn't even majoring in music. His drive has been toward the educator of children.

This is Judy Dunlap, wife of James E. Dunlap Jr., the band director at the University of Arkansas at Monticello.

"Yes, he's a good musician. A lot of bass drummers don't read music but Bill does. I don't know how many people have tried to get him seriously into music."

But there is the other thing.

"Our three children adore him," she said.

James King grew up at Pickens in the home of his aunt, Mrs. Mildred Coleman. Outside his hospital room at the University Medical Center Wednesday, she was saying the same thing.

"For awhile James was torn about what to do about the music. And maybe he's wished to himself he could have gone into it more. But ever since he's been growing up, he's had in mind teaching young people. There were eight children in our house. He couldn't turn back on that. Whichever way, I'm very proud of him."

The trouble began in May, a lung congestion. James went to the school nurse a time or two, and then to a doctor who sent him to the hospital at Little Rock. Knowing that money was short, the Dunlaps pursued and acquired a small amount of help from the school's insurance program.

The stroke occurred as doctors were coping with the lung condition. It was severe, leaving James paralyzed on one side. Friday, he will have been at the Medical Center, Room 3-B 24, for five weeks. He listens well but talks with difficulty. He has lost about 75 pounds.

James King is 21.

At Monticello they have started a little fund for him, at Union Bank and Trust Company.

How About a Fried, Smothered Bear Steak?

Some friends on Greers Ferry Lake made a present to the Paul Huffmakers of what was purported to be a two-pound bear meat steak.

The gift caught Mrs. Huffmaker unprepared.

"I don't know what I expected, but this was not it."

Somebody suggested that Mrs. Huffmaker soak the bear steak in a vinegar solution. She did that and then began to fry it.

"It had to be bear for sure, if I remember anything at all about visiting zoo bear houses in the summer."

Mrs. Huffmaker changed courses, electing to smother the bear steak.

"The longer it cooked, the more I was convinced that this bear had been previously smothered."

As a last resort, Catherine Huffmaker "swissed" the steak. This fogged up the kitchen windows, and sent Paul Huffmaker outside in a prolonged search for something, not bear tracks.

Finally Mrs. Huffmaker set the bear steak free.

"I do not want any more bear meat. Small wonder that some of our country's original inhabitants were painted as rebellious souls."

Probably about 10 pounds of salt would have helped the steak.

And a thick sauce of hot peppers and chinaberries.

Ken Parker got to reminiscing recently about a big polar bear escape in the Ouachita Mountains.

This was about 30 years ago. A circus truck overturned on a mountain road and several animals went free.

Within a day or two, all the wild animals were rounded up, except for some monkeys and a polar bear named Whitey.

The monkeys have not been heard from.

Whitey was not so lucky.

Ken Parker, then working the *Arkansas Gazette* State Desk, recalls that a reporter went to the Game and Fish Commission with some questions.

The reporter was advised that the moment Whitey escaped he became a ward of the Game and Fish Commission. Furthermore, in that no polar bear season ever had been established in Arkansas, it would be against the law for anybody to kill Whitey.

Parker recalls:

"The same day the article appeared, some people around Mountain Pine spotted Whitey and shot him. They loaded the carcass into a pickup truck and started in to report their feat. But they stopped at some general store to show off the bear."

Somebody at the store had the newspaper article.

"A couple of days later we got rumors of the kill and learned further that, wishing to destroy the evidence, the hunters had dressed out the bear, cut it up and distributed bear roasts throughout the countryside.

"Polar bear recipes apparently were scarce in that area, and it seems that improper cooking causes an odor that not even a hungry Eskimo could abide.

"For a week we tried to reach someone in the area who would confirm the polar bear kill, but no one was answering the phone. The best reports we could get indicated that all the residents of the community had decided to visit out-of-town relatives while airing their houses."

The largest bear ever eaten in Arkansas weighed 2,000 pounds, apparently gaining 1,700 after he died.

The bear, initially the pet of a Russellville man's children, grew up and had to be dealt with.

A permit was obtained to kill the bear. Around and about, the prospect of eating some bear meat caused considerable excitement.

Our man Leland DuVall was in the area.

"This was back when beef was selling for about 25 cents a pound. The man at Russellville agree to sell his unusual bear meat for $1 a pound."

At his death, the bear weighed about 300 pounds.

DuVall recalls, "The last I heard that bear had turned out about 2,000 pounds of meat."

"You Have to Understand Bear Meat"

Mrs. Paul Huffmaker's opinion of cooking bear meat is that it is a close encounter of the worst kind.

We reported that some friends gave a bear steak to the Huffmakers.

With her head mostly out the kitchen door, Mrs. Huffmaker fried the bear steak. The smothered it. And finally "swissed" it.

Then she returned the steak to freedom.

"I do not want any more bear meat," said Mrs. Huffmaker, understanding at last what caused certain early Americans to go on the warpath.

But Carl Pennington say, no, bear meat is delicious.

"You have to understand bear meat. The older it gets, the fresher it tastes."

Pennington speculated that the steak cooked by Mrs. Huffmaker was fast-frozen.

We asked her about that.

Mrs. Huffmaker said, "It wasn't frozen fast enough for me."

But Carl Pennington, who got it straight from some Indians in Wyoming, insists that bear meat must be allowed to hang around.

"The trick is to age the meat as long as possible, then cook it just before it spoils."

We asked how long that was.

Pennington said, "If you waited too long, you'll know it."

We once got some bear information from an Indian in Wyoming.

This was after a raft-ripping on the Snake River.

A small party of cowardly souls was cast up on the bank to shiver and await rescue.

In addition to the cowardly souls, the party also included a native guide, a fellow from Moose, Wyoming.

Dense forest came virtually to the water's edge.

We asked the guide whether bears lived in there.

"Black and grizzly," he said.

How did one tell them apart?

The guide said, "Run for the nearest tree. If you manage to get up, it wasn't a grizzly."

Back in December, when Arkansas had its first authorized bear hunt in 56 years, Josephine Graham went through her bear recipes.

Josephine Graham is a woman of many talents—cooking, writing, painting.

"As a very small child, I helped my grandmother at Christmas make and decorate plum puddlings. She showed me the old cookbook—a collection of handwritten 'receipts' in faded ink. The plum pudding called for bear or beef suet.

"I remember well a brown stain on the old sheet of paper of the cookbook—I imagined the stain looked like a bear. I picked up a pencil and added ears and eyes to the stain to make it look even more like a bear. My aunt came along and said not to scribble up the old recipes."

Here is an old recipe for pot roast of bear:

"Place haunch or chuck of bear meat, salted and peppered, in a covered roasting pan with an inch of hot water and ¼-cup of melted bear fat. Roast in hot oven, 400 to 450 degrees, basting every 15 minutes, until tender, from two to four hours. Remove meat from roaster. Stir in flour and extra salt and pepper to browned fat in pan, and add hot water to make gravy of proper consistency. Serve with hominy grits, boiled onions and swamp cabbage."

And this is for Mrs. Paul Huffmaker:

"Hang rib steaks of bear as long as possible without spoiling. Brush with salt and pepper and melted bear fat or olive oil. Broil over live oak coals about 20 minutes, turning twice. Serve with baked sweet potatoes and coleslaw."

We Finally Know What Happened to Whitey

Thanks to Donald Poe, a lawyer at Waldron, we finally know what happened to Whitey, a polar bear that escaped into the mountains of Western Arkansas.

Most of the details have been missing for about 30 years.

Donald Poe writes, "I trust I am not too presumptuous to add my connection and knowledge of Old Whitey's demise."

Poe remembers the excitement and sense of danger.

"Old Whitey escaped from the overturned animal truck on United States Highway 270 east of the towering Bald Knob.

"The owner and manager of the carnival, traveling from Mena toward Mount Ida, Montgomery County, appeared shortly after the mishap. He was very anxious to instigate a search for the fleeing animal. He informed the people that Old Whitey was dangerous and advised that if the bear was sighted, they should use caution in any attempt to recapture him, but without letting him escape further. He wanted the bear killed to protect human beings and other animals. The entire countryside was aroused. A reward was offered by the owner and manager for his body, dead or alive."

Then came a Sunday morning, the day before deer season opened. Donald and Florence Poe and their children were backing out of their driveway, on their way to Sunday school and church.

A pickup truck occupied by three men pulled into the driveway. Poe got out of his car to meet the men. They were Bill Biggs, Almond Biggs and Hubert Sims.

One of the men said, "Donald, we are fixing to make camp in the deer woods this afternoon and we happened to think that that old white bear is still loose. Would it be all right if we killed it?"

Lawyer Poe's initial reaction was that the bear was a domesticated animal. Considering that the owner had offered a reward for the bear's body, Poe reasoned that killing the bear would be within the law.

Then one of the men spoke out:
"Aw hell, let's tell him we have already killed and skinned the bear."

Poe knew the men and regarded them as outstanding citizens.

"I advised the men to place the hide and meat in cold storage, which was done at Waldron. For the next few days several contacts by the Fish and Game Commission were made with me as the attorney for the men who participated in the killing of the bear. On my part, there was no attempt to keep the identity of the bear's killers.

"An uncle of one of the men came by my office and left me a package of the bear meat."

Eventually the Game and Fish Commission dropped its pursuit of the polar bear matter.

"There was no attempt to destroy any evidence," Poe says. "The Commission gave up because they could not sustain their claim on the evidence and law."

Poe's brother, W. E. Poe, taught agriculture at Alma High School. He called up and inquired about the bear meat.

"We are coming to see you today and would like to have some of it."

Florence Poe knew nothing about cooking bear meat, and she got no help from her sister-in-law, Daisy Poe Hamilton, a home economics teacher.

Donald Poe recalls the day the bear meat was served:

"When my brother and his family arrived, all doors and windows were opened, and the smell, odor and aroma of bear meat filled the house. Neighbors [there were many] put in their appearances to find that bear meat was cooking. There were many who tasted and stepped back saying, 'I have tasted bear meat.'

"Florence and I took my brother and his family to the restaurant for our meals that day.

"No one ever came forward with a recipe for cooking bear meat. My recollection of cooked bear meat is that it was too sweet for my taste and it was tough as shoe leather."

Just "Dropping In"

James Jones, the retired school superintendent at Hope, got a telephone call the other night from a woman who invited the Joneses to come over and eat homemade ice cream.

"We'll be right there," Jones said.

He hung up and told his wife, Ruth, "Come on. The Seymours want us to eat homemade ice cream."

The Joneses drove the few blocks to the home of their friends, Fay and Francile Seymour. It was Sunday evening, getting on toward 8 o'clock.

"I see the preacher's here, too," Jim Jones said, noting a familiar station wagon.

The Joneses went in. Sure enough, there was Rev. Ralph Hale, pastor of the First United Methodist Church, and his wife and teen-ager. And the Seymours.

Everybody was glad to see everybody.

"The preacher let us out early tonight," Mrs. Seymour said, laughing. Jim Jones is a big kidder, but having missed the evening service he did not pursue this observation.

Ruth Jones couldn't help noticing that Francile Seymour was scooping ice cream from a Yarnell's carton. She reasoned that her husband probably messed up the details of the telephone invitation.

So everybody sat around the kitchen table, eating ice cream and enjoying the get-together.

In the Jones house, out on South Main Street, the telephone was ringing off the wall.

The preacher's family left first. After about a two-hour visit, the Joneses got up to go. The Seymours walked them out to the car.

"I'm just so pleased that you all dropped by," Francile Seymour said.

Ruth Jones got into the car with a heavy feeling. As her husband drove them away she said, "We weren't invited."

"What?"

"We weren't invited to come over here and eat ice cream."

"What do you mean we weren't invited?" Hadn't Jim Jones taken the call himself?

Ruth Jones stared through the windshield, shaking her head. For one thing, Francile served store-bought ice cream. There was certainly nothing wrong with that; Yarnell's is fine ice cream. But for another thing—the worst thing— people who invite you over never walk out to the car and say how nice it was of you to "drop in."

Jim Jones would get to the heart of this. He drove home and did what had to be done. He made his wife telephone the Seymours.

"I can't do it," Ruth Jones protested.

"We've got to find out one way or another," Jones said.

They learned the worst. The Seymours could not have been sweeter but, no, they had not invited the Joneses over to eat ice cream.

"You've got to call somebody else," Jones said.

"I can't do it," his wife said.

"You have to. Somebody is waiting for us to come over and eat homemade ice cream."

It was 10 p.m. By 10:30 Mrs. Jones had telephoned all over Hope, waking up friends to talk about homemade ice cream.

She could take no more of it.

"If anybody else gets called tonight, you'll have to do it."

Jim Jones made the decision that probably enough persons had been waked up. The Joneses went to bed.

"What happened to you all?"

This was Monday morning, down at Stephens Grocery Company where in retirement James H. Jones works a few hours every day. The question was from his Stephens colleague and friend, Merlin Cox.

Cox explained how he and his wife had sat round the night before waiting for the Joneses. Then they began telephoning them. A little before 10 p.m. they gave up the calling.

"We figured maybe you two were out driving around somewhere, looking for some homemade ice cream."

Crystal Clear Concentration

We need to clear up an impression about our friend, James H. Jones, the retired school superintendent at Hope.

The matter came up here that Jones got a telephone call the other night, an invitation from friends to come over and eat homemade ice cream.

Jones misidentified the voice. He got his wife, Ruth, and they drove unannounced to the home of other friends. For two hours the Joneses sat around the kitchen table, eating the wrong people's ice cream.

"I'm just so pleased that you all dropped by," the lady of the house said, out at the car.

The discovery and ensuing flurry of telephone calls made at home turned into a nightmare for Ruth Jones.

James H. Jones has taken it in stride. It is a good thing. There isn't a stride he can take on the streets of Hope without somebody's calling out, "Hey, Jim, how about coming over tonight for some ice cream?"

But this leaves an unfair impression. It suggests that Jones does not keep his mind on business at hand. Nothing could be further from the truth.

Consider golf, and the personal concentration required by that game.

When Tom Duncan first moved to Hope the superintendent took him to the Country Club for a round of golf. Actually there was a foursome. Albert Graves and Hugh Reese were along.

But Jim Jones was the perfect man to go around with Tom Duncan. Widely respected, the school official was less likely than almost anybody to try to fleece the new man. At least not on his first day at the course.

The day went splendidly. So far as we know, the subject of alligators was not even brought up.

Hempstead County, many will remember, was the original home of Big Arkie, the 12-foot alligator who lived so many years at the Little Rock Zoo.

Veteran Hope golfers are good about pointing this out to a new player. Their sense of history asserts itself the first time the new man steps into the woods to look for a wayward golfball.

But there is no indication that alligators even got mentioned during the round, unless Jim Jones himself put the question at ease—"Partner, while you're in there forget all that talk about alligators."

So Jones and Duncan went around the 18 holes together, riding in Jones' cart. Then they got with Albert Graves and Hugh Reese in the clubhouse for a glass of iced tea and fellowship.

That same night, down at the Town and Country Restaurant, they had a big banquet of some sort, probably Rotary.

James H. Jones was going through the buffet line when a young fellow greeted him with a smile and a, "Hi there, Mr. Jones." The young man moved toward the superintendent with his family.

"I'd like for you to meet my folks," he said.

A school superintendent meets a lot of persons in his time, persons who grow up to become former students.

Jones looked at the young man, trying to summon a name to go with the face. He shook hands warmly and said with a large show of old mentor's interest, "Well it's sure good to see you again." He added, "Where are you now?"

Tom Duncan pulled himself together to explain how he had just moved to Hope.

"We played 18 holes of golf today, Mr. Jones. I rode in your cart."

So anybody who knows the demanding game of golf cannot fault Jim Jones' concentration.

Some Folks Just Don't Talk in the Morning

He looked to be between three and four-and-a-half, just old enough to dress himself in the dark and get his shoes on the proper feet.

It was still dark when the walking man found him. They were near the postoffice, the Forest Park Station, on Kavanaugh Boulevard.

"What's your name, son?"

Son wasn't saying.

"Where do you live?"

The strangers stood in the street, man and boy, a Norman Rockwell painting meagerly illuminated.

The boy said okay. He was in fine spirits for a child with no name and no address, out before daylight.

Joe Humphrey goes to work early at the Forest Park Station. He described it all later to his wife. We are indebted to Mrs. Joe Humphrey for this account.

"This man came to the postoffice door with the little boy. He said he couldn't just leave him out there in the street. Now what was anybody going to do?"

The Postal Service took over.

"Now, then, son. Hi there. What's your name?"

Son wasn't saying.

"Where is your house, son?"

Somebody came up with a doughnut. Things got festive.

Mrs. Humphrey says:

"The boy was having a great time of it. He ate the doughnut and laughed and talked with the men. But they couldn't find out anything about him."

Duly summoned, the police arrived as day broke.

"Hello, son. What's your name?"—a real policeman.

"Where do you live, son?"—with a real gun.

Mrs. Humphrey relates:

"This child obviously was smart enough to know his name and where his house was. But he was just the coolest youngster the men ever saw. He wouldn't tell them anything about himself."

The police left with the happy youngster.

Work went on at the postoffice. But not easily.

"The men realized they didn't know a thing. Not even the name of the gentleman who found the little boy in the street. The whole thing just walked in on them."

After awhile they had to know.

"The men telephoned the police station and learned the good news. Apparently when the parents missed the youngster, they got excited and called the police. Everybody was back together with no harm done."

And the mystery?

There was no mystery.

"The boy was leaving home. He finally said he'd had all of that five-week-old baby he could stand."

Millers Are Into the Security Market Now

His name was Mat Miller.

Was and is.

Judging from the reaction, it makes sense to update his story.

Some give it little credibility that a four-year-old boy would get out of his bed in predawn darkness, dress himself and then without so much as a "so long" strike out on his own to find a better life.

A life not eroded by the howlings of a new baby sister.

The report a week ago was that a youngster, name unknown, was found before daylight not far from the postoffice, the Forest Park Station, on Kavanaugh Boulevard.

Mat Miller was lone wandering, but not lost.

A frustrated adult led the way to the postoffice door, where the two were admitted.

Inside, the youngster was subjected to a doughnut and interrogation.

He was having too much fun to rat on himself.

Nor could the police, once they arrived, wear him down.

The precise moment at which Mrs. Patrick Miller's hair stood on end is not clear.

It was when she arose at 5200 Country Club Boulevard, about six blocks away, and could not find her small son.

Pat Miller, an officer at T. J. Raney and Sons, investments, was away on a dove hunt. His hair did not stand on end until later.

After a week it is more or less back in place.

Mat Miller's dad says:

"We're grateful to a lot of people for getting him back to us—the man who found him, the postoffice folks and the police. We're also proud of Mat. He's a very capable little boy."

So maybe his baby sister, Marian, has been an occasional pain since arriving three months ago. But the real reason for Mat's departure was not learned until he was safely back home.

His dad says:

"Mat had slept all he wanted to. He got to thinking about the Safeway store on Kavanaugh. They have the good bubble gum. He just got dressed and went."

Mat Miller, by the way, is not four. He is two years and 11 months.

"You ought to see the security on the door now," his dad says. "It looks like a New York City apartment."

Husband Saves His Own Neck

Running late for an appointment, Phil Moore got quickly out of his car at the entrance to the Donaghey Building and held the car door open while his wife, Carol, slid over to take the wheel.

Moore leaned in for a farewell smooch, withdrew and, slamming the door, turned away.

That sounds like a whole series of actions.

Actually it was all one smooth motion.

Until the car window slammed on the end of Phil Moore's tie.

His head snapped back and his eyes shot out, or felt like they did, the way eyes shoot out when people see Casper the friendly ghost.

"It was impossible to describe," Moore would say later. "Even worse than the pain was the immediate consideration of my wife's driving habits. She takes off in a hurry."

Fortunately, Carol Moore used a second to adjust the car seat.

Hearing the urgent rapping on the window, she quickly rolled it down and released her husband.

Moore staggered backward into Seventh Street, clawing at his collar with both hands.

This takes a lot longer to tell than it took to happen.

Inside the car, Carol Moore took one look out there and then buried her face in her hands, leaning forward on the steering wheel.

The victim got his collar loosened and moved in close to console his wife.

She wasn't crying. She was trying to smother her laughter.

Subsequently, others tried to smother their laughter.

There was the doctor's receptionist, when she filled in the line "Nature of Accident."

Then the X-ray technician. The precautionary neck films revealed no damage.

And the doctor, himself, who said, "Phil, I'm proud of you. So many young fellows go to work these days without wearing ties."

Moore says of his mishap:

"There is no understanding how it happened. Maybe the wind created by slamming the door fanned my tie up in the air. I couldn't do it again if I tried a thousand times."

He won't try even once.

By the way, we are grateful to Phillip Moore Sr. for what he describes as Phil Moore's "Seventh Street necktie party."

It was the elder Phillip Moore who some years ago locked himself up in the carport storage room.

He wasn't freed for more than an hour, that began when the rest of the family came home and found an assortment of neighborhood dogs gathered around the storage room door, barking at whatever was making all the noise in there.

At that time young Phil Moore said, "Dad, locking yourself up in the storage room is the dumbest thing I've ever heard of."

Phil Moore's Latest Dilemma

For the record, Phillip W. Moore, general agent for Great Southern Life Insurance Company, is not the same Phil Moore who gave himself whiplash by slamming his necktie in a car door in front of the Donaghey Building.

Phillip W. Moore might as well be.

People have been calling up to say how amused they are at his zany behavior, and to wonder about his new wife, Carol.

"Please share with your readers that I, Phil Moore, am still happily married to Beverly."

It was the other Mrs. Moore, Carol, who narrowly avoided serious laughing injuries when her husband, the other Phil, slammed the car door on his necktie downtown.

The tie got caught at the same moment Phil Moore was turning away from the car.

Mrs. Moore was sitting in the car, about to drive off, when her husband set up an urgent whomping on the window. He was pointing at his throat and his eyes were sticking out.

That was not Phillip Moore of Great Southern Life, who says:

"People who have the same name often create problems for each other. Phil Moore is not a very common name but people tend to change it for me. Phil Moore becomes Philmore, Filmore, Bill Moore or Phillip Morris—you know that old cigarette. I don't think they sell that old thing any more."

At any rate.

"I hope Phil and Carol Moore haven't been mistaken in print or otherwise for Phil and Beverly Moore. If they have I hope they were as flattered as we were."

From Jonesboro, Elizabeth Fetterly sends her sympathies to the victims of the East Seventh Street necktie incident.

"I sympathize especially with Mrs. Moore for the flak she has undoubtedly taken since her fit of helpless laughter was broadcast in your column."

Mrs. Fetterly has been caught in that painful situation.

"My fit came at the end of my one-and-only night-sail when my husband attempted to show off his newly achieved sailing talent by dropping sails at just the right moment in mid-basin so he could still maintain enough way to gently nudge the dock and step ashore in full glory from his exploit."

Unfortunately, Mrs. Fetterly's husband was farther from the dock than he thought when he stepped off the boat.

"I saw his head clear water with an unlit cigarette dangling wetly from his lips and, knowing he was a strong swimmer, fell prey to that same helpless laughter and had to grab a stay to keep myself from falling in.

"For weeks all I got was muttered remarks about the sadistic tendencies of females."

Those tendencies, whatever they are, work in merciful ways as well.

"The same thing saved me from a teary morning when my baby boy left for the school bus on his first day [after being up-and-waiting since before dawn] and tripped over a low bush in the yard."

Elizabeth Fetterly turned 180 emotional degrees, from bawling to holding her sides behind the front door—"where he couldn't see me, I'd had enough trouble with his dad."

Finally, some sympathy for the main victim.

"My sympathy also goes to Phil Moore because I know all too well that feeling when you're the one who has inadvertantly triggered such a reaction in someone else."

Mrs. Fetterly says she has spent a good deal of her lifetime being cajoled back into a better humor.

Somebody has forever been saying, "Oh, come on, Liz. I'm not laughing at you. I'm laughing *with* you!"

Liz has had a haughty sniff for that.

"How can it be *with* me when I'm not laughing?"

Word of Shep Fields Sends Buzz Through Ballroom

When word went around that Shep Fields was in the ballroom, things happened.

Not that the ladies tore their clothes. Or threw themselves through plate glass.

But a respectful buzz ran through the crowd where hundreds were dancing to the music of the Jimmy Dorsey orchestra.

"Shep Fields! Where?"

Over there! The knowledgeable pointed across the huge ballroom of the Excelsior Hotel.

"He's over there in the corner."

Shep Fields of the Rippling Rythms. A giant among giants. His music achieved its romantic effect when he stood close to the microphone and blew through a straw into a glass of something.

This one woman, an apparent imbecile, could not remember Shep Fields. Being only 40, she couldn't remember anything of quality.

"Name me a song he played."

It didn't matter what Shep played. Every song was seven saxophones blowing through mineral water.

Shep Fields made Lawrence Welk sound drug-crazed.

And here he was, sitting quietly in a corner, on Jimmy Dorsey night at the Excelsior.

Word is whispered that Jimmy Dorsey and Shep Fields did not get along.

That's why nobody was getting on the microphone and calling Shep to the bandstand.

In small groups, music lovers go over there, to the corner, to pay their respects to Shep Fields.

The unannounced bandleader, white-haired and goateed, is dignity personified.

A woman of about 70 comes back from over there.

"He kissed my hand."

Seventy is her weight. Her age is only about 60. A blue corsage matches her hair.

"He made my evening."

Already she has danced to the old Jimmy Dorsey favorites "Green Eyes" and "Tangerine" and, somehow, "Song of India" and "Mack the Knife." The music of her life, as they say at radio station KAUL.

And now Shep Fields has kissed her hand. She shows where the goatee touched.

You could knock her over with a soap bubble.

Other ladies go to the corner and return showing the backs of their hands. Some take their hands home early, rather than do something to them.

During a break in the hand-kissing, James O. Powell, editor of this newspaper's editorial page, drops over to Shep Fields' corner to verify a recollection.

"Didn't you play the Shalimar Casino at Fort Walton?"

Shep says, "Oh, yes. We played the Shalimar."

Powell says, "I thought so."

He does not explain that at the time he was down there in Florida writing editorials, trying to shut the casinos down.

Vonnie Hewitt goes over to get a photograph of Shep Fields, a nice addition to her Sunday report in the society pages.

The man could not be more accommodating.

Somebody asked whether we had been over to shake hands with Shep Fields.

It had not been our pleasure.

When you are practically a Solid Gold Dancer there is no getting away from the demands of musically crazed women.

But there was something else, too.

It has caught up with us, days later, as we go through a book of show business facts.

It says here that Shep Fields, the band leader, died September 23, 1981.

That was before last Saturday night.

Who was that hand-kissing giant of a man?

Notable Appearances Can Be Deceiving

A surprise appearance at a Little Rock dance by the old-time bandleader Shep Fields brought to mind an impromptu performance in the same town by the great Irish-born American tenor John McCormack.

The appearance by Shep Fields was a surprise because he died in 1981.

That failed to diminish the enjoyment of hundreds who were dancing the evening away at the Excelsior Hotel.

One by one they took refreshments over to visit with Shep, discussing old songs, photographing him and getting their hands kissed.

In the harsh light of several days later, a woman conceded, "Well, he didn't actually say he was Shep Fields."

Retorted her friend, "No, but he never said he *wasn't*, either."

John McCormack's unscheduled appearance in Little Rock was briefer but more spectacular.

It was the late Joe Wirges who loved to recall the astonishing performance of the great tenor, McCormack.

Wirges most frequently was described as a hard-bitten police reporter. In truth he was a lover of fine music, with emphasis on polkas.

Persons who have grown up with television have to imagine what it was like before then.

The world's heroes were just as big—no, bigger—but nobody particularly knew what they looked like.

Dizzy Dean, on his way to spring training in Florida, stopped off long enough to horse-collar a great semipro baseball team in McGehee.

The McGehee team never knew it was their hero whose fastball blew their clothes off.

At midafternoon Joe Wirges stopped by the *Arkansas Gazette* on his way to the police station.

It was one of the luckiest days of his life. At least for a few hours.

"About the same time I came in a very distinguished-looking gentleman walked into the newsroom. He was alone, not looking for anything particularly."

Lo and behold, the man introduced himself as John McCormack.

The great tenor himself!

You could have heard a metronome stop at the other end of the building.

"Mr. McCormack was between trains. He said he just wandered in, killing time, because he liked to visit newspapers. In fact, he very much liked newspaper people.

"Somebody ran out of there and got Mr. Heiskell."

Memory dimmed what the actual song was.

Nothing would do, before he left, but that John McCormack stood up on the city editor's desk—they helped him up there—and sang a song for his newspaper friends.

Maybe it was "Danny Boy."

Or it could have been, "I'll Take You Home Again, Kathleen."

Whatever, when the great tenor finished there wasn't a dry eye in the newsroom.

Joe Wirges knew personally that he would never be the same again.

Just as quickly as he had appeared, John McCormack got down from the desk and went his way.

Next morning Wirges clipped the article that appeared in his newspaper. Something to preserve the moment forever.

"Our article told how John McCormack had come by between trains and favored newsroom employees with a song. It was really a nice piece."

The *Arkansas Democrat* was an afternoon newspaper.

That day it printed, without comment, a small article at the bottom of Page 1.

Wirges said, "Their article told how the day before John McCormack gave a concert in Sydney, Australia."

Big Bill Made It as a Teacher

Dumas—His family and friends gathered here in the late morning Wednesday to say goodby to James Nelson (Big Bill) King.

Big Bill's church membership was at Pickens, a few miles down the road where he grew up in the home of his aunt, Mrs. Mildred Coleman, and with a bunch of other children.

But the church at Pickens is small and somebody had the feeling that maybe 200 or 300 persons might come to Big Bill's funeral. So permission was asked for use of the First Baptist Church of Dumas.

When the printing order for the programs came to the *Clarion* office, a fellow got on the phone and called over at First Baptist. He had a fine feeling about Bill, himself, but he wanted to double check and avoid an extra printing bill for somebody, in case the copy he had received was a mistake.

The situation was that, well nobody of Big Bill's color had ever had a funeral service at First Baptist.

The Church replied that, well, it was about to happen because Big Bill's service was going to be there, and the programs should be printed up.

So it was that persons of Big Bill's color had the church Wednesday and the first thing they did was turn around and open the doors to persons of no color, and help as many as possible find seats.

More than 800 came to say goodby.

In a geographical sense, James Nelson King never ranged far from Pickens. But for a man of only 21 years, his age when he died Saturday, he had a long reach.

He was recruited out of Dumas High School, an honor student, by James Dunlap, the band director at the University of Arkansas at Monticello. Dunlap greatly admired King's ability and showmanship as a bass drummer. By midway through his first football season on campus, Big Bill was an established favorite with UA-Monticello fans.

In his sophomore year he got a standing ovation from the fans, and the opposing band itself, after a half-time performance at Arkansas Tech. Last year he was in intercollegiate circles the "living legend," the pride of the Boll Weevils and the whole conference.

This fall, he would have been a senior, closing in on what he wanted most—a degree in elementary education. He wanted to teach young people, and he was a hero to more than a few already, children of UAM administration people and faculty who sat and stood here Wednesday.

James Nelson King was a hero, Rev. R. Willis told the gathering, because he knew how the real game was to be played. Mr. Willis said:

"Some people in this life knock a lot of balls over the fence and run around the bases all their life, but they never really score and—why?—because they didn't touch first base. This young man knew where first base is, and that is to believe in God. He knew it and he touched it."

And in the process he reached out and touched a lot of people. William Gray, Big Bill's principal at Dumas High, said standing outside the church afterward, "He made things easier between people, between the races. Not because he set out to, but just by being himself."

To most of those standing outside, what had happened didn't make any sense. It was Rev. R. L. Whitten, the pastor of nearby Watson Baptist Church, with a white congregation, who tried to find some.

"I went to see his aunt when I heard, and she asked me why—if Bill had been called to teach, as he said he was—why had he been called home so soon. I told her some people can teach us more in a few years than others can in 100."

Medically, there was too much to turn around. First, there was the lung infection that forced him into the hospital in the closing days of the spring semester; then, in the hospital, a massive stroke that left half of him paralyzed.

That wasn't all, either. His doctors found that Bill King, had a heart that was very large. Everybody here Wednesday knew that. But they also found that the heart was far older than his 21 years. Maybe a few suspected that, too.

CHARLES ALLBRIGHT   147

Old Aunt Head With Holler Eye Great Fun

As the game of hide-and-seek was played back in the old days around Moreland, in the hills of Pope County, the person who was It leaned against a tree, squinched his eyes up more or less and counted to 100, generally skipping the 70s and 80s, then shouted to the outer limits of earshot:

> Bushel of wheat,
> Bushel of rye,
> All ain't hid—holler I!

Anybody who couldn't hide by 100 generally was too sorry to play, although that did happen occasionally. Somebody out there would holler—"I!"—trying to sound like he was somewhere else.

At which time whoever was It leaned against the tree again and set a record for counting to 50. Then this final shouted warning:

> Bushel of wheat,
> Bushel of clover
> All ain't hid cain't hide over!

The game was on.

Wherever hide-and-seek was played, it was played something like that, although we can no longer remember what warning words were shouted leaning against the trees of suburban McGehee.

Suburban in those days, as in these, meant a bus ride to school. Only back then there were fields in between.

The game was called hidengoseek. Or that is the way we heard it.

Our man Leland DuVall grew up playing this game in the hills around Moreland, north of Russellville.

DuVall is moving along now toward the early maturity of a man who has passed 60. It is just now dawning on him, and maybe not completely, what was being shouted back there years ago as he crouched motionless in a Pope County thicket, waiting for somebody to come find him.

What everybody else heard was, "All ain't hid—holler I!"

What DuVall heard, crouching, was, "Old Aunt Head—holler eye!"

It added a lot to the game. Especially after dark.

"I can shut my eyes and see her now," DuVall says.

He means Old Aunt Head with the holler eye.

"I knew she was out there someplace."

If it got dark enough a person might go in and volunteer to be It.

That was not all.

"When they hollered, 'All ain't hid can't hide over'—that's not what I heard."

What young DuVall heard was, "Old Aunt Head can't high Dover."

DuVall knew about Dover, a community not far over the mountain.

Like her holler eye, Old Aunt Head's not being able to high Dover—that added a lot to the game.

"It never occurred to me to ask what any of that meant," DuVall says. "The important thing was I knew what to do when the time came."

At Bauxite they played mostly kick-the-can.

Kick-the-can precipitated a heated foot race between hider and seeker. A tin can was set up at a designated home base. If a hider could swoop out from some place and kick the can first, then everybody who had been caught was set free.

There was glory in swooping out and kicking the can.

Our man Mike Trimble doesn't recall what words were hollered at the start of a game of kick-the-can at Bauxite.

He does remember, though, the time Lawton Higgs swooped out from someplace and on the dead run launched a mighty kick that would set everybody free. He remembers that because Lawton's little brother, Zack, had put the tin can over a stob.

It's Ottzen Free! No, It's Oxen Free! No . . .

Bob Hicks, the KTHV-11 man, wants something cleared up about the game of hidenseek:

"Your recent column on hidenseek ignored one facet of the game which was quite common where I grew up. When It failed to locate hiders he could allow them, in the interest of saving time, to return to the tree without penalty.

"It would communicate this message by yelling what I remember was 'Ollie Ollie Ottzen Free.' Since your column appeared I have spent untold hours trying to figure it out.

"Can you help?"

We were going to explain this earlier but two things came up.

One was we didn't know how to spell Ollie Ollie Ottzen Free.

The other was we never knew what it meant.

We still don't.

Bob Hicks will understand that it is one thing to get up and explain politics or relativity to a learned audience. With hidenseek, though, somebody is going to stay awake and insist on some facts.

The first time we ever heard anybody yell Ollie Ollie Ottzen Free—if indeed that is what they yelled—the first time was shortly after we moved to Little Rock from McGehee.

A person just arrived from a smaller town, and a natural gulper at that, does not ask city youths what is being yelled. The newcomer will do anything to avoid the appearance of a fool.

The first time we heard anybody holler Ollie Ollie Ottzen Free we ran through the back end of a garage, climbed a small tree, crawled under some doorsteps and got a drink from a hydrant, all more or less simultaneously.

"You're It!" the city youths yelled, all in high good spirits.

We ran to the tree with joyful leaps, pretending it was what we had always wanted.

That was in June. We were still It when school started.

It is an ignorant person who tries to hide being a fool. A person should go ahead and be himself.

Years later, in the freezing light of dawn on an Army drill field, we learned this lesson again. A Sergeant Holcomb commanded our squad of eight men in a shrieking voice:

"Mungummmeree—*wahd!*"

Nobody understood what was ordered, but when Sergeant Holcomb spoke something had to happen. Our squad looked like the Bowery Boys trying to get away from the truant officer: Three did about-faces. Two presented arms. Two fell down. Personally we marched off smartly at a right oblique.

"What did you fools think I said?" Sergeant Holcomb roared, having rounded everybody up.

We fools didn't know.

"What I said," Sergeant Holcomb roared at the top of his voice, "was Montgomery Ward!"

We fools got to drill two extra hours, freezing and missing messcall. It was what we had always wanted.

The sergeant might as well have hollered Ollie Ollie Ottzen Free.

"It's not *Ottzen* Free," somebody advised us, trying to help our old friend, Bob Hicks. "It's *Oxen* Free."

Somebody else said that didn't make any sense.

"It makes the same sense as *Ottzen* Free. It's what you yell when you're sick of not finding anybody and you're about to go home."

Then what was Red Rover?

"Red Rover was when you threw the ball over the girls' outhouse at school."

Somebody else said, no, that was Annie Over.

If everybody will meet down at the vacant lot we will get this straightened out.

Maybe It Should Be "Allzoutsinfree"

Bob Hicks ought to be ashamed. Hick is It and can't hide over.

It was Hicks, the KTHV-11 man, who didn't know what Ollie Ollie Ottzen Free meant. Imagine that!

We tried to explain it and now there is trouble all over.

For one thing, Bob Hick's wife called him a name.

For another, no sooner had we cleared up Ollie Ollie Whatsis when a woman telephoned from Pine Bluff. She was identifying herself as a Mrs. Thomas L. Somebody when a male voice hollered at her in the background.

"Hush up!" Mrs. Thomas L. muffled, "I'm on the telephone."

But the male voice hollered, "You don't know what you're talking about. It's ollie, zollie"—the phone went dead.

Would the folks at Pine Bluff check on their neighbors?

What about Morris Young? Young's mother grew up at Adona. When it comes to hidenseek she knows what she is talking about. Morris Young's mother-in-law, Cynthia Thomas Ashcraft, grew up at Sweet Home and she also knows what she is talking about. Unfortunately, when it comes to Ollie Ollie the two ladies are not talking about the same thing. Young wouldn't call it an argument but there was no way he was going to get home free.

Leona Littlefield of Conway: "Ollie Ollie comes from all ye, all ye outs—in free!"

Mrs. John Baumgardner, who played hidenseek in Texas and at Fort Smith: "It's bee, bee, bumblebee, all that's out's in free."

Carolyn York, "It's not hidenseek. It's hidengo seek. Hidengo is one word."

Sue Rownd grew up playing the game at Grady: "It's Ollie Ollie Ottzen, I can't see. Or, no. Maybe it's Ollie Ollie Ottzen one two three. Anyway, everybody can come in free."

Theresa Rhodes lives at North Little Rock but she grew up at Leachville: "Some of you people are not old enough to know how to play the game."

Mrs. Cecil Garrison of Conway: "How old is that man who doesn't know about Ollie Ollie—you know? He must have been pretty young when he played."

Bob Hicks of Little Rock: "My wife called me a dummy. I think."

David Neaves: "They didn't say Ollie Ollie in Oklahoma. I didn't hear that until I moved to Little Rock." Neaves heard it from the Treasure Hills gang.

Hazel Sweeney: "It's because a little kid doesn't know how to say, 'All yallsoutsinfree!' "

Eloise Hamilton, who grew up at Fordyce: "Ollie Ollie hollers better. You can't say all-who-are-out-come-in-free. Nobody hollers that."

Jack Graham of North Little Rock: "Ollie Ollie Ottzen Free means all ain't hid can't hide over." (Graham called back later to ask what he had said. Advised of his interpretation, Graham said, no, that's not what he meant at all. He meant everybody got in free.)

Pearl Lawson, who played at Newport: "You know how people mispronounce things. I do the same thing. It should be allzoutsinfree."

Carl Kittrell, now at City Hill, a one-time player at Augusta: "I never knew or cared what Ollie Ollie meant. We just knew what to do when the time came."

Lee Crownover, who grew up in Cleburne County, one of nine children: "I don't know about some city folks but if you grew up in a family like mine you couldn't say something foolish without being called on it. Ollie Ollie or whatever, it had to make some kind of sense."

Lori Cockerell said it meant you got in free.

Marian McRae said whatever they yelled at Hope, that's what it meant.

Joyce Cross, who played at Charleston: "That was the last thing we said. It meant the game was over."

Bob Hicks: "Plake I never mentioned it."

Do what?

"*Plake*. You know, like plake you're a cop. It's what we said instead of 'play like.' "

We had to tell him, no, it was not plake. It was *plike*. As in plike you're no account and I'm Buck Jones.

Hicks: "No wonder I always got chosen last."

In Some Places It's Chalky Corners

The name of the game was chalky corner.

Unlike hidengoseek, chalky corner required some elaborate equipment.

A piece of chalk.

Otherwise you needed the same two things. Young folks who ran out of the house with supper in their mouths. And the approach of dusk.

George Russell played chalky corner at Ozark. That was in the 1930s. In the 1980s, living at Pine Bluff, Russell believes somebody could amass a fortune wrapping pieces of chalk in the scrawled-out rules of chalky corner. Then giving them away.

Not all fortunes are measured the same way.

As a reader named "Gran" writes— "Modern kids would never believe the fun kids had in those days."

Which is partially explained by Mrs. J. D. Norris of Dumas.

"When I was a child in Oklahoma, what we said was, 'All sowt sin free.' This had nothing to do with a license to sin. Kids playing hidenseek are not much concerned with grammar. Come to think of it, kids are not much concerned with grammar, period."

At Ozark it was chalky corner.

George Russell recalls: "You played chalky corner in teams, with the first bunch leaving out 10 minutes ahead of the other. Second bunch had to find the first, following the directions of chalk arrows. We didn't have many sidewalks at Ozark back then, so we mostly drew arrows in the streets."

At a critical point the chalk arrows pointed off in several directions. Then the fun began.

"The first bunch could stay out there a long time without being found. The big idea was to take girls along. We were—how old? Seven or eight. We hid out there in the dark with these girls, waiting to be found."

Russell said he never made sense out of what to do about the girls.

"I still don't know," he says.

Dr. W. Adolph Owings, before he became a professor of history at the University of Arkansas at Little Rock, played Red Rover at Sebastian, Texas.

Other things occurred in between, like World War II, but they were irrelevant. Dr. Owings told us:

"I can't help you with Ollie Ollie Ottzen Free, but I'm glad somebody came out of the closet and asked what it meant.

"About Red Rover, though, your sources are giving you bad information. Red Rover and Annie Over go together. You said it this way, 'Annie over, Annie over—Red Rover come over.' "

Whereupon somebody threw a ball over the girls' outhouse on the schoolground, to somebody waiting on the other side.

And if somebody was in the outhouse?

"If a girl was in there," Dr. Owings said, "you made sure the ball bounced on the roof."

Red Rover in Minnesota was something else. Rev. Paul W. Sipes, retired and living at Hot Springs, describes it:

"You formed a human fence, linking arms, and called for somebody on the other side to come over. If this person could run fast enough to break a hole in the fence, he got to take somebody back with him."

Red Rover set Paul Sipes on the road to the ministry.

"I learned early that violence was not a life for me. Being not only small but slow, I got thrown back every time as far as I had run."

Personally we retired from Red Rover, Minnesota style, the day they let one of our teammates—he could fly—break through right in front of a tennis court backstop. The backstop was mesh wire.

We haven't seen Waffles Jeeter in probably 40 years.

Who's This Fellow, Ollie, Anyway?

Quinby Smith of Mountain Home wants the simple truth about us and Ollie Ollie Ottzen Free. Smith writes: "Breathes there an Arkansas boy with soul so dead that he never to his buddies hath said, 'All that's outs in free'? Of course you knew this all the time."

But Connie Irwin of Magnolia says, no, the truth doesn't count. When she played hide and seek at Kansas City 60 years ago the give-up cry just as often was, "All's out up a tree!" Some dull-witted player, not noticing the slurred words, would show up and get caught.

Ward Turley of Little Rock: "I never did figure out who Ollie was because in all my life I never played Hidenseek with anyone named Ollie."

Ann Allen, now of Benton, grew up at Whelen Springs: "This was hollered loud and clear in a sing-song rhythm: 'Honey, honey, bee ball, bee ball. I can't see y'all, see y'all.' I can't vouch for what it might have meant. Anyone whose father was a carpenter who liked to talk about his work at home, and didn't realize until she was grown that a 'tubafor' was a 2 by 4 can't be much on phonetics anyway."

Mrs. Fern G. Heard, 74, of Cherokee Village: "All the, all the Urchins in free. I'm from up Chicago way, and believe me some of the places us kids hid while playing the game were out of this world. Do you know what a 'swill box' is?"

Mrs. Russell Rydin of Mountain Home: "Evidently none of your readers has a Swedish background. I grew up in a Swedish neighborhood in Chicago. We all knew the call was—'Ole, Ole, Olson Free.'"

Mrs. Ward Conklin of Little Rock: "Apparently it takes a native of Minnesota to give the true words. Growing up in St. Paul it was uniformly said, 'Ole Ole Olson Free.' One of those Scandinavians must have migrated south, and the Southern drawl erased the original."

Mrs. George Goza of Little Rock spent her girlhood in Wisconsin: "The cry Ollie Ollie Ottzen Free must be known to kids all over the country (though my husband never heard it growing up in Georgia)."

Clarence Wisowaty lived and worked at Chicago, but now is retired and "enjoying the good life" at Mountain Home. He says it all depends on what part of the country the words are hollered in: "Now try the cry of a salvage material buyer, with his horse and wagon in the alleys of a big city— 'Rexoline!' (pause) 'Rexoline!' You had to be from the neighborhood to know that the man was hollering, 'Rags—Old Iron!'"

Anybody who got run over by Arnold (Boots) Simpson when he was playing football at Augusta won't believe this but Simpson, who was all-state, insists it was "Honey in the beeball, I can't see yall!"

Mrs. Nellie Puckett of Little Rock: "Allis head in 10 feet of my baste is caught. Almost wish we could plike a kid again."

Sue Ann Overstreet of Bentonville: "All-e, all-e out's in free."

Mrs. Stephen Brown of Little Rock: "In California we said, 'All the, all the ox in free.'"

Mrs. Violet Pickford of Mountain Home: "Deciphered it means All & All, Search & Free. Pronounced Allie, Allie Urchin Free."

Peter Neathery of Little Rock: "Could it be in German, 'alle alle aus sind frei'? The only trouble is that 'frei' is pronounced like the English 'fry.'"

Mrs. Lillian Balch Ogden of Little Rock: "It is olot olot oltzen. That is the way we called it at Balch (Ark.) as I was growing up some 50 years ago."

Anybody still confused can consult our associates in these areas:

Mrs. Louise Zermatten and Bette S. Miller at North Little Rock, Mrs. J. C. Martin at Concord, Mrs. Harold M. Hansen at Mountain Home, Helen Hunt deLeuw at Eureka Springs, Lorne W. Davis at Glenwood, Jo Ann Campbell at Fort Smith, Susan Wallace at Harding University, Alberta R. Conyers at Batesville, Ruth Jennings at Russellville, Sherry Snow at Searcy, Marcia Morris at Newport and Rose Burrow at Ozark.

The 1980 Hidengoseek Olympics will be held in Arkansas.

News From Land of "Pleonasm"

At Fayetteville the other day E. C. (Ernie) Deane put on his hat and went over to see Vance and Mary Randolph, a thing Ernie did with frequency and profit back when he was writing this newspaper's Arkansas Traveler column.

Vance Randolph is a folklorist above whom there are no folks in this state. Mary taught Chaucer for years at the University of Arkansas, which was all right with Ernie Deane, too.

This time Deane went calling on the Randolphs to find out what a "pleonasm" was, although he did not know it at the time.

Now, all of a sudden, the old Traveler is writing to us about our "pleonasmistic activity." With a hat brim that wide a man can get airborne in a hurry.

Hat brim, Ernie will tell us, is a pleonasm.

The same as *widow woman*.

And also *cash money*.

"A pleonasm is a redundancy," Vance Randolph told our old friend and mentor, assuring him that it was nothing nasty. "It is simply the matter of using more words than are necessary to express an idea."

Because Vance has made plenty of cash money knowing these things—many have read his book *Down in the Holler*—Ernie pursued like a hound dog.

Hound dog, he will tell us, is a pleonasm.

The same as *free gift*.

And *true fact*.

And *grape vineyard*.

And *razorback hog*.

But what is the language for?

Ernie says: "Some friends of mine up in the Kansas City area have been married better than 40 years. She's originally from Joplin, Missouri, and he's from down at Texarkana. She still breaks up when he says something about the cook stove."

For a person to say *cook stove*, Deane points out, falls in the area of pleonasmistic activity.

But it also makes clear where you want the biscuits kept warm, which is not on the bathroom heater.

Ernie says:

"I can vouch that those of us who came from cotton country talked quite differently from Ozarkers, and from city people, too." (Deane is a relative newcomer to the hills, not having arrived there until 1930.)

"In the Ozarks, for example, if you said a fellow was *hipped* it meant he had fallen off of something, probably a mule, and injured himself."

And down in South Arkansas?

"Down there if you said a fellow was hipped, it meant he had gone overboard on some subject, more than likely religion."

But old differences can melt away.

Ozarkers and old flatlanders should become linked, Deane says, joining hands against a common foe.

The common foe is a young person who runs off and hides, or falls down laughing, when one of his elders says he is going to see somebody like the tooth dentist.

"Tooth dentist," Vance Randolph told Deane—which is how this all started—"a tooth dentist is a pleonasm."

Right, Deane said.

Saying tooth dentist might be colorful and expressive and all those other old-timey things, but it also served, and still serves, the useful purpose of making one's self understood, Randolph said.

It left no doubt about which dentist was going to do the work, Deane said.

The whole thing left him refreshed.

"Let the young folks laugh," Ernie says, and he told the same thing to readers of his "Ozarks Country" column. "Let them laugh if grandpa's choice of words doesn't meet today's standards. I find the old ways preferable to some of the new."

Like, specifically, he had been sitting there trying to figure out whether this was a pleonasm: "Hey, man. I mean, wow, you know."

Even with his hat on, nothing had happened.

Sliding From Oxymoron to Superfluous Redundancy

In Sarah Coleman's English class at Mabelvale Junior High School they're having a high old time with the oxymoron.

This is a personal challenge for Sarah Coleman, herself. It was the English teacher's mother, a nurse, who was fretting recently about a friend's poor health habits.

"If he doesn't watch it, he'll wake up in a coma one day."

Adults are always waking up in comas.

One of the Mabelvale students brought from home the oxymoron that every time he asked his parents about going on a certain outing, they replied, "Absolutely maybe!"

Which describes the expansion plans of a Little Rock corporation, also run by adults. Those expansion plans, we read in the announcement, are *tentatively definite.*

Or maybe they are *definitely tentative.*

A fellow teacher walked by Sarah Coleman's room at Mabelvale and stuck her head in.

"We asked her to tell us her favorite oxymoron."

The teacher said, "I don't know about oxymorons." She added, "But I can name several mega morons."

Mega, presumably, for *mighty.*

To review once again, an oxymoron is a combination of contradictory or incongruous words.

For example, prior to an evening newscast, Jack Graham read the words on his television screen in North Little Rock: "Coming up . . . Snow."

Graham says, "I'd like to see that."

To see snow come up, you run the film backwards.

Somebody in Mountain View submits the oxymoron *broiled fryer.*

Or could it be *boiled friar.*

Also *gun control,* a word combination that is pointedly foolish.

"The ultimate oxymoron," observes George Fisher, "is *Charles Allbright.*"

Mr. Fisher is a Little Rock man who sits around all day, fully grown, drawing pictures. He erases a lot.

From Kay Fish, an English teacher at Little Rock Central High School:

"Your January 18 column incorrectly identified the phrase *false illusions.* It is not a oxymoron; it is simply redundant.

"Redundancy is a malady of our language of which there are many examples. *Free gift* and *false bravado* come easily to mind."

And from Ken Forrester, between sips of wine:

"If you will give it further thought, I believe you will agree that *false illusions* is not an oxymoron but rather is a superfluous redundancy.

"The most common superfluous redundancy is *Jewish rabbi.* And that (to use the next most used superfluous redundancy) is a true fact."

Cliff Bracy of Batesville is wondering whether his *genuine naugahyde* den sofa qualifies for anything.

"I hope so, because it sure is ugly."

John L. Ward, the Conway editor, contends that to be genuine such a sofa must contain the hydes of seven naugahs.

But that is only partially on Cliff Bracy's mind.

"What really bothers me are these repeated reports of *shrinking inflation.* Admittedly I do not understand economics, any more than the experts do, but in the current state of things just the opposite seems to be happening. My economic shrinkage is inflating."

Bracy can only guess at the outcome.

"Maybe we are witnessing one of those *rare phenomenons* so often written about and spoken of. I have never seen a phenomenon that wasn't rare. In fact, they are so rare I've never seen one at all."

But nowadays anything is possible.

"As my radio preacher told me this morning, driving along, we are living in times that are *very unique.*"

Mildred Farrell of Benton marvels that her Aunt Rose, who lives up in the bootheel of Missouri, apparently has survived what could have been a terminal case of the oxymorons.

The community newsgatherer up there

reported about Aunt Rose in her weekly column:

"During her bout with the flu, Rose Matthews enjoyed visits from all her children, 12 grandchildren, her prayer group, many covered dishes and more telephone calls than in memory."

And those were only while Aunt Rose was conscious.

Mildred Farrell reports, "She also enjoyed all those folks who came to the door, and then left before she could stagger out of bed and let them in."

From a shy observer in Pocahontas:

"Does the item in the *Gazette* newsbriefs count as an oxymoron? It has that Linda 'Wonder Woman' Carter had a *private* wedding with only 250 guests.

"If that is a private wedding I'd hate to see her if she had a semi-private hospital room."

C. Spencer Morris of Little Rock:

"There is no need to stir up more oxymorons than necessary. However, I felt this should be documented in the edible oxymoron category, or inedible as my father-in-law calls it.

"Dr. Morris says it's the most con- founded item he's ever experienced in his 82 years—*turkey ham*."

It sounds good, says Bob Armstrong of Searcy, but sooner or later you have to evaluate the phrase *free trade*.

"Before it's over," Armstrong notes, "*somebody* is going to pay *something*."

He also suggests *rules of war* and *fair fight*.

"And a *rolling stop*, unless it's on ice. Then you're talking about a *sliding stop*."

Considering the street's serpentine meanderings, Ann Nicholson is fascinated by a Little Rock billboard that instructs motorists, "Straight Ahead on Cantrell."

Sondra McKelvey of Clarksville, reading from her Agriculture Department booklet on how to grow mushrooms at home:

"Most amateurs will find it very diffi- cult and disagreeable to prepare a suitable compost from a small heap of manure."

The Department's solution?

"Use sterile manure."

John Fincher, in the secretary of state's office, reflecting on the president's recent State of the Union address:

"I know it is an abomination, but is a *bipartisan negotiating committee* an oxymoron or a redundancy? Or both?"

Judi King of North Little Rock lost concentration and missed the important development when she heard a 10:15 p.m. weatherman disclose, "The weather, by this same time tomorrow morning, is going to . . ."

Judi King says, "My mom and I were too busy giggling and didn't hear what the weather was going to do."

Probably the best oxymoron example of all time, according to Tim Stillings of Jonesboro, is the *Internal Revenue Service*.

Stillings says, "If this appears in the *Gazette* and I get audited, I'll let you know."

Judith Long of Little Rock:

"I noted the tag on a pair of women's trousers in a local department store read *Size 18—Petite*."

James M. Buffington of Lake Village:

"To my way of thinking the most common redundancy is *have got to*. Even Mr. Clinton used it three times on televi- sion while fighting for better schools."

Up in Mountain Home, Everett Wheeler caught the important part of that weather forecast.

It called for "a pretty decent snowfall."

Wheeler says, "I have seen *pretty* snowfalls, but none I would consider *decent*."

When Vic Fleming checked in at Washington National Airport for his return flight to Little Rock, the airline spokesman told him the flight had been canceled.

But there was nothing to worry about.

TWA would fly Fleming to St. Louis. There he would catch his flight, Flight 1277, where it was "reoriginating."

Vic Fleming thought that over.

"I was not about to show my ignorance by asking how something, anything, could be *reoriginated*."

What he was coping with, Fleming concluded, was in fact *preorigination cancellation.*

That, and more.

"TWA did this deed without prior notice to the passengers (unilaterally). Also, the reoriginated flight was taking off at a later time and in a city hundreds of miles away."

Fleming began to perceive an oxymoron of supersonic proportions.

By the time he boarded his flight in St. Louis, the Little Rock man had pondered his situation across time zones. He explained it to the stewardess.

"I told her how privileged we all were to be experiencing first-hand a unilateral multi-phasic inter-city time-delay post-preorigination cancellation reorigination."

So why did the stewardess practically fall into the aisle laughing?

Jean Williams of Fort Smith read it in a newspaper article about gardening:

"The University of Arkansas has developed this red grape, also seedless, and you can buy the seeds from Blossom Berry Nursery in Clarksville."

Jean Williams says, "I'm not one for oxy's, but this is sorta far out."

Horticulturally, it is easily explained.

The seeds were canceled only after the red grape had been reoriginated.

Jim Elder, the radio sports wizard, found a memo waiting for him when he got to work Monday morning at station KARN.

Elder has been pushing sales of home computers for one of his sponsors, Computerland.

The memo was from a station salesperson.

Something had gone wrong in the scheduling of commercials.

The memo said, "Due to computer error we missed several Computerland spots."

From Bob Stroud, a lawyer in Batesville:

"I submit what may be the only one-word oxymoron:

"Permanent."

That's permanent, as in beauty shop.

Stroud explains, "I just had a permanent six weeks ago, and I need another one already."

From Hardy Peacock of the P and W Oil Company of Dumas:

"The oxymoron has intrigued me to such an extent that I remain constantly on the alert for bigger and better examples.

"While visiting South Argenta on business I had occasion to cross the Main Street Bridge and observed what can only be described at least in North Little Rock as an oxymoron."

What Peacock observed has withstood the years.

"Considering the ever-interesting Casey [Laman] and the peace-loving, uncontroversial Honorable Mayor Thompson (not to mention roses), the sign outside City Hall that states *RESERVED MAYOR* seems a classic."

The oxymoron, as is widely known, is a phrase that contradicts itself.

Either that, or the phrase is just downright squirrelly.

As in, "Accelerate your banking through our drive-in window."

Or, "The police said Fortensen was legally drunk."

Presumably Fortensen was free to go. Powered by his own fumes.

Such phrases are of special interest to keen-minded newspaper persons. Masters of words.

As Rev. Paul Sipes, retired in Hot Springs, points out, "Keep the oxymorons coming. I know you will because your newspaper tells us it has the most complete coverage. I notice that on some days it is *more complete* than on others."

From Marion Stanwich of Mountain Home:

"Thank you for printing my oxymoron— Internal Revenue Service—last April.

"Now, with a very sad heart, I submit another one:

"Peacekeeping in Beirut."

The oxymoron jumped out at Howard Watson from a Little Rock radio station newswire:

"The 14 Grenada hospital casualties resulted from United States friendly fire."

Our man George Fisher is filled with hope by what the military calls its *build down.*

An unsigned reader credits *Parade* magazine with *selectively promiscuous.*

And gives an oxymoron to boot: *Monogrammed sweatshirts.*

It is far too late, according to Mrs. Clyde Findley of Crossett, to try to stir up anything with the oxymoron.

"People have no more idea than a betsy bug what they are saying or hearing. I hear things now that in my girlhood would have been uproarious. Now people don't even blink an eye."

Mrs. Findley's neighbor changed dog food recently

"He told me it has a meatier taste than before."

Paul W. Klipsch, the sound reproduction wizard from Hope, has a seven-year collection of oxymora. The things come from every printed and spoken source imaginable.

Pick a favorite:

"Daylight Savings Time."

"The four corners of the globe."

"Blackberries are red when they are green."

"Foot-operated hand brake."

"Hand-operated foot feed."

"Thirty-minute lunch hour."

"Round ice cubes." Also "melted ice."

"Effortless exercise machine."

"Pushbutton dial telephone."

"Original copy" (from *Wall Street Journal*).

"Roll-on spray deodorant."

"Smaller half."

"Routine emergency landing."

"Automatic stick shift."

"Liquified gas."

"Two-hundred-and-fifty per cent reduction" (Monsanto accomplished it).

"First annual."

"Green blackboards."

"Happily married."

"Soooo Pig!" Baffles Some Yankees

Visiting with family in the East, Mrs. Sarah Patterson of Little Rock found herself taking a break in the snack bar of a place called Mystic Seaport, an old shipyards attraction in Connecticut.

Imagine her pleasure when she saw walk into the place a man and two boys, about 12 and 10, the youngsters wearing Razorback T-shirts.

Mrs. Patterson, who is 69, couldn't wait to get over there. She approached the youngsters, dropped into a half-crouch and ripped off a rousing hog call.

The youngsters looked at her weirdly. Then they looked at each other. Then everybody looked at each other. Mrs. Patterson's *Sooo Pig!* still echoed through the snack bar.

Somebody had to say something. It turned out to be Sarah Patterson.

"That's the famous yell that goes with those shirts," she explained.

To which the father, moving protectively toward his sons, replied in precise and serious Eastern tones, "Their uncle sent them these shirts."

The Arkansan might as well have yelled fish for sale.

Still it worked out all right. Mrs. Patterson insists she was not the least bit embarrassed about it. And the Easterners moved away apparently relieved that they hadn't caught anything.

Baiting the Yankees in Old Boston

An impromptu hog call that left natives blank-faced in a Connecticut snackbar reminded Stephen E. Sundin that strange things can happen where people gather in Eastern melting pots.

It was Mrs. Sarah Patterson of Little Rock who called the hogs in Connecticut. She was inspired by two youngsters who walked into the snack bar wearing Arkansas Razorback T-shirts.

The youngsters didn't run but they got plenty wide-eyed. Their father moved in protectively and told Mrs. Patterson in serious tones that the T-shirts were gifts from an uncle in faraway Arkansas. The Hog reunion was over before it started.

Stephen Sundin is from Old Mystic, Connecticut, but he tells of an incident at Boston.

Sundin says two visitors, obviously Southerners, were spending the evening in a Boston bar, and things got late and soggy. Out of nowhere one of the Southerners yelled in a challenging voice, "I hate Yankees!"

Sundin describes the bar's reaction:

"One can only imagine their astonishment when the entire place erupted in a resounding cheer followed by a round of applause for the visitors."

Whether the Rebs ever understood is doubtful. Much of the talk in Boston bars is about the baseball Red Sox, and Red Sox fans know no greater hatred than their own for the New York Yankees.

Joe McGee tells about the ultimate cool of a Razorback basketball fan.

This was back on that Saturday afternoon, March 17, when Arkansas went against Indiana State in the televised regional finals at Cincinnati.

The action was hot and heavy, McGee says, when the doorbell rang at the home of a friend of his at Conway. The man shot four feet out of his chair.

Coming down, he backed toward the door, unable to take his eyes from that on which practically everything in the civilized world rode.

At the door were two young church fellows. The Razorback fan could not believe his eyes.

Could they come in?

He was very busy, the fan croaked.

It would take only a small amount of time.

The Conway man could not believe his ears. (He could believe one of them. Sidney was doing something.)

McGee says: "It seems these young men were earnest about wanting to make their presentation, and nothing he said was making any difference."

Something happened on the television set—he could not tell what—but the Razorback fan was pushed to the brink. His voice went from croaking to firm:

"Listen, I think I should tell you that I'm very happy with my own religion." Then he added, "Although right now I'm about to lose it."

That seemed to do it.

Jumper Fell As Fat Lady Hit Big Note

Texarkana—Our friend Dawes, drinking coffee here in the Kings Row Inn, observed that his wife had obtained tickets to an operatic presentation in Dallas. He certainly was looking forward to attending.

"My wife got tickets, too," sighed Dawes' cousin, also named Dawes.

The second Dawes sipped wistfully, revealing little excitement about the trip to Dallas.

"You don't understand opera," said our friend Dawes.

"I never claimed I did," said the second Dawes.

But that was not entirely so. For years he had dressed up and pretended.

"This heavy-set singer was finishing her song and was falling down on the stage, I don't know, dead or something, and just at that moment—I had my portable radio with the earpiece—just at that moment Sidney Moncrief sank a 360-degree fall-away jumper that beat Baylor, and Baylor is who I never could stand."

As Sidney came down, Dawes (the cousin of our friend) went to the rafters.

Disgraced, he had stumbled out of the Memphis auditorium, his radio disconnected in the excitement, but with the cord still dangling from his ear.

"My wife and her mother wouldn't come outside until 30 minutes after everybody else had gone, and they wouldn't speak to me for a month."

Since that night he had enjoyed operas without a radio, when possible telephoning at intermission for scores.

The second Dawes greatly admired his cousin. He took no pride in his own ignorance of the arts. But he was getting older every day.

"I'm tired of pretending to like things I don't like," he said, "and I'm just as tired of acting like I don't like things that I really do."

Our friend Dawes observed that it was a free country.

But his cousin went on, "No, it's not a free country. If it's a free country why do I hide to watch 'Dance Fever'?"

He watched that television program on the sly every Saturday night.

"If you ask me 'Dance Fever' has got just as much entertainment value as an opera, there's just as much hollering and falling down, and the numbers don't last half as long."

Moreover, "Dance Fever" had other appeals not associated with opera. The second Dawes was on the verge of saying what those appeals were when the waitress came with more coffee.

The man appeared to plunge into confession.

"If I didn't know better," he said, "I'd even think I liked country singers."

"Like Glen Campbell?" his cousin said.

"No, not like Glen Campbell. Like the guys with the greasy hair and the shiny shirts. *Those* country singers!"

He had lived a lifetime of lies.

"Let me tell you something. I even liked the food in the army. But you can't come out and say a thing like that. You've got to howl about army food, like about the food at school, or the food that comes out of a machine. Everybody howls about it, and then everybody goes home, all these gourmets, and what do they eat? Lord! Who knows?"

At work, the second Dawes confessed, he hid in the men's room when he ate dime-store candy. "The really cheap kind. It tastes like medicine. I love it."

His cousin observed that it was a free country.

But the second Dawes wasn't even listening.

"I'm supposed to throw up my hands when my kid dumps ketchup all over his eggs. Horrors! Don't do that, son! Here, enjoy some of this quince jam. He doesn't want any damn quince jam. I don't either. I want ketchup on my eggs!"

Our friend Dawes stirred and left—"It's not the profanity. It's the ketchup on the"—he could not complete the thought.

As we left the second Dawes was still talking. To himself. Vowing what all he was going to do with his new life. When he got back from Dallas.

Fans Straightened Out After Hogging Wrong Seats

At Razorback football games in War Memorial Stadium, John and Kara Lee Ford sit in the south end zone.

Section 16. Row 44. Seat Nos. 7 and 8.

Coaches call these the best seats in the stadium.

"From high up in the end zone you can study the line splits," coaches say. "And watch the guards pull."

John and Kara Lee Ford, along with other nonscholarship donors, hog these great seats while coaches are forced to see what they can from midfield and from the pressbox.

Being Razorback fans, the Fords can't wait to get there.

Saturday night, with the Ole Miss kickoff drawing near, Kara Lee and John Ford scaled the south face to Row 44.

They worked their way in from the aisle, to seat Nos. 7 and 8.

Those seats were occupied.

The Fords checked their tickets. They inquired, "Is this 44?"

The people sitting there said no.

"This is Row 43."

Kara Lee and John Ford returned to the aisle and moved up a row.

Those seats were taken, too.

"Is this Row 44?"

People sitting there said no—"This is 45."

Like the 13th floor in a tall building, Row 44 had disappeared.

John Ford is 6 feet 3½ and weighs in the neighborhood of 215 pounds.

He stood his ground between Rows 43 and 45 (seats No. 7 and 8) trying to sort things out.

Nobody was budging. Except for Kara Lee Ford. She retreated again to the aisle.

Something was different.

"The aisle was painted red, and the row numbers were white. I didn't remember it that way from before."

A person with the best seat in the house is not likely to forget.

"It was right about then," Mrs. Ford says, "that this gentleman from about 10 rows up shouted something down."

What the gentleman shouted sounded like a Simon Says.

He shouted, "You sit where your feet go!"

It is unfortunate that what ensued was not recorded on film.

You sit where your feet go.

Kara Lee Ford says, "It sounded strange, but I figured out what this gentleman meant."

He meant that according to the way things were set up, if your ticket said Row 44, then you put your feet on the area so designated.

From the aisle, Mrs. Ford could see that the people did not have their feet on "44." They had their seats on "44."

This could revolutionize seating procedures worldwide.

"All right, children, recess is over. Return to your feet."

"Let's go to the movie early, dear. We'll get good feet."

Kara Lee Ford got the message to her husband: "You sit where your feet go."

High in the south end zone conditions were getting right for E. F. Hutton to make a pronouncement.

Kara Lee Ford did not believe what she was seeing.

"All you people are right," her husband said, addressing Row 43.

He turned to those who thought they were on Row 45.

"Now you people, and everybody from here on up"—John Ford raised his hands, pushing backward and upward against the night—"you are all wrong."

Start the music.

Ten rows stood and retreated upward.

Apparently all found seats. There is no record that a row of fans disappeared over the top.

Dean Witter Doesn't Make the Homecoming Game

Naturally, everybody remembered the name of the old Razorback cheerleader—they would not forget one of their own—but nobody could quite get his face in mind. Or recall the year he led the soooies.

The cheerleader was named Dean. Dean Witter.

Willie Oates of Little Rock got her group together, as she does every year for the homecoming game. These are old Hog cheerleaders who go back to Fayetteville to lead the alums in yelling one more time.

This year's roll call was impressive:

Bobby Harlan of Fayetteville, 1956; Dick Trammel of Rogers, 1958; Marty Schaufele of Little Rock, 1971; Gene Toland Gibson of Dermott, 1941–43; Jim McClellan of Little Rock, 1962; Johnny Jackson of North Little Rock, 1967; Lisa Monroe of Little Rock, 1972; John Keel of Cincinnati, 1966; Tansil Stout of Little Rock, 1975; and Willie Oates, Arkansas Razorback cheerleader, 1938–41.

Oh, and Jo Neva Light Menefee.

Willie Oates explains, "Jo Neva was to call me back if she wanted a ride up to Fayetteville."

Willie was not at home when Jo Neva telephoned. Mrs. Oates was off at a meeting of some sort. Dr. Gordon Oates wrote down the message:

"Jo Neva called and said she would see you at practice at the amphitheater at 1 o'clock Friday."

Included was a telephone number Willie Oates was to call if she changed the practice time.

Also included was the name of Dean Witter.

On Friday at the amphitheater in Fayetteville, Willie Oates asked around to see whether anybody had see Dean.

"Dean who?"

"Dean Witter. You know him, don't you?"

Oh, sure. They knew Dean. Everybody had heard of Dean. But they couldn't place his year. And his face kept not materializing.

As it turned out, Willie Oates concludes that the only person at practice she didn't ask about Dean Witter was Jo Neva Light Menefee.

Came Homecoming Day.

"We took off for the field. It was a miserable day of rain and very cold weather, and we looked like a bunch of drowned rats.

"Right before half-time the announcer came on the loudspeaker and introduced all the alum cheerleaders who were on the field."

Apparently, 1972 sounded like a good year to have had Dean Witter lead yells. He got introduced along with Lisa Monroe.

Willie Oates says that Jo Neva Light Menefee went into near convulsions.

"She just got hysterical and started screaming—'There isn't a person here by the name of Dean Witter!' "

The homecoming crowd acknowledged Lisa and Dean with applause.

"That's the name of the company I work for!"

Willie Oates says by then all the old cheerleaders were out of it, so far as composure was concerned.

"We all went into convulsions of laughter and are still laughing."

Along with her list of returning cheerleaders, Willie had turned over the telephone message from Jo Neva.

The homecoming crowd was cheering the stockbroker.

Of course, by that time Arkansas was well on its way to thrashing Texas A and M. The man on the PA system could have announced, "Fish for sale!" and got a standing ovation.

Getting all Keyed Up

A week ago last night the Brad Tedfords poured out of War Memorial Stadium, jubilant with everybody else, only to find that they had locked the keys up in their car.

Fortunately, they were prepared for just such an emergency with two spare sets of keys.

One spare set was locked up in the glove compartment and the other was back home at Fayetteville.

After an exchange of family pleasantries, Tedford circled the car several times, trying to see a plan somewhere. Seeing none, and not optimistic about locating a locksmith within hours, he broke a window.

The crunching was achieved simultaneously with the appearance of a man wearing some kind of uniform.

Mrs. Tedford writes:

"I don't think he was a policeman, but he was awfully concerned about seeing Brad break the window. He took our license number, even after we convinced him that the car was ours, and watched us closely as we drove away."

It didn't dawn on the Tedfords until later why all the concern about their own car. An insurance claim.

"My family was in the insurance business for years," Mrs. Tedford says, "and I want to commend the man, belatedly, for recognizing a situation that could have resulted in a false claim. He can be assured this one won't."

Well, the uniformed men who keep order around athletic events in Arkansas have a history of being helpful.

We recall a similar situation some years ago in which a public official from Lawrence County left in the middle of a basketball tournament at Barton Coliseum and made the same dreary discovery about his car keys.

Standing there on the parking lot, he had picked up a large stone and drawn it back to smash a window in his new Cadillac when a state trooper appeared.

"You'd better not do that," the trooper advised him. "Somebody might get the wrong idea and try to give you trouble. I'll do it for you."

The man was grateful and stood back. Just as the stone crashed into the Cadillac's window he made a second discovery. This wasn't his car.

"That ought to do it," the trooper said.

The Lawrence County man said that sure would do it, all right. And with the trouble all fixed, he thought he'd just go back in and watch the rest of the game.

Midshipman Delivers Game Prayer

The United States Navy is in Little Rock today to play the University of Arkansas a football game.

The situation poses a special challenge for Maurice E. Roberts of North Little Rock.

Mr. Roberts is a retired navy captain. In the mid-1970s he was senior chaplain at the Naval Academy.

He recalls a special evening.

"It was the night before the traditional Army-Navy game and spirits were high as the 4,000 midshipmen gathered in the world's largest dining room for their evening meal. However, all stood behind their chairs and there was complete silence when the chaplain began the 'prayer,' which precedes the evening meal."

That silence didn't last.

When in his prayer Captain Roberts petitioned, ". . . and if tomorrow against Army we should lose . . ."

Four thousand voices shouted in unison, "No . . . No . . . *No.*"

To this date it is the only prayer at the Naval Academy that the Midshipmen have interrupted.

Captain Roberts notes, "The writer of Ecclesiastes has written: 'There is a time for everything.' "

He notes further, "The time to pray to be good losers is not the night before the Army-Navy game."

And that isn't all.

Signing off "written with a red face," Captain Roberts declares, "This chaplain is not going to make the same mistake when he leads Navy's pre-game religious service here in Little Rock Saturday.

"I love the Hogs, but *Go Navy.*"

Maybe NFL Should Try Church Plan

Printed in *The Tower*, weekly bulletin of Pulaski Heights United Methodist Church:

"We will have only a 30-minute telecast this Sunday, 11 to 11:30, as we have been pre-empted by the NFL Pregame Warm-up Show."

When is religion going to learn?

Nobody competes in this league—this is the 1982 season!—with the same old game plan.

Get in there and mix them up. Call church at 12 midnight. Next week kick off at 4 a.m.

The NFL will get so confused, it'll be October before they can come up with an all-night Pregame Warm-up Show.

At that time schedule Sunday services for Tuesday noon.

We know a man who thought the churches should start buying television time on Sunday, religious spots between the Miller Lites and the steel-belted radials.

"But only if the Saints are playing," he cautioned.

He has not seen the Saints play. Saints fans wear paper bags over their heads to avoid being recognized in the stands.

No, a different church game plan is needed. If it works the NFL will take the plan over. Then church can be resumed at 11 a.m. Sunday.

On the abbreviated Pulaski Heights telecast this morning Dr. James B. Argue's message will be "The Rejected Gift."

Most of it can be offered if Dr. Argue employs a brisk two-minute drill at the finish.

Pew-Passes, Astroturf May Help Defeat the Devil

In the week following Arkansas's rout of Texas on television, a power came over Rev. Larry D. Powell and he perceived the total solution.

Yes! The pews *could* be filled.

The devil *could* be confronted by superior numbers head-on.

Mr. Powell is pastor of Oaklawn United Methodist Church in Hot Springs.

In the church's weekly bulletin, "The Pulpit and Pew," he revealed to his congregation:

"In a local place of business I chanced to overhear two matronly ladies exchanging remarks about the Razorbacks' big win over Texas."

One of the ladies said, "How about that game?"

The other said, "Oh, I was so angry when it was announced that we were going to play on TV. I just knew we were going to get on there and make fools of ourselves again."

Fools indeed!

Mr. Powell said of that game, "Forget the official ratings. Arkansas was No. 1 in the universe."

There had been casualties.

"Reportedly, 10,000 fans lingered in Fayetteville to celebrate well into the night, more than 70 were arrested for being too wobbly on their feet, and bars were locking people 'in' to help police contain mayhem."

Through it all the minister began to perceive a solution.

He is no newcomer to the fray.

"I have been a card-carrying Razorback fan for a long time. When we lived in Georgia, the Hogs played Texas on TV. When Bobby Crockett caught the pass that put the Horns away, the outburst in the parsonage was so great that our oldest boy (now married, but about 3 at the time) ran outside, frightened and crying at the commotion."

The solution was coming.

"I was at the first Big Shootout when President Nixon's helicopter landed behind the south end zone where we were sitting.

"I was at Little Rock when Texas lost in a torrential downpour, and the victory was so sweet that nobody wanted to leave after the game. It was glorious, even while pouring rainwater out of my boots."

Yes! He saw the solution.

"I think I've finally learned something about loyalty, support and enthusiasm. I think I know how preachers can fill up their pews."

The Rev. Larry D. Powell Plan offers eight points: "1. If we can figure out some way to get the devil to take on the appearance of Texas, we stand a chance of getting serious about doing battle with him.

"2. We can tear out all the carpeting in the sanctuary and replace it with Astroturf.

"3. We can sell season pew-passes.

"4. After hearing thousands of screaming, eager fans call the Hogs, we need to adjust our 'Call to Worship' accordingly.

"5. Inasmuch as multitudes of people are willing to spend six or eight hours getting to, watching, and leaving a game, not counting travel time to and from home, it occurs to me that our worship services are not nearly long enough.

"6. A referee could roam the aisles at church to blow the whistle (in the ears of sleepers), and those who daydream or whisper could be penalized by moving forward five pews.

"7. We need a scorekeeper. If the preacher scores a point, the people say 'Amen.' If he makes an incomplete pass, the people can shout 'Boo-hiss.' At the end of the service, 'Amens' and 'Boo-hisses' would be tallied to see who won.

"8. Ask Orville Henry to write the pastor's articles in the midweek newsletter to get everybody as hyped up for worship as he does for a big game."

If somebody had only put horns on the Houston Cougars.

Mr. Powell will stick with his game plan.

"The Hogs return to action again this week. And so do we! Be in your 'position' this Sunday and let's go for the victory!"

The Carter Boys or Hogs' Holtz: Why Worry?

While his wife shopped, Ted Upton passed the time visiting with friends who happened into the Ozark Mall at Harrison.

A fellow Upton has known from the early days, a mountaineer, came by and started a conversation with, "What do you think about this mess the Carter boys are in?"

Ted Upton knows a lot of Carter boys.

"I haven't heard," he said.

The old friend said, "Why, don't you know about the mess Jimmy and Billy are in?"

Upton said, oh, those Carter boys. He explained:

"I'm kind of like Lou Holtz. The things I have no control over, I just don't worry about."

The old friend seemed to like that.

He abandoned politics and said, "Now who is this feller you call Lou Holtz?"

It can't happen this year because that football game will be played at night.

But last year when Arkansas played Texas, two Arkie canoeists got caught high up on the Buffalo River, out of touch.

Linda Fulbright says the outdoorsmen were up there only after an argument in the first place.

"One threatened to cancel the trip, but the other one said, no, they could take a radio and listen to the game on the way down river."

Coming through the bluffs, their radio reception went out. Mrs. Fulbright describes a downstream plunge that must have been a nightmare.

Too late, she says, the Razorback fans emerged at a spot where a man and woman sat up on a hillside. The canoeists came out of the water like desert rats stumbling toward an oasis.

"Who won the game? Who won the game?"

The man and woman looked at each other. Then the woman said:

"I'm not right sure. But I think it was Berryville."

After a 500-mile drive through Northwest Arkansas, as August 1980 burned its way onto the calendar, we can say without question that the two greenest spots in that mountainous quadrant of the state are within the municipal limits of the city of Fayetteville itself.

And not a shade tree at either location.

No other green has survived the summer quite like the artificial surfaces on which the Razorbacks play football and baseball.

Always Room for One More

Outside the west stands of War Memorial Stadium, in the crush of humanity surging in for the season opener against Vanderbilt, a man lost his ticket.

One minute the ticket was there. The next minute it was gone.

It happened when he jumped from the tailgate of a station wagon that was plowing slowly through the festive crowd. Somehow the ticket pulled out of his back pocket and disappeared down there among all those feet.

The man was borne away from it like flotsam on a tidal wave.

Better to have lost the station wagon.

There were cool heads in the party. When the station wagon was parked its occupants went in a group to the stadium office and told the horror story. It was horrible enough to be logical. And there was this. The tickets held by the group were numbered sequentially. Any stranger who showed up to sit among them obviously would not be the ticket's original purchaser.

Wonder of wonders, the man walked into the game without a ticket.

Everybody in the group knew what would happen. The ticket outside would be found by a professional wrestler, some guy about 6 feet 5 and weighing 260, and he would come into the stadium with the ticket and demand the seat. Maybe he would clean house.

But what is a crushed skull on the night of a Razorback football opener? The man without a ticket vowed to make a stand.

He got his chance.

She was not 6 feet 5, or hostile. She was most attractive, strikingly turned out in middle years, a bit weary after a climb of 57 rows, but obviously concerned only with finding the seat that matched the ticket she was consulting.

The station wagon group became aware of her presence. As she reached the precise spot, the man whose ticket she held felt relief and sadness.

"Ma'am, I know what you're looking for. That's my ticket. I lost it, and I'm as sorry as I can be, but you can understand that I'm not going to give this seat up."

The woman sighed. "Oh my," she said, or whatever a person says when she has climbed 57 rows and her husband, as she explained, had just paid somebody $20 for the ticket, and the kickoff was near and. . . .

"We just fooled around this year and didn't get our tickets in time." Everybody in the group sighed, truly sympathizing. "I guess I'll have to go down to the lounge and listen to the radio."

The lounge?

Yes, the Razorback lettermen's lounge. It turned out the woman was the mother of Charlie Daniel, the one-time Arkansas fullback and defensive hawk who, although a thorough-going gentleman, was remembered by everybody in the group as having left lumps on Razorback opponents all over the Southwest Conference.

She would do nothing of the sort!

"We've got plenty of room here," somebody said. With Mrs. Charles Daniel protesting, everybody said, "Yes," and started scrunching together, hearing none of the protests and insisting that she sit down and watch the game with them.

Which is how it went.

Which proves that no matter how crowded the stadium gets, there is always room for one more. If she is good-looking and her son played for the Razorbacks.

Unclassified Ads Tout Goods, Services

Jodie Jones and Mrs. R. H. Holderby, both of Bentonville, have been good enough to show us how telephone directory messups can be corrected with affirmative action.

Dr. John W. Cain was left out of the new Fayetteville-Springdale phone book. The omission was fixed up with a two-column advertisement, heavy type, in the Rogers *Daily News*.

The ad identified Dr. Cain as a "Podiatrist—FOOD SPECIALIST".

Two days later, in another corrective ad, Dr. Cain became a foot specialist.

Classified ad in the Fayetteville *Northwest Arkansas Star Shopper:*
"Lost: Old, white, miniature, female. Cindy. Lost around Rock & Locust St. Call 443-0164 or 443-9274."

Quoting the high temperature listings in this newspaper:

> *Portland . . . 72*
> *Raleigh . . . 90*
> *Reno. . . . 900*
> *Richmond . . . 91*
> *St. Louis . . . 91*

If you can't stand the heat, stay out of Sin City.

Under the headline "Pet Predicament Perturbs Populace," an article in the *Fairfield Bay News* alerts residents that they must start keeping their dogs up, or else.

It could be scarier.

The leash law will be enforced by Police Chief Joe Nipp.

John L. Ward found it among the classified ads in the *Faulkner County Record:*
"1976 Chevy half ton, 4-wheel drive pickup with wench. Heat, air, tilt steering, $3,800 firm."

Ward notes, "Not a bad price for a truck with a wench included, and *firm* too!"

John Bunch of Fayetteville was impressed by the scope of this yard sale, advertised in the classifieds:
"FIRST TIME yard sale: Two family,

clothes of all sizes, dishes and lots of miscellaneous. Thursday through Sat. 8 to 5 and Sunday 8 to 12."

Sounds like a winner, all right.

Where is it?

Legal Notice:
"Sealed proposals will be received by Arkansas State University in the Purchasing Department * * * until 10 a.m. June 25, 1980, for Furnishing and Installing a Loafing Shed on Arkansas State University farm land * * *."

James E. Griner of Jonesboro wonders what a loafing shed is.

The last time we checked, a loafing shed was part of the architecture of a country store. It was, in fact, the front porch of the store.

The owner furnished the porch with feed sacks, on which individuals sat to discuss matters of importance.

To construct a loafing shed on its property, Arkansas State University needs only to put up a phony store front and then add the real porch to that. People do not go there to buy anything.

Severe winter weather was hard on trees in Conway.

It produced this caption, appearing with a photograph in *The Log Cabin Democrat:* Dead Live Oaks.

Classified ad from the *Press Argus* in Van Buren:
"Grandson wants small dog. Grandma wants a boy, and housebroken."

C. L. Birch of Tillar found it in the *Desha-Chicot County Shoppers Guide:*
"FOR SALE—Two black coon hunting mules weight app. 500–600 lbs. Gentle, good riding, good ride in woods, and one big size Jack for breeding—phone 664-3678."

C. L. Birch cannot put it together.

"I can go along with bird dog, fox hound, deer dog, hog dog and cat dog, but I can't find the handle on 'coon mule.' "

We will explain it. But first Birch will have to describe the "cat dog."

Dianne Metzler of Bryant feels the political commercials taking hold of her family.

Her 4-year-old son, Michael, came to advise her, "President Raisin is on TV."

Mrs. Metzler concludes, "I guess that means the GOP ads are fruitful."

Pastor Figures "Parimutuel" Advantages

Hot Springs—He watches them on their way to the track, Rev. Larry Powell does, from his study at Oaklawn United Methodist Church in Hot Springs.

Oaklawn Church is across the street from Oaklawn Park. Could somebody make that the other way around?

"I was just thinking," Mr. Powell says, "why couldn't we incorporate some of the racing spirit into our worship services? After all, with our present average attendance on Sunday mornings, it would take us three years and two months to equal Oaklawn's attendance last Saturday."

That was two Saturdays ago.

"They must be doing something right over there. They had over 43,000 in attendance and the 'handle' was over $4 million."

It is the enthusiasm that stirs the minister.

"Most abandon their cars as quickly as possible [sometimes with the motor left running, and occasionally forgetting where they park] and briskly shuffle toward the track, head down, leaning forward, excitedly discussing favorite horses with their companions, or thumbing intensely through *The Racing Form*."

How, on its day of the week, to get people to storm the doors of Oaklawn United Methodist Church?

Mr. Powell proposes an action-packed Sunday to stir up things on his side of the street:

(1) DAILY DOUBLE: Correctly guess the liturgical color of the day AND the name of the choir anthem. WIN first place position in line at the church's next pot-luck supper.

(2) FEATURE: Correctly guess what text the minister will preach on. WIN a new Revised Standard Version Bible and 500 Green Stamps.

(3) 7TH DAY DERBY: Correctly guess the exact amount of the morning offering (or 'handle'). WIN a book of blank checks to use when making out your 10 per cent to the church, plus a new felt-tip pen.

(4) SPECIAL: Worship bulletins will be numbered. WINNING number receives tape of the pastor's sermon and free church parking for one year.

"Oh well," he concludes—and turns to Ecclesiastes, "The race is not to the swift."

From Catfish Ice Cream to Formal Levi's, Signs Say It All

A sign on an elevator in the Pulaski County Courthouse instructs, "This Elevator's Capacity is 10 Persons."

Beneath that, handwritten apparently by somebody unhappy with his advocate's performance in court, is this:

"Or Four Fat Attorneys"

On a trip with her husband, Mrs. Lee Hudspeth saw this sign in a cafe window at Springfield, Missouri:

UNDER NEW MANAGEMENT—WE FIRED THE OLD COOK.

This sign, says Jack Reeder, at a small boarded-up cafe near the water's edge at Bull Shoals:

OUT TO LAUNCH

Sign in the window of the Hillbilly Gift Shop in Eureka Springs:
"STORE HOURS—Open When I Get Here. Closed When I Get Tired."

This large sign advertising employment opportunities outside The Shack restaurant on Cantrell Road:

MANAGEMENT
JOBS
AVIABLE

None too soon, either.

On a morning walk, Dianne Woodruff and Carol Williams saw the sign at 2100 South Broadway.

The sign said, "Arkansas Medical Assistant Traing School."

It did not look just right.

The walkers went around to the other side of the sign.

Around there it says, "Arkansas Medical Assistant Trainig School."

Our man Jim Bailey read it on the big message board outside a chicken specialty restaurant in Prescott:

WE FRY IT RIGHT
HELP WANTED

The sign was on a shop door in Memphis, where Melissa Taylor of Jonesboro went looking for sheet music:
"Sorry. Bach in a minuet."

James E. Griner of Jonesboro, visiting in a Little Rock hospital, was intrigued by large-lettered signs appearing at several doors:

FIRE EXIT
KEEP CLOSED

Billboard of the times, on an approach to downtown Clarksville:

FORMAL WEAR RENTAL
LEVIS $10.95

Frank Kinney couldn't believe it, so he photographed it, a restaurant and gift shop sign outside of Forrest City that offers CATFISH ICE CREAM.

Eighth Street Baptist Church in North Little Rock is located at 821 Hickory Street.

This sign admonishes shoppers who enter the Nelson Leather Goods store in Eureka Springs:
NO PANTS
NO EARMUFFS
NO SERVICE

The motion picture house on the Jasper square is called Buffalo. Not Buffalo Theater. Not *The* Buffalo. Just Buffalo.

Information at the door says, "Open 7:00. Start 7:30."

But here is a message taped to the door:
"Film has not come in—Maybe tomorrow."

Jack Graham of North Little Rock saw the sign in a front yard in Greenbrier:
"YARD SALE FRI. AND SAT.—Sale to be Held Inside of House."

A sign outside Lewis Bros. General Store minces no words:
"This Place Protected at Night With Biten Dogs and Automatic Shotguns."

Roadside sign on Highway 10 near Danville: WORMS 32 CENTS EACH

Eloquent poster, with a telephone number, placed on a utility pole near Mount St. Mary:
"LOST Old black dog."

Sign in a yard in western Little Rock:

BABY SETTING NIGHT OR DAY

With special rates for larger broods.

Irene Rensch of Clarendon saw the sign at the cashier's counter in Stuckey's near Galloway:
"These Free Matches Are Now 3 Cents."

On the marquee, outside Tucker Coliseum at Arkansas Tech University:

ATU vs. UAM
And
Jehovah's Witnesses
Oct. 20

John Harris observes, "That's going to be a long day for ATU."

On a large sign outside First Baptist Church in Murfreesboro:
"Lord Fill My Mouth With Worthwhile Stuff—Stop Me When I've Said Enuff."

Menu offering at the Timbers restaurant in Murfreesboro:
"Chili (in season)."

From Mary Catherine McSpadden of Mountain View:
"Would you believe that AETN is a regular carrier of oxymorons?"
It's right there in the program notes, every Sunday at 3:30 p.m.: *The All New This Old House.*

Warning sign at a coin-operated laundry on Main Street in North Little Rock: ALL CARS WILL BE TOLD OFF.

We are contemplating a belated career in concrete.
Our man Bill Lewis had some work done at his house. The work took two hours. It cost $200.
On the receipt the concrete man wrote, "Pade."

In listing some favorite Western Arkansas place names, we forgot to mention a community establishment on the highway between Dardanelle and Danville.
The Slo-Fork Grocery Store.
Also, Hacker's Garage.

Warning sign, according to Bill Hurt, at a roadside establishment on Highway 5 southwest of Little Rock:
"No Horses Allowed on Parking Lot"

A reader found it in this newspaper:
"French Handsewing by Machine."

Mildred Watson travels six Southeast Arkansas counties for the March of Dimes. A sign reader, as most traveling folks are, she was struck by this combination of offerings outside a small roadside business north of Lake Village:

HOT COFFEE
SANDWICHES

Plus:

COLD BEER
WORMS

But some really fascinating signs are lining a 13-mile stretch of highway south of Monticello. The shoulders are extremely narrow and rough along this stretch.
At least twice a mile, on 28 different signs, motorists are warned "NO DRIVING ON SHOULDERS."
Mildred Watson was driven almost to breaking the law.
"I can't imagine anyone in their right mind and very few fools who would ever think of driving on those shoulders . . . but I must admit, reading all those signs brought out the devil in me and I was sorely tempted to drive over there just to see what would happen."

Jack Monk reports a new T-shirt.
It said on the front: "TITAN II DAMASCUS 0"

James Foss took a picture of a sign at a watermelon patch near Nashville. The sign said:
"EXPERIMENTAL MELONS. Will Turn Your Mouth Green."

Foss says the experiment obviously is a long-term thing.

"The same sign has been going up on that place for years."

We would print James Foss' picture of the sign except for some unexplained photographic deterioration.

The picture has turned green.

There's Something Strange About This Wedding

Running late, Jack Cross of Fayetteville made it into a pew just before the bride headed down the aisle at a Fort Smith wedding.

The ceremony was traditional but the participants were downright strange.

Afterward, because of a quick getaway planned by the newlyweds, the reception line formed at the church door to greet guests as they emerged.

Jack Cross was trapped in line right up to the bridegroom's mother before he found room to break and run for daylight.

The smiling mother extended her hand and said, "I've misplaced you among Bill's friends."

Cross said he understood. "It's been forever since Bill and I have seen each other."

Actually it had been longer than that.

Cross drove 65 miles across the mountains to sit through the wrong wedding.

We heard recently about a Little Rock man who attended a large wedding over in Nashville, Tennessee.

The man was a house guest of the bridegroom's parents.

He over-celebrated and late at night found himself wandering in a disoriented state in an upstairs hall of the palatial house.

He found himself by knocking over a small writing desk and sending ink in all directions.

Next morning the guest saw a trail of his own handprints on both sides of the hallway, running a considerable length of it.

Unable to face anybody, he quietly departed the house.

So much for the unhappy part. From here on it gets rotten.

Conscience stricken, the man went back in two weeks bearing candy and flowers for his hostess.

A maid showed him to a large sofa, where he sat uneasily waiting for his hostess.

Uneasily and uncomfortably.

After some minutes the man stood up, turned and discovered that he had been sitting on a miniature poodle, the hostess's prized pet.

The small creature did not survive the sitting.

This time the wedding guest fled the house in what has been described as absolute horror.

If he ever went back again we have not heard about it.

Pastor in the Lock-up? Well, Sort of

Rev. Paul Sipes is preparing a note of sympathy for Rev. John Turner.

It was Mr. Turner, pastor of Pulaski Heights Christian Church, who at church time on Sunday morning got stuck in a ground-level dog's door, trying to get into, or out of, his locked-up house.

Paul Sipes is retired and living in Hot Springs.

"Many good people will not forget the morning that services in our church in Kansas proceeded without their minister, me, although I was trying as hard as John Turner to be with them."

Mr. Sipes was trapped in a small room that adjoined his church office.

The organist ran through half a hymnal before the minister faced the fact that there was no other way out.

"I began kicking on the door, knowing full well the racket would resound to the back of the sanctuary and probably frighten the congregation half out of its collective wits."

When the kicking started, the organist played louder. And faster.

A voice came from beyond the door where the minister was trapped—"Who's in there?"

Paul Sipes identified himself.

"Oh yes, Brother Sipes." The doorknob was tugged several times. The voice said, "You stay right where you are, Brother Sipes"—then went away.

It took three ushers ten more minutes to liberate their preacher.

Word had preceded him to the pulpit. Mr. Sipes arrived to a crescendo of organ music and looking into a sea of contorted faces.

He told the congregation, "Since we're running late I'll dispense with the announcements except to say that the building committee will meet immediately after services to discuss installing a new lock on the pastor's washroom door."

What was left of services went about as reverently as you would expect.

Panic Strikes Choir Loft In Pocahontas

John Malone teaches social studies at Pocahontas High School. On Sunday he sings in the choir at First Methodist Church.

Malone was there last week when Betty Griffith got up to sing an offertory solo.

"As she stood to sing and opened her music she noticed half of it was not there."

The soloist wheeled and left the choir loft, heading for the choir room in the manner of one running but not appearing to.

The door to the choir room was locked. John Malone takes us there:

"The organist is faking it and the plate is being passed. Choir member Marvin Wells arrives with the key."

They get the door open and Betty Griffith disappears into the choir room. The search is on.

"The organist is playing and the plate is passing. The music is found right where it was left."

Can somebody slow the ushers down?

"Betty runs back to the choir loft, catches breath and sings solo."

So it all got squeezed in. Whew!

Betty Griffith's offertory solo was "He Was There All the Time."

Inside a wooden outhouse facility on a place near Timbo the caller is greeted by this ornately lettered message:

"Congratulations. You are now a member of the Birch John Society."

A Cross-eyed Bear and a Palm Leaf Fan

Next to the universally loved Round John Virgin, the most famous creature never to exist in all of religious music would have to be the cross-eyed bear.

Round John, as everybody knows who knows "Silent Night," is there in the manger every Christmas when little children begin to sing about the mother and child, holy infant so limber and wild. Sleep is heavenly please.

The cross-eyed bear, on the other hand, has not been that well thought of at all.

Paul Meers, for one, remembers that when he was a child the bear curled his hair with fright.

"This was at a brush arbor meeting in the woods up north of Batesville. I was about 4 years old and everybody started singing, 'The consecrated cross I'd bear.'"

That was scary enough, but simultaneously a woman in the congregation felt the power come over her.

"It was Aunt Sarah Jane," Meers says. "The minute everybody sang those words Aunt Sarah let out one of her shouts, and I knew it was all over."

Meers remembers being scooped up by a protective grown cousin, at whom he kept shouting, "Where's that bear?"

It was a useful experience.

Many brush arbors later, young Paul was able to sit still when Aunt Sarah Jane went down to the front and started whamming his father on the head with her palm leaf fan.

"My father was a dignified man. He wouldn't wear a collar and tie, but he was a deacon and he sat down on the front row with the other deacons, a dignified man."

Under the power again, Aunt Sarah left her pew and went down and started whopping Paul's daddy and shouting, "Walter Meers, God bless those old gray hairs. Your mother has gone to glory and you'll go there too before long."

Paul Meers was especially proud of his daddy that day.

"It wasn't easy, being hit on the head and hollered at like that, but he stayed dignified."

Tom Glaze, the chancellor, tells us about a young friend of his, Ashley Laser, who went down front with the children on Sunday morning for the young folks' sermon that the Presbyterians do so much good with.

Ashley is 10 and Judge Glaze describes her as being "very bright."

Here is how that inspiring moment went:

"The sermon was on tithing. The minister asked Ashley to hold out her hand and he placed 10 animal cookies in her palm. He asked her to consider how many of the cookies she would return to him if she knew that she might be rewarded for her giving."

Ashley didn't have to consider at all. She gave all 10 cookies back.

The minister was delighted and told the congregations, small and large, as much. That this young person would return all she had so that—he was in the process of saying that when Ashley volunteered:

"I don't like animal cookies."

Nobody thought Lory Buie was listening when the older folks were talking about how much they liked their preacher.

Mrs. Turner Buie said, "You know, he doesn't preach but about 20 or 25 minutes. I like his sermons so well I hate for them to end." Lory, 6, said she hated it too.

That surprised everybody.

"I sure do," the youngster said. "About the time I get to sleep I have to get up and walk out."

Afterword

In my opinion, the Arkansas Traveler column has managed to do subtly at least three important things for the *Arkansas Gazette.*

First, it is a constant reminder that the paper is as old as the Traveler. The *Gazette* is and always will be tied to the state's past and at the same time devoted to covering the events that most likely will shape its future.

Secondly, the column has had as its goal reaching and reporting about persons who are not necessarily newsmakers. By giving space to such persons, the *Gazette* sends the message that it is interested in all the citizens of the state and that the news is not exclusive to meetings and politics.

And, finally, during the Allbright years, the gentle humor of the column has established the fact that nothing goes down with your morning coffee better than the Traveler column and the *Arkansas Gazette.*

David B. Petty
MANAGING EDITOR

Epilogue

A student on the campus at Fayetteville asked me whether I had ever considered writing anything serious. It made me flinch. Serious like what?

This young man spoke of writing that fell somewhere between shedding light and grieving on Mr. Faulkner's "universal bones."

Imagine my relief. He had described the Arkansas Traveler column.

The secret is that there is no writing to it. Simply hold up a mirror, and the lights of Arkansas become reflected in it. The lights, and the darks as well. When a county judge picks up a stone, from the parking lot at the coliseum in Little Rock, and smashes his automobile window to get to his keys, and with the glass still tinkling realizes he has the wrong car—that grieves on some bones.

In the middle of our explaining this, the university student excused himself and went away.

The point is that the people of Arkansas get up every day and write the Arkansas Traveler column. The four of us—Deane and Lancaster and Trimble and Allbright—each has held the mirror the best way he knew how.

So will the next.

Charles Allbright